27 (28)

MASS
MEDIA

MASS MEDIA

Systems and and Effects

W. Phillips Davison
Professor of Journalism and Sociology

James Boylan
Adjunct Associate Professor of Journalism

Frederick T. C. Yu
Associate Dean and Professor of Journalism

All of Columbia University

Praeger Publishers
New York

Photographs on the following pages reproduced by permission of: Magnum: 70, 104
(Burk Uzzle); Rapho Guillumette Pictures: 158 (Alice Kandell); Rapho/Photo Researchers, Inc.: 130 (© Bruce Roberts); and UPI Photo: 42.

ANNENBERG

HM
258
D29

Published in the United States of America in 1976
by Praeger Publishers, Inc.
111 Fourth Avenue, New York, N. Y. 10003

© 1976 by Praeger Publishers, Inc.

Library of Congress Cataloging in Publication Data

Davison, Walter Phillips, 1918–
  Mass Media : systems and effects.

  Bibliography: p. 220
  Includes index.
  1. Mass media. 2. Communication—Social aspects. I.   Boylan, James R., joint
author. II. Yu, Te–chi, 1921– , joint author. III. Title.
HM258.D29   301.16'1   74–31000
ISBN 0–275–33680–8
ISBN 0–275–89140–2 pbk.

Printed in the United States of America

UNIVERSITY of PENNSYLVANIA
THE ANNENBERG SCHOOL
OF COMMUNICATIONS
PHILADELPHIA PA 19104

PREFACE

Mass media are frequently blamed for encouraging violence, contributing to a decline in morals, and causing many other ills in our society. With almost equal frequency they are praised for opposing tyranny and corruption, for providing entertainment for all, and for making enlightenment available on a scale hitherto unknown. We are said to be suffering from an overload of information—that no human being can cope with all the messages dinned into his ear; yet there are also loud complaints that the public is uninformed about matters that should be of concern to everyone. Some observers see the citizen as manipulated or narcoticized by the press; others assert that the media are distrusted, disbelieved, and disregarded. "I never believe anything I read in the newspapers," is a familiar refrain.

Why so many contradictions? One reason is that the mass media are complex and diverse; to generalize about them is to invite error. Another is that people are even more complex and diverse; no two individuals are affected exactly the same way by what they see, or read, or hear. The interaction of minds and messages produces a bewildering array of phenomena.

Not all contradictions can be explained, nor can the effects of communications be predicted with confidence. But some explanations and some predictions are possible. More balanced evaluations of the media and their effects can be made if we know something about the way they developed, how they compare with media in other countries, what forces determine the nature of their content, and how they have been observed to affect the people exposed to them.

That is the aim of this book—to present an introduction to the history of the mass media in the United States, an overview of information about their functioning and effects, and a brief comparison of the American media system with other media systems.

We hope that the discussions in the following pages will be relevant to readers, viewers, and listeners in general; that increased familiarity with the processes and effects of mass communication will make them more able to enjoy and profit from the media. Those who are already involved in journalism or in some other branch of mass communication will already be familiar with some of the material presented here, but they may also find new perspectives on their

v

work by seeing how it is viewed by researchers from outside their field. Students interested in the mass media as a subject for academic pursuit may use this book as an introduction to the field and to several of its component parts: media history, international communication, media sociology, and the uses and effects of communications.

The volume's content and the system of references used are designed to allow readers to pursue each major subject dealt with as much or as little as they wish. Those who want a general picture can confine themselves to reading the text; there are few footnotes or technical terms to disturb them. Readers who would like to explore one or another subject somewhat more thoroughly will find suggestions for further reading at the end of each chapter. These brief listings are confined to books easily available in most libraries, since a full bibliography of all references used has been included at the end of the book. Students with interests in specific aspects of mass communication may wish to track down some of these sources and can then use them as leads to still more information on the topics selected.

We are heavily indebted to the authors whose works we have cited or quoted. We particularly thank Professor Wilbur Schramm, formerly of Stanford University and more recently of the East-West Center, for permission to use some of his research that is in publication. In addition, a vote of thanks goes to our students over the years, whose questions and observations suggested much of the content of the volume, and especially to Mary A. Nelson, Annette L. Miller, Mary Shepard, and Nelson A. Navarro, some of whose contributions have been incorporated in the text. Numerous organizations have been helpful in providing background or statistical information, including Response Analysis, Inc., of Princeton, New Jersey, the Motion Picture Association of America, and the American Association of Advertising Agencies; our thanks to them all.

Even more, we are indebted to our respective wives—all of whom happen to be professionally engaged in some branch of communication—for their criticism and encouragement. As is fitting in an era when the status of women is being reevaluated, none of them typed any of the manuscript. To them the book is affectionately dedicated.

W. Phillips Davison
James Boylan
Frederick T.C. Yu

CONTENTS

Chapter Three
Media Sociology
How Content Is Shaped

PART TWO   EFFECTS

Chapter Four
Communication Channels
What Information Is Available ?

INTRODUCTION

We are immersed in the mass media. The television set in the average American household is turned on for more than six of every 24 hours. On a normal weekday, more than three-quarters of the adult population reads a newspaper. Some 62,000 periodicals are available in the United States and Canada. Nearly all families have at least two radios—one in the house and one in the car. Not everybody reads books, but those who do have their pick of about 40,000 new titles a year from American publishers. Billboards, posters, phonograph records, mimeographed newsletters, handbills, not to mention films and other theater amusements, all compete for—and often get—our attention.

That we are enormous consumers of the mass media can hardly surprise anybody who lives in the United States. But most of us are less conscious of the fact that we also may help to shape what the mass media are and what they offer. We do this indirectly by tuning in particular programs, by buying certain advertised products, by reading one newspaper or magazine rather than another, by buying a certain paperback off the drugstore display rack. Market researchers and sales managers are constantly monitoring public preferences and reporting their findings to newspapers, magazines, broadcasters, and advertisers. Just as media content may influence our behavior, our behavior determines, in part, the media content that is offered to us.

A smaller proportion of the public attempts to affect media content more directly, by such means as writing press releases for organizations to which they belong, by writing or telephoning an editor (an "offensive" remark on television is likely to draw a barrage of telephone complaints), by taking part in radio talk shows or television interviews, by sending protests to government officials or agencies, by joining groups advocating specific changes in the media, or even by demonstrating noisily in front of a newspaper office. Another segment, several hundred thousand persons, works full time in shaping media content. These are the professionals employed in some branch of the communications industry and in advertising or public relations.

1

THE MEDIA IN OUR LIVES

The aim of this book is to help readers become more intelligent users of mass communications, to be more effective when they want to influence the media, to make appropriate career choices if they should decide to work in communications, and, as citizens, to be able to encourage the kind of communication system that will best serve the public. To perform effectively in these roles, a media consumer needs a broad spectrum of knowledge. It is useful, for example, to gain an understanding of how media came to assume the shape they have today. What political, economic, and technological influences were involved? How did the media come to serve some of society's needs and neglect others? What does the history of mass communication institutions tell us about the possibilities of change in the future?

Just as important is an acquaintance with media sociology—that is, the study of influences at work on media content. Researchers have probed such questions as: What determines the prominence of various kinds of material in the media? How does an editor decide to use a given piece of material and discard another? Who or what wields the real power over media output?

It is useful, in thinking about American mass media, to compare them with systems operating in other countries. The world is a laboratory in which we can study many types of publishing and broadcasting, and can observe how well they satisfy varied requirements. For instance, those who have worked to develop public broadcasting in the United States have paid close attention to the British Broadcasting Corporation, as an example of a system publicly owned but not government controlled.

There is a further reason for studying communication systems of other countries. A prime issue of our day is whether differing societies can live together peacefully and productively on this planet. We may be more likely to find ways to cooperate with global neighbors if we understand them, and we are more likely to understand them if we know how their mass-media systems work, and why their picture of the world, as presented in their media, differs from ours. We would also like them to understand us, and consequently would like to know how to overcome the barriers that restrict communication between peoples.

One major question involved in studying mass media centers on the availability of information. That is, what messages travel along what channels? What are the varying characteristics of these channels, which include not only the print, sound, and pictures of mass media, but the whole range of interpersonal communication. We need to know how these person-to-person channels affect mass-media communication.

Another important field deals with the ways we receive information. Why, for example, do we remember one news story and not another? How do people deal with a flood of communication? How does the principle of selectivity operate?

Still other work on the effects of communications makes it possible to improve predictions about the impact of media content: Will Candidate A win the election because he has more money for political advertising than Candidate B? Is a child who likes to watch violence on television going to develop aggressive behavior patterns? Can starting a community newspaper stimulate civic pride? Gauging communication effects is not an exact science, and many kinds of effects remain to be explored, but those who are familiar with what *is* known will usually be able to make more accurate predictions than those who are not.

A surprising number of the major issues facing us today involve the mass media. The operation of the American political system, even the very ability of the government to govern effectively, depends in part on the printed media and broadcasting. The Watergate scandals were but one glimpse of the deep involvement of the media in processes of government. Moreover, unless members of a political opposition can communicate effectively with the public, they have little hope of winning power.

The functioning of the economic system also depends in part upon the media. The mass media are one means used by manufacturers and merchandisers to call goods to the attention of consumers. In addition, the media themselves constitute a substantial industry, the well-being of which has some bearing on the health of the economy.

Finally, the media rank with the educational system as a prime means by which society transmits its culture and values from one generation to another. It is important to consider how well the communication system functions and in whose behalf, for what it transmits will help determine the shape of American society in years to come, as it has in the past.

SOURCES OF KNOWLEDGE ABOUT COMMUNICATION

The mass media are studied by journalists and journalism researchers, as well as by psychologists, sociologists, market researchers, political scientists, historians, economists, anthropologists, and others. There is also a branch of social science called "communication,"[1] which studies the media as well as other information channels. Communication researchers, who are now represented at most major universities, make use of theories and techniques of the other social sciences, and have also developed some theories and techniques of their own.

One of the first of the modern communication researchers was a political scientist, Harold D. Lasswell, who described the communication process as, "Who says What, in which Channel, to Whom, with what Effect?" (Lasswell, 1948). In accordance with this formula, communication research is often divided into the study of sources (who), content (what), channels, audiences (whom), and effects. Lasswell also developed techniques for describing media content quantitatively and was one of the originators of modern content analysis (Lasswell, 1946). His doctoral dissertation on propaganda in World War I is still read today and has recently been reprinted (Lasswell, 1927).

Other branches of science have contributed, too. Physicists, chemists, and engineers are concerned with the development of new technologies for broadcasting and printing. Some of these boggle the mind. Home video terminals, which permit the user to ask a question of an information source such as a computer and to obtain an instant response on the video tube, are already available at about $1000 each. They probably will become less expensive as demand for them grows. Publications of the future may be produced by ink-jet printing, in which tiny droplets of ink are hurled toward the paper through oscillating nozzles. A computer-controlled electronic field forms these droplets into letters or numbers at speeds of up to 150,000 characters per second. This process is still experimental.

Mathematicians and physicists have developed "information theory," which deals with relationships among components of communications systems: for instance, between a channel's capacity and the volume and quality of signals flowing through it. (How many conversations can be carried on one telephone circuit without unacceptable distortion?)

Journalists who study the media are mainly concerned with professional standards—thoroughness, fairness, and independence. They

---

[1] "Communication" is usually used to denote the *process* by which meaning is transmitted from one person or group to another, and as an adjective. The word "communications" (plural) usually refers to the messages themselves. Thus, one could speak of communications that deal with communication. We wish there were a shorter word.

are concerned, too, with the relationship of media with all levels and branches of government. If one is interested in the question of freedom of the press, one of the first places to look is in the literature of journalism. Several professional periodicals keep a critical eye on journalistic performance and on press-government relations. The *Columbia Journalism Review,* which is the largest of these, is a useful source for students of the mass media.

Psychologists have investigated not only the mass media, but also communication in small groups and even in dyads (groups of only two individuals). They are principally concerned with the ways people learn, how and why their attitudes change, and the role that communication plays in relations between them. Much of the psychological research on communication has been carried out in laboratories. For instance, several matched groups of subjects may be exposed to films or recorded messages that vary in only one important respect, and the different effects of these stimuli on the subjects' behavior are carefully observed. This makes it possible to draw inferences about the power of different types of message content to influence people.

Sociologists are more likely to make use of public opinion surveys in studying the effects of communications. They are interested in the structure of the media, too, and in the ways that this structure and various outside pressures influence media content. These questions are often investigated through intensive case studies of publishing or broadcasting organizations. Sociologists have given attention to the degree to which journalists are influenced in what they do by media owners and managers, by the publics for which they are writing, and by the norms of their own profession. Market researchers, who are concerned primarily with the demand for products and the effects of advertising, make use of both psychological and sociological research techniques.

Political scientists are interested in the role that the mass media play in the political process. They have conducted numerous studies of the influences of political propaganda on the way people vote, on the part played by the mass media in the decisions of political leaders, and on press-government relations.

The findings of social scientists about the mass media and the communication process in general are published in the books they write and in their own professional journals, such as the *American Journal of Sociology,* the *Journal of Personality and Social Psychology,* or the *American Political Science Review.* They also publish in the journals devoted specifically to communication research, which include the *Public Opinion Quarterly,* the *Journalism Quarterly,* and the *Journal of Communication.* There are also some excellent journals published abroad; for example, *Gazette* in Holland, *Publizistik* in Germany, and *Communications* in France. The findings of market and advertising researchers are most likely to appear in the *Journal of Marketing Research* and the *Journal of Advertising Research.*[2] Two new journals, *Communication Research,* edited at the University of Michigan, and *Communication,* edited at Simon Fraser University in Canada, were started in 1974.

While we hope that this book will be a useful introduction to the field of mass communication for students who are contemplating careers in the media, as well as for members of the public who deal with the media in their daily lives, our primary concern is with conveying an understanding of *why* mass media communications take the forms they do, and what kinds of effects they may have on different audiences. We think that an understanding of the forces that influence mass media institutions and content, and of the role the media play in our individual and collective lives, will contribute to an understanding of the society in which we live. And we hope that this knowledge can be put to work in finding solutions to issues now confronting the mass media and society as a whole.

Part I of this book is concerned with media systems: how they developed in the United States, how they function in other countries, and how the news content of the principal American mass media is shaped. Part II focuses on effects of communications: what messages are available to us, how we select certain ones for attention, and what happens as a result. An epilogue discusses some of the choices we face as a result of the development of mass media: choices that will affect our personal lives and the world in which we live.

---

2 For a much more complete listing of journals devoted to communication research, see *Aspen Handbook on the Media,* published by the Aspen Program on Communications and Society, 770 Welch Road, Palo Alto, California 94304 (1975–76).

SYSTEMS

Part One

Biologists frequently think of living creatures as systems that are composed of interrelated smaller systems. The cells of the body have a life of their own, but they also make up larger units that are called tissues or organs. The organs, in turn, are parts of a still larger system— the biological individual.

Social scientists, too, make use of the concept. They see individuals as components of systems called families or tribes, or as building blocks for churches, political parties, or factories. These groups and institutions make up comprehensive systems that we call societies. A change in any one of the smaller systems is likely to cause reactions in the larger system, just as restructuring of the larger system is likely to cause changes in the subsystems. The various units are interrelated and interdependent.

The mass media, together with much simpler systems such as face-to-face conversation, make up the communication systems of societies. Media systems affect government, education, the economy, and other systems, and are affected by them. The way in which communication systems and other institutions are interrelated has been documented by historians, who have noted, for instance, that the relative stability of the Egyptian and Roman empires was ensured in part because a light and relatively cheap paper-like substance— papyrus—was available to them. This meant that the central governments could keep records more easily, send orders swiftly, and coordinate the actions of myriads of officials in widely dispersed communities. The ancient empires that had to rely on clay tablets and stone engravings for records and messages were more likely to dissolve into smaller units (Innis, 1950). In modern times, the availability of radio and television has tended to increase the power of central governments still more. A prime minister or a president can now appeal to the voters of a whole nation via the broadcast media; it is no longer so important for him to cultivate the support of local political leaders.

7

Media systems are made up of interrelated subsystems. What goes on in the editorial office of a newspaper affects what happens in the printing plant, and both are affected by the behavior of subscribers, advertisers, news sources, and many other groups. We often think of broadcasting stations or newspapers as being located in particular buildings. It would be more accurate to say that some of their subsystems are housed together, but that others may be scattered over larger areas. Yet all these subsystems comprise a working whole.

The following three chapters examine mass media systems from three points of view. The first traces the evolution of the mass media as we know them. in the United States today. In the next chapter, our system is contrasted with the media systems in other countries. This chapter also illustrates the way that different media systems are related to different political and economic institutions. The final chapter in Part I examines the structure and functioning of the American mass media and describes how the various component parts of this system help to shape the content of the news and information that influences and is influenced by the larger social system.

CHAPTER ONE
The Age of
Mass Media

So plentiful, so relatively inexpensive, so easy of access is the intake of communication products in industrial nations today that it is hard to recall how slim that diet once was. As late as the end of the eighteenth century, most communication remained—like other products of the artisan—one of a kind. People could hear an address or a sermon, but only if they were within earshot. They could see a painting if they traveled to the place where it was hung. They could witness drama or hear music, but the performance, once given, was gone forever. They could learn a piece of news on the day that it happened only by word of mouth.

The one capability of multiple communication 200 years ago was the printing press, which had come to Western society in the mid-1400s. But the technology of the press had advanced little in three centuries. Its pace was restricted not only by the slowness of setting type by hand, but by the laborious processes for inking and pressing the type surface on the paper. Both the variety and volume of what might come from a press was severely limited, and even among those able to read, there was hardly a surplus of reading matter—skimpy two- or four-page newspapers, a few primitive magazines, and individually issued books, pamphlets, and broadsides.

The instruments of abundant communication came into existence in a society that learned—as it became increasingly industrialized, technology-minded, affluent, and urban—to produce goods identically and plentifully. Although mass communication (like other consumer products) has been slow to reach many of the world's poorer peoples, industrial society—and the United States in particular—has brought into being what some would call a surfeit of consumer communication. In America, long-term prosperity, a literate public created by universal education, and a quota of inventiveness (or willingness to borrow inventions) combined to produce the outpouring that the historian Daniel Boorstin has called "the Graphic Revolution"—the multiplication of "man's ability to make, preserve, transmit and

9

disseminate precise images—images of print or men and landscapes and events, and of the voices of men and mobs" (Boorstin, 1962:13).

The range and volume of these images now is staggering. In the United States alone, the mass-media output includes not only 60 million copies a day of newspapers, but an average of 40 million periodicals printed each day, an average of more than 3 million books a day, television stations on the air for a total of possibly 12,000 broadcast hours a day transmitting to sets turned on for perhaps half a billion hours, and radio stations broadcasting as much as 100,000 hours of programming to sets receiving a total of (at a wild guess) a billion hours a day. Nor do these totals take into account such other communication products as cable television output, phonograph records and tapes, film, and miscellaneous other communications offered by mail, retail display, signboards, leaflets, or dirigibles.

Obviously, a communication industry of such dimensions can supply every member of a public in a city, a state, or a nation, if the consumer chooses to purchase or receive the product. Indeed the attainment of such capability is one way of measuring the emergence of a mass medium. Crudely speaking, the mass media have come into being in the United States only in the last century, an era that can conveniently be called the Age of Mass Media. Before the 1880s, there was a steady expansion of the output of printed media, but they still fell short of being able to reach an entire mass populace. In that decade, there emerged America's first true mass medium—the popular urban daily newspaper. At an increasing pace, then, other media joined the first—the popular cheap magazine, film, pictorial journalism, radio, phonographic sound, and finally television and its variants. As Boorstin has observed: "By a giant leap Americans crossed the gulf from the daguerrotype to color television in less than a century. . ." (Boorstin, 1962:13).

How did this rapid growth come about? How did the media become so abundant? How was society able to absorb so many new types of communication so swiftly? The narrative that follows attempts to supply answers.

THE URBAN DAILY NEWSPAPER

As little Eohippus was to the horse, so the early American newspaper was to its bulky descendants. The first regularly published American newspaper did not begin until 1704, considerably after its English predecessors and nearly 70 years after the arrival of the first printing press in Massachusetts. John Campbell's *Boston News-Letter*, moreover, was scarcely a full-scale newspaper but the translation into type of letters the publisher had been painfully copying out by hand. The *News-Letter* and its successors for 80 years were weeklies; there were no dailies until the 1780s. Well into the nineteenth century most newspapers were limited to four pages and to small circulations.

This is not to say that the role of the early newspapers was negligible: Even with circulations of but a few hundred copies, newspapers of the 1760s and 1770s played a major part in marshaling public opinion for the struggle against Britain (Schlesinger, 1958). The port cities, which were the sites of most of the early papers, depended on the weekly issues for commercial and shipping data. Moreover, in the days before the telegraph, the exchange of newspapers between editors constituted an important means of inter-urban communication (Pred, 1973).

The modern newspaper began to develop with the Industrial Revolution's substitution of steam power for human muscle. Steam-driven presses increased output and made possible the offering of daily newspapers in quantity. The most distinctive product of the change was the medium called (for its popular price) the penny press. The master innovator of the penny press was James Gordon Bennett of New York; his *Herald,* founded in 1835, foreshadowed much of the modern character of American newspapers. Dubbed by one biographer "the man who made news," Bennett actually could be called more appropriately the man who made news into a readily salable consumer commodity (Carlson, 1942). Unlike predecessor papers, which relied most heavily on information arriving from elsewhere, Bennett's first resource was the city of publication. His was the first paper to "cover" a city, to send reporters to Wall Street, to the churches, to society events, and especially to the courts, which yielded rich returns in human waywardness and wretchedness. Bennett further spiced the paper with stunts and occasional hoaxes. His innovations shocked traditionalists, but his was the most widely read paper in America at that time.

Bennett's paper, run for profit, was a harbinger of the press to be; but before mid-century most of the newspapers retained the traditional character of the American press, which was political. Although privately owned, many newspapers of that period owed their existence to support by a political party, faction, or individual. Later historians have tended to scorn this old political press. In fact, it could at its best provide high-quality political discussion in a framework understood by the reader; if the reader did not like the particular setting, he could try another newspaper. The newspaper now considered the most distinguished of the early nineteenth century, the *National Intelligencer* of Washington, was supported by patronage but still offered thorough coverage of the seat of government (Ames and Teeter, 1971).

That age also produced American journalism's great editorial writers, who made their newspapers into lengthened shadows of their own opinions. Horace Greeley, founder of the New York *Tribune*, exerted great public influence before the Civil War, especially through the nationally distributed weekly edition of his paper. William Cullen Bryant, now remembered in classrooms as a poet, was better known in his own time as the voice of the New York *Evening Post*, whose policies he shaped for 50 years.

The age of thunderers drew to a close when the great debates of the 1850s ended in the clash of arms. The events of the Civil War were a vivid illustration of what the journalist-historian James Parton wrote immediately after the war.

> The word newspaper is the exact and complete description of the thing which the journalist aims to produce. . . . An editorial essayist is a man addressing men; but the skilled and faithful journalist, recording with exactness and power the thing that has come to pass, is Providence addressing men. (Quoted in Starr, 1954:351)

By 1861, the voice of Providence could be carried at the speed of light over thousands of miles of telegraph wires; instantaneous, long-distance transmission transformed the handling of news. Newspapers could now offer near-instant gratification of the public's great news-hunger; they fed readers extra editions and multiple editions, as the wires brought in the latest from the battlefields. In the war years, the total circulation of New York's twenty-odd dailies swelled to a level near mass circulation—425,000 copies a day in a city of 1.5 million (Lee, 1937).

The day was not far off when a single paper would command that circulation. The next level in newspaper growth was achieved within two decades after the Civil War, thanks to a combination of economic, social, and technological opportunities. Curiously, these developments provided at the same time for increased standardization and increased innovation in the newspaper business. There were laments for the death of "personal journalism"—that is, the influence of the great editorialists—at the same time that a new class of entrepreneurs was putting a highly individual stamp on their enterprises. These new men had political ideas, but their first object was to seize the largest possible audience. Their methods were called the "new journalism" (not the same brand as the new journalism of the 1960s).

Its earmarks were flamboyance, activism, primitivism, and a sometimes spurious air of excitment. At the same time, its production and distribution rested on the type of standardization becoming common in other mass-production industries.

That standardization came about through a changeover in newspaper production to devices that are still in use today. The Mergenthaler Linotype, culmination of a century of effort to develop an automatic typesetting machine, instantly tripled the rate of composition over handsetting. By 1880, newspapers also had available presses that used cast forms, rather than the type itself, mounted on cylinders that printed on continuous rolls of the new, inexpensive wood-pulp paper. Fast-drying inks and contrivances for cutting, folding, and bundling papers also speeded output. Newspapers at last had dropped the fetters of eighteenth-century methods.

For the first time, newspapers could produce many pages in many editions a day. This capability had enormous implications for the business, for it opened the way not only to more lavish and varied display of news and features, but to more and bigger advertisements. Advertisers could be sold large quantities of space at modest rates. The newspaper began a shift characteristic of many later commercial media—from dependence primarily on what its readers paid to dependence on what its advertisers paid, based on the number of readers claimed. Thus readers could be offered the newspaper at a rate below cost because they became to a degree part of the sales talk to advertisers (Lee, 1937).

Despite an air of romantic chaos in the newsrooms, the urban newspaper industry began to resemble other forms of big business. Labor was increasingly divided by specialty. The crafts of newspaper publication, once embraced in a single typographical union, subdivided into typographers, stereotypers, pressmen, deliverers, and others. On the news side, reporters could still be jacks-of-all-trades, but their output was put through industrial processing by editors who brought the material into line with the paper's requirements and wrote headlines of a character suitable to the paper.

Standardization increased on the inter-newspaper level, too. The telegraphic news services, which had started before the Civil War, offered news inexpensively to hundreds of newspapers. Because the presentation of such news had to avoid giving offense to clients of many political shadings, wire-service news became carefully nonpartisan and identified with the credo of "objectivity." In practice, this meant that reporting of politics or social issues became bland and carefully restrained, while news of events—catastrophe, violence, war—could be reported with less restraint.

The increasing demand for entertaining, as well as informative, reading matter was also met by mass distribution, through the syndicates, or wholesalers of feature material. Small papers were able to receive such material on prepared printing plates, from which they sawed off what they wanted to use—hence the term "boiler plate" for cheap, standardized newspaper matter. Syndicate material was not necessarily without merit, however. The most notable pioneer in the field, S.S. McClure, roamed the world to sign up serialization rights of leading novelists.

Such was the groundwork for the new journalism of the 1880s and 1890s. Its coming merely awaited innovators who could use these advances most effectively. Three in particular appeared in quick succession, and each left an imprint on the American newspaper. It is tempting to place Joseph Pulitzer, Edward Wyllis Scripps, and William Randolph Hearst among the robber barons of that gilded age, but they do not truly belong beside Morgan, Rockefeller, or Carnegie, for they sought a somewhat different impact on society beyond being rich. Not primarily interested in personal fortunes (indeed, Hearst already had one available), they professed to seek to speak to and for the new urban masses. Human motives being largely impenetrable, historians have been unable to decide in these cases which was the uppermost motive—the desire to speak for the people or the use of the people's causes as an avenue to power.

Pulitzer was the eldest. An immigrant from Hungary, he settled in St. Louis, where he created the *Post-Dispatch* in 1878 by combining two older papers. (This is the sole newspaper property remaining in the Pulitzer family.) Five years later, at the age of 36, he bought the New York *World,* a faltering derelict. Almost at once, he began to build the paper into a showcase that seized the attention of the growing city, particularly the hundreds and thousands of Pulitzer's fellow immigrants who were swelling the poorer neighborhoods. Pulitzer gave them a paper that promised simple excitement, entertainment, and advocacy. His headlines and illustrations (no photographs until the 1890s) were vivid. The editorials called, in direct language, for justice for those oppressed by predatory interests. He sponsored promotional stunts, the most spectacular of which was bringing the Statue of Liberty from France to New York harbor. So pleased was Pulitzer that *The World* adopted the statue as its own symbol. Always the focus was on *The World*—what *The World* had done, how many people were reading *The World,* what titillation might be found in *The World* that day. Soon the paper grew from a circulation of 15,000 to half a million, and was the biggest in America to that date. However, unlike Scripps and Hearst, Pulitzer did not use his success to build an empire; nearly blind in the years from *The World's* early success until his death in 1911, Pulitzer tried only to ensure the continuation of his two newspapers. But *The World,* losing money, was sold by his heirs in 1931, and closed (Swanberg, 1967).

Twelve years after Pulitzer's arrival, there appeared in New York a newcomer who not only could outdo Pulitzer at Pulitzer's own tricks but was also an empire builder. William Randolph Hearst, a Californian backed by a mining fortune, had built the San Francisco *Examiner* up by consciously aping Pulitzer. In 1895, at the age of 32, he purchased the New York *Morning Journal,* a near failure. Hearst's success was even more spectacular than Pulitzer's; he not only gained by such innovations as color comics, but also hired away much of Pulitzer's best talent. For nearly three years, he did his best to promote a war with Spain over Cuba (whether he actually brought about the war is a matter of historical dispute) and called the resulting conflict "the *Journal's* war." The war proved an immense circulation builder, and Hearst's morning and evening *Journal* had press runs totaling 1.25 million one day in 1898.

Hearst had won his success with what was dubbed "yellow journalism"—probably in honor of the Yellow Kid, a comic-drawing character Hearst had bought away from Pulitzer. Hearst did not blink at coloring, stealing, or even faking the news; he did not hesitate to appeal to jingoism and a variety of other cheap emotions; and the tone of discourse in his papers often fell to mere abuse. Eventually, Pulitzer decided to withdraw from the kind of contest Hearst required, and Hearst ruled as the master of sensationalism for more than two decades.

Moreover, Hearst's impact was far wider than Pulitzer's. He was a pioneer in establishing a national chain of newspapers; he set up new papers in Chicago, Boston, Los Angeles, and other cities, and ultimately founded or acquired more than twenty. As the chain grew, he branched into mass-production aspects of journalism to keep its need supplied—a wire service, International News Service, notorious for a time for pilfering news; numerous feature services, many of them collected under the umbrella of the big, successful King Features Service; and a syndicated Sunday supplement, *The American Weekly.* Moreover, he also moved into magazines, news and feature film, and radio. By and large, these enterprises were highly successful, and might have endured to this day had Hearst been reasonably prudent about his enormous personal expenditures. As it was, his properties underwent a severe crisis in the Depression of the 1930s and were sharply trimmed. Hearst's day had long passed when he died in 1951 (Swanberg, 1961).

The third of these innovators never became as notable a public figure as either Pulitzer or Hearst. Edward Wyllis Scripps was a member of a Detroit newspaper family; he branched out on his own by setting up a series of afternoon penny papers, mostly in Midwestern cities. Most of these have survived as part of the Scripps-Howard newspaper group. Scripps sought mass circulation for what he believed were honorable purposes; in his hardbitten, eccentric way, he had a concept of the newspaper as the university of the unschooled, and his newspapers espoused causes that got little notice in the business-oriented newspapers. Under his successor, Roy Howard, their orientation became more conventional. Like Hearst, Scripps tended to expand—his enterprises included a wire service, the United Press (which ultimately absorbed Hearst's International News Service and became United Press International), and feature services, notably the Newspaper Enterprise Association (Knight, 1966).

Although they led the way in expanding newspaper audiences, the Pulitzer, Hearst, and Scripps patterns of popular journalism scarcely dominated the entire field. Many papers resisted the gaudy displays of yellow journalism. A few marked a new path—that of attempting serious journalism for a mass readership—a rejection of the British confinement of affairs of state to elite newspapers. One pioneer in this respect was Adolph S. Ochs of Tennessee, who appeared in New York a year after Hearst. He took still another rundown paper, the New York *Times,* spruced up its appearance, and started to build it slowly, on the basis of expanded, comprehensive news coverage. It became a paper of national and international reputation and far outlived both Pulitzer's *World* and Hearst's *Journal* (Berger, 1951).

Nonetheless, the Hearst-Pulitzer successes illustrate a key phase in the growth of mass media. The new journalism led the way in expanding the media audience—in converting nonreaders into readers—and in setting the pace for what was, nationally, a spectacular leap in newspaper circulation. Late in the 1880s, in fact, daily circulation crossed an imaginary line that can be taken as marking the start of mass-mediahood: For the first time newspapers distributed on a given day totaled more than the number of urban households in the United States. This crossing cannot be taken literally, of course, for it did not mean that every household was buying a newspaper, nor that all city newspapers had become mass newspapers. What it signifies is that production and consumption of newspapers had reached the point where, conceivably, an entire urban populace could be supplied if it so desired.

Moreover, the new journalism arrived in ways that anticipated each major new expansion of the media audience over the next 80 years. In each case, there would be simplification and popularization of materials, an appeal to immediacy or excitement, and an enhancement of the directness of the material. The line drawings and big headlines of the new journalism were more direct than the columns of tiny-lettered prose in earlier newspapers, at the price, of course, of specificity and detail in content.

The urban newspaper itself went through a second phase of such broadening four decades after the new journalism arrived. The new phase could be called "crimson journalism," to show its advance beyond the yellow brand; the more common term for it was "jazz journalism," a term preserved in the title of a book about the species (Bessie, 1938). It is probably most readily understood as the era of the arrival of the tabloid, a term that once meant a small pill and came to be applied to the half-size newspaper page, convenient for handling on crowded mass-transit facilities.

Aside from their size, the most obvious characteristic of the new tabloid newspapers of the 1920s was their exploitation of the photograph. The halftone technique for high-speed publication of photographs had been available since the 1880s, but newspapers had been slow to realize its potential. The change in attitude was signified in the original name given the tabloid founded in New York in 1919 by Joseph Patterson—the *Illustrated Daily News* (later shortened to *Daily News*). One of its imitators, Bernard Macfadden's *Evening Graphic* (nicknamed the "porno-graphic"), created a new art of sorts in halftone techniques, gluing and airbrushing together composographs (as in "composite") to produce scenes at which no photographer had been, or could be, present; one high point was a view of the deceased tenor Enrico Caruso greeting his admirers in heaven. Readers did not necessarily need to believe such fakes; they were simply part of the day's news game, and millions played.

That game was called, in the slang of the day, "ballyhoo." In a time lacking major war or domestic crisis, the press had to create its circulation-building excitement with the big buildup, the created news event, a syndrome that created a symbiotic relationship between newspapers and the young public-relations industry. Frederick Lewis Allen, chronicler of the 1920s, described the process:

> The national mind had become as never before an instrument upon which a few men could play. And these men were learning . . . to play upon it in a new way—to concentrate upon *one tune at a time.* . . . They discovered—the successful tabloids were daily teaching them—that the public became excited about one thing at a time. Newspaper owners and editors found that whenever a Dayton trial [the Scopes "monkey trial" of

1925] or a *Vestris* disaster took place, they sold more papers if they gave it all they had—their star reporters, their front-page display, and the bulk of their space. . . . The result was that when something happened which promised to appeal to the popular mind, one had it hurled at one in huge headlines, waded through page after page of syndicated discussion of it, heard about it on the radio, and was reminded of it again and again in the outpourings of publicity-seeking orators and preachers, and (unless one was a perverse individualist) enjoyed the sensation of vibrating to the same chord which thrilled a vast populace. (Allen, 1931:189–90)

The biggest news, or quasi-news, events of the 1920s thus were such easily publicized and artificially dramatic occasions as lurid murder trials and heavyweight boxing matches (Bent, 1927).

Although jazz journalism did not crash with the stock market in 1929, its excesses became less frequent and less apparent. Gradually, even the jazzier American newspapers became more solemn and mellow. Only one of the three New York tabloids of the 1920s has survived, and even the *Daily News* is far less sensational. Yet the new journalism of the nineteenth century and the jazz journalism of the twentieth left their mark on the way newspapers conduct themselves and in the way media seek audiences. Many of their premises remain enshrined in the media—the dominance of sports in the most widely consumed media, the idea that a medium can best communicate excitement by becoming overwrought and a little unbalanced itself; and the axiom that casual violence or sex ought to be the basic ingredient of news. These earmarks, it must be said, are less those of newspapers now than of media that have come later and have captured even larger audiences.

MAGAZINES: A NATIONAL MEDIUM

Although newspapers developed trade associations and unions that linked them as a national industry, they remained largely local in news coverage and audience. But a national medium began to emerge before the end of the nineteenth century. Like newspapers, magazines had had colonial ancestry—small, ephemeral publications with limited readership. The general run of magazines of the first three-quarters of the nineteenth century were somewhat larger and sometimes more permanent, but still limited in appeal. Specialized periodicals, in such fields as agriculture or business, were increasingly plentiful; general magazines, such as *The Atlantic Monthly* (founded in 1857), tended to be literary in emphasis. The closest approach to a widely popular magazine was *Harper's Weekly,* which pioneered in pictorial journalism; its large, ornate engravings, based on battlefield photographs and sketches, remain the best-known images of the Civil War.

The development of a large-circulation national magazine waited on many of the same factors that produced the urban newspapers— technological advance, a potential audience, and attractiveness to entrepreneurs. There were two additional circumstances that worked especially to prepare for magazine growth. One was federal legislation in 1879 establishing advantageous rates for mailing periodicals; there was thus assured a means of cheap, reasonably prompt national delivery.

The other was more complicated: Mass production and improvements in transport had made possible the offering of quantities of identical goods nationwide under a single, striking name; specialty home products led the way—Royal Baking Powder, Sapolio soap, Baker's Chocolate. At the same time, retail chains began to expand across the country—A & P and F.W. Woolworth, for example. Such products and businesses could advertise in individual newspapers, but they might be able to reach audiences more efficiently through a single national medium. Magazines proved to be that medium.

The first need was a new kind of magazine to command an appropriate national audience of consumers. Neither the small circulation literary publications nor the thriving dime-novel species were appropriate. The first successful candidate came along after 1883, the year Cyrus H. K. Curtis founded *Ladies' Home Journal.* In six years under the editorship of Mrs. Curtis, the magazine grew to a circulation of 440,000; under her successor Edward W. Bok, it approached a million before the turn of the century. The *Journal* was the first of a hardy genre—the women's service magazine.

The popular general magazine, directed at the entire family, sprang into existence on October 2, 1893—or such is the date fixed by the historian of magazines, Theodore Peterson. On that day, the publishing entrepreneur Frank A. Munsey announced that the magazine named for him would cost but a dime a copy, rather than a quarter. Peterson states the principle that made possible this seemingly reckless step:

> One could achieve a large circulation by selling his magazine for much less than its cost of production and could take his profits from the high volume of advertising that a large circulation attracted. (Peterson, 1964:7)

Munsey carried a step farther the shifting of the economic burden of publication from reader to advertiser. Munsey and his imitators were rewarded by reaching both new readers for magazines and advertisers who had not used magazines before. In the case of *Munsey's,* circulation grew tenfold, to 500,000 in two and a half years. Almost at the same time S. S. McClure was launching *McClure's* in the teeth of the 1893 depression; he too prospered as soon as he cut his price to ten cents.

Although the cheapness of the new magazines, combined with a wider range of articles and fiction and (for that time) plentiful illustration, led to initial successes, a second wave of expansion took place through a change to more exciting, more controversial journalism. As early as 1900, *McClure's* published a notable series of articles on the underworld; in January 1903, it offered articles exposing municipal corruption, corporate greed, and labor union abuses. This form of journalism was later called by President Theodore Roosevelt, who deplored it, "muckraking," after Bunyan's man with the muckrake who never looked up from the filth underfoot; a more appropriate contemporary term was the "literature of exposure." Other magazines joined in, as did newspapers, book publishers, official investigative commissions, and politicians. The country went through a period of turning inside out nearly every American institution, including the press. Muckraking was a stimulus to the major political impulse of reform progressivism in the period (Filler, 1939).

As part of the history of magazines, however, the muckraking era represented a brief, if celebrated, phase of transition. Exposure proved limited in possibilities and in audience appeal. Whether through reader weariness, the flagging of editors' ingenuity, or corporate censorship, muckracking in magazines declined before World War I. The leader, *McClure's,* went into a fatal decline, but the national magazine field as a whole moved swiftly from the older levels of circulation to new highs. In the muckraking days, the content of magazines had occasionally conflicted with the tone of the advertising; the magazines of the next period offered content that was much better adapted to the mass market, for it appealed to a broader audience than the somewhat intellectual muckraking, and it soothed and attracted, rather than troubled, the growing crop of national advertisers.

The magazine of the New Era—with a positive, rather than a critical, outlook—was exemplified in the supremely successful *Saturday Evening Post.* Curtis had bought the old publication in 1896 for only $1000. In the early years of the twentieth century, under the editorship of George Horace Lorimor, the *Post* had largely ignored muckraking in favor of an outlook that defended things as they were. Even before World War I, its weekly circulation approached 2 million; afterward, it added a million more. More indicative, its annual advertising revenue quadrupled between 1912 and 1922, reaching a peak of $28.3 million. By the end of the twenties, the *Post* was often enjoying million-dollar issues, with more than 200 large pages. The *Saturday Evening Post* formula under Lorimor glorified and comforted the business, middle, and white-collar classes with fiction (which included several enormously popular series), articles that emphasized a conservative point of view, and editorials that fitted the business ethic of the 1920s. The magazine was edited and printed with polish; it made a colorful, substantial, and inexpensive purchase for readers (Peterson, 1964).

This formula, imitated with modifications by other general and women's magazines, led the industry into full mass-mediahood in the 1920s. No one magazine could reach as great a share of the nation's households as, say, an urban newspaper could reach in its own city. But the two dozen magazines of a million or more circulation in existence in the mid-1920s had a combined impact that compared favorably with that of newspapers, since their circulation amounted to more than 40 million in a country of fewer than 30 million households.

So swiftly did the magazine audience expand in the 1920s that there was room for considerable variation on the basic formula. Working from copies of magazines and newspapers in the public library, De Witt and Lila Acheson Wallace pasted together a magazine of reprints that offered to select the best for readers who did not have the time to read much. The *Reader's Digest* was enormously successful—even though it imposed the entire cost of production on readers by spurning advertising, a policy that did not change until 1955. Eventually, the *Digest* became the most widely read magazine in the United States (with a circulation of 16 million), as well as the American magazine most widely read abroad (9 million more). Starting at almost the same time as the Wallaces, two young Yale graduates, Briton Hadden and Henry R. Luce, brought out a terse, smartly written weekly magazine of news; after a struggle, *Time* became the germ of a publishing empire built by Luce after Hadden's early death.

Such magazines as the *Post*, the *Digest*, and *Time* were the success stories, but in general the national magazine field has been one of great change and perishability. The years from the end of World War I into the 1950s marked the heyday of the general mass magazine. The chief index of their health, the expenditures by national advertisers in their pages, continued to rise until 1960. At that point, competition from two new sources began to cut into advertising support: (1) The most generally consumed products—foods, personal products, appliances, automobiles—drifted ever more swiftly to the even more general national medium, television; (2) Specialized magazines, whose audiences could be defined more precisely as to interests, age, affluence and geography, began to cut in on the general magazines, which were still trying to offer a little of everything to a large, undifferentiated audience.

A preliminary shock frightened the magazine industry as early as 1956, when the Crowell-Collier publishing combine closed its two general magazines, *Collier's* and *The American,* as well as its *Woman's Home Companion.* The 1960s and early 1970s were strewn with further catastrophes, most notably those of two photography-based magazines of the 1930s, *Life* and *Look.* Finally, after a decade of travail, the kingpin, the *Saturday Evening Post,* also fell, and brought down with it the whole Curtis publishing domain. In their place were newcomers offering something different. The most important new circulation leader was hitched to the new competition: *TV Guide* eventually passed *Reader's Digest* simply by printing television schedules and articles about television. Others, led by *Playboy,* thrived by offering more in sexual content than could be seen on commercial television or, for a time, in films.

Even with the death of the dinosaur general magazines, it could not be said that the national magazine had lost its audience or its place in the advertising economy. Rather, there was a shift to a new, more varied base, and possibly one that would prove more healthy. No one magazine now soaks up so great a proportion of national advertising as once did the *Saturday Evening Post* or, later, *Life.* Like newspapers, magazines went, in a rather genteel way, to lowest-common-denominator editing to enlarge their mass audience. Like newspapers, they also had a second phase of expansion resting on the use of photographs. Pictorial journalism did not represent a truly different medium, but it brought elements into periodical publishing that deserve separate consideration.

THE PHOTOGRAPHIC MEDIUM

The printed word, however simplified, presents barriers to a mass audience. The primary barrier, inability to read, was overcome in large part in many nations by publicly supported education. Even so, vivid typography and colorful writing of an event cannot alter the remoteness of prose; words may enhance, interpret, or illuminate an event, but they do not pretend to be a representation of the event itself. Mass magazines and newspapers tried early to supplement words with pictorial representations of an event. The yellow press used ever-larger line drawings, splashes of color, and, finally, gaudy four-color printing in the comic section—hardly a form of reporting itself, but for decades the appetizer for the Sunday paper.

By the turn of the century, means were widely available for better representations of reality. Photography had been advanced enough by the 1860s to record men and events of the Civil War, but publishers of that day lacked the means to reproduce the photographs. That came with the half-tone process, a system of printing photographs from a plate engraved with tiny dots. Newspapers neglected the halftone for more than fifteen years, but began cautiously to use it in the 1890s.

Pictorial journalism gained momentum with the introduction of the gravure process, a system of applying ink from recesses in the printing plate that offered good quality reproduction on a large scale. Before World War I, newspapers began to issue gravure sections that were collections of unrelated amusing or striking photographs. Sometimes a group was arranged to fill a page on one topic or event.

Just as important as the technical improvements was the growth of editorial versatility in handling photographs. There began a gradual evolution from media that used pictures as a form of decoration or illustration toward a new species that would use photographs as the primary means of communication, with only such text as was necessary. The origins of this form of exposition can be traced back to the reporter Jacob Riis, who used slides of his photographs of the New York slums in the 1880s as his primary arguments for housing reform. In the muckraking years, the photographs of Lewis Hine in pamphlets and magazines documented the evils of child labor.

The photographic story or essay finally came into its own in the 1930s. There was a series of popular photographic books, each devoted to a single major topic. Time Inc.'s *Fortune* magazine began to integrate photographs and text in new ways. Then in 1936 the same company brought out *Life* magazine, which projected pictorial journalism into mass consciousness. Although much of *Life*'s phenomenal appeal stemmed simply from striking, effective display of timely or unusual pictures, it also became the first American magazine to rest its content primarily on picture essays—the presentation of an extended piece of subject matter through photographs and minimal captions. For the first time, talented documentary photographers—such as those who had been recording rural poverty for the Farm Security Administration—had a mass outlet. The impact of *Life* was enormous; its publishers could not keep up with demand and had to limit circulation arbitrarily. Soon *Life* predictably inspired a multitude of less capably edited picture magazines, only one of which, *Look*, came to aspire to comparable quality and duration (Stott, 1973).

Despite its great initial popularity, magazine journalism based on photographs proved to be a transitory phenomenon lying between the old print media and television. By the fifties, when people could have their appetite for pictures satisfied by television, which supplied images continuously and immediately, *Life* and *Look* made the familiar change, shifting away from their initial "pop" approach toward more restraint: They used more prose, and emphasized quality color illustration of cultural, scientific, and historical subjects. Nonetheless, their advertising base, like that of the old type of general magazines, eroded; by 1972, both were gone. The still photograph continued to hold its own as a news and documentary form, but it was no longer profitable as a separate medium.

PICTURES WITH MOVEMENT

Just as the mass-reproduced photograph gave a more realistic impression than the line drawing, so moving photographs seemed more real than stills. Out of the same period of innovation that helped bring mass newspapers and magazines into being came the early motion pictures. Edison in the United States and Lumière in France experimented in the 1890s with showing brief slices of reality—workers leaving a factory, strollers in a park, an athlete in a tiny studio. By the turn of the century, brief motion picture films of news events were on public display, and represented a level of pictorial journalism ahead of what could be seen in the printed media at the time. News film of the Spanish-American War in 1898, however, was consistent with the tenets of yellow journalism—the embarkation of troops (to ringing cheers from the audience), an episode showing a Spanish flag being torn down and the Stars and Stripes raised, a battle of Santiago faked with models. The enthusiastic reception of such crudities hinted at the enormous power of film (Barnouw, 1974).

In a decade or so, film was on its way to becoming a mass medium of a kind distinctly different from printed publications. Unlike periodicals, it was not distributed to individual consumers; its mass reproducibility was used instead for distribution of prints at a wholesale level. Because, once the peep-show phase was past, people saw film in a theater setting, it was thought to be more a branch of the theater arts than a mass medium. In fact, it had characteristics of both.

Film maintained its closest relationship with the mass media through its journalistic aspect, the newsreel, a regularly issued pot-pourri of news and feature film. The French concern, Pathé, showed the first regularly scheduled newsreel in the United States in 1911; it was soon joined by American companies—Vitagraph, Selig-Hearst, Fox. As it continued, the newsreel took on highly stereotyped forms, greatly influenced by the newspaper people among its first organiz-ers. The format is described by Raymond Fielding, a recent historian of the genre, as "the fragmented succession of unrelated 'stories,' the titles composed in the manner of front-page headlines, and the prac-tice of beginning each issue with the major news event of the day, followed by successively less important subject matter" (Fielding, 1972:135).

By the mid-1920s, the silent newsreel was reaching most of the general film audience, which was estimated at 40 million persons a week attending 18,000 theaters. Such popularity was tribute to the impact of film. Despite a history spotted with fakes and fictionaliz-ing, news film maintained its credibility because people literally be-lieved their eyes.

For such a primitive form, the newsreel had a long life. It was of course enhanced by sound, starting with coverage of Lindbergh in 1927. The 1930s brought an influential variation on the format in the *March of Time,* issued by Time Inc., which devoted an entire film to a single current subject. In the same decade, there came into being urban theaters devoted primarily to showing newsreels. Even when television doomed movie-theater news, the Hearst newsreel held on until 1967, having lasted, remarkably, more than fifty years.

SOUNDS IN THE AIR

While photography and film were making new appeals to sight, the immediacy of mass sound reproduction and distribution was also becoming possible. Communication by wire preceded radio, and early attempts at mass sound distribution were made by telephone; however, the telephone did not press beyond a few such experi-ments as long-distance transmission of a concert. Thereafter tele-phone facilities were used primarily for private communication, al-though telephone lines were eventually used to distribute broadcast signals at the wholesale, rather than the consumer, level.

The 1890s, which saw the early motion-picture experiments, also witnessed the first attempts to send wireless signals and voice trans-mission. In addition, the phonograph, which would serve as the first vehicle of mass sound distribution and would later become a valued adjunct to broadcasting, appeared in primitive form. The two inventions were combined for the first time on Christmas Eve, 1906, when Reginald Aubrey Fessenden, a scientist at the Westinghouse Company in Pittsburgh, broadcast a record of a woman singing as part of an experimental program.

As early as 1909, ancestors of what later became radio stations were sending out programs, but not until the end of World War I did stations with regular broadcasting schedules appear in any number. For those members of the public who bought or built primitive crystal receiving sets, an experience of striking immediacy and novelty was in store. In 1920, some of them heard the national election returns over KDKA, Pittsburgh, hours before the morning newspapers were printed. The next year, they could hear one of the great sports orgies of the decade, the Dempsey-Carpentier fight. By the end of 1922, 690 stations had gone on the air. Equally important, the foundation had been laid for the commercial basis of American broadcasting. On August 28, 1922, a New York station owned by the American Telephone and Telegraph Company offered broadcasting's first paid commercial, for a housing development in Queens, New York City.

Radio moved rapidly toward greater variety in programming and heavier commercialization. Before the 1920s were gone, programs had become known by the names of their sponsors: the Eveready Hour (the first program series), the Cliquot Club Eskimos, the Ipana Troubadors. In 1928 WMAQ, Chicago, offered a program that became radio's first "classic"—*Amos 'n' Andy,* a comedy program by two whites playing stereotypical black characters. Immediately popular (among whites), the program was syndicated to other stations and won an audience estimated at 40 million, an immense jump toward giving radio the status of a universal medium.

Behind the exuberance and outward disorder of early radio was taking place the organization of a new media industry, devoted not only to broadcasting itself but to supplying the equipment necessary for home reception. The national radio industry first took shape around a curious creation called the Radio Corporation of America, which was formed by three major companies seeking to dominate international radio communication and the sales of receivers. RCA acquired the Marconi radio interests in America, and, with them, David Sarnoff, a Russian immigrant who had already foreseen the great potential of broadcasting. Young Sarnoff was given command of RCA in the mid-1920s and guided the company to leadership, not only in radio, but in production of electronic goods and later in television.

But Sarnoff's first creation was network radio, with the founding of the National Broadcasting Company in 1926. There had been hookups of stations before, to permit all to broadcast the same program, at first for such special events as the Democratic National Convention of 1924, and later for entertainment of a more customary kind. NBC pioneered in offering programs on a continuing basis to affiliated stations, which cooperated not only for the sake of getting the programs but for a share of the fees paid by advertisers to the network. The attractiveness of this arrangement led to network dominance in broadcast programming that has now extended over 50 years. Sarnoff, in fact, had intended that this dominance would be exerted by NBC alone. He brushed off a group of outsiders who sought a role in NBC programming, and thus inspired the founding of NBC's chief rival, the Columbia Broadcasting System, under William S. Paley.

Another force creating order in broadcasting was the government. Earlier media had been touched only lightly by government, as a rule; newspapers, magazines, and film were checked somewhat by state laws on libel and obscenity, and films were starting to attract censorship locally, but they had no federal code governing their existence. Radio came from a different background: Because of its importance in military, naval, and international communication, it had been all but nationalized by the federal government in World War I. Even afterward, the government maintained a semiproprietary interest, to the extent of having for a time a seat on the RCA board.

Thus it was not surprising when the Department of Commerce, under Secretary Herbert Hoover, stepped in to regulate radio frequencies. A permanent setting for regulation came into being with the Federal Radio Act of 1927, and its amended version in 1934 created the present Federal Communications Commission, which must license every outlet that goes on the air, on the theoretical contention that the commission oversees air waves that belong to the public. In practice, this has become a convenient fiction that has permitted government to keep broadcasting from operating with the kind of freedom enjoyed by print media, for invariably the FCC reviews not only engineering criteria but alleged fitness of owners. One measure of its effect is that radio, and broadcasting in general, has had almost no overt political orientation, in contrast to the printed press (Barnouw, 1966).

With the 1930s, radio was ready to emerge as a new mass medium, joining newspapers, magazines, and film in commanding a large audience. By the mid-1930s, the 20 million-plus radio sets in operation began to approach the number of nonfarm households in the country. With this growing audience available, advertisers flocked in, and radio became, economically speaking, primarily a channel of advertising. Network radio began to compete seriously with magazines for national brand ads.

The 1930s and 1940s were radio's great era. A people shaken by the worst depression of the industrial age seemed ready to turn to newer, more direct media for assurance; newspapers were under attack as unreliable and backward-looking. Films grew, but radio grew even more emphatically in the face of hard times. Politicians were among the first to recognize the power of radio to reach people in their homes and to persuade them, as if in one-to-one conversation; such orators as the Rev. Charles E. Coughlin and Senator Huey Long won national followings via the microphone. But the master of the medium was President Franklin D. Roosevelt, whose quiet, matter-of-fact Fireside Chats on the air were sources of reassurance and information for the public.

Radio also began to expand its own information functions. Stations tried to present news better than they had in the 1920s, when the commonest form of reporting was pilferage from the local newspapers. Publishers, seeing a possible new form of competition, tried to block radio's access to news agencies, but succeeded instead in freeing radio from its dependence on newspapers. Gradually the networks developed news organizations of their own, beginning the evolution from one-man-band operations into full worldwide staffs of correspondents. Soon radio reporters and commentators became far better known than their print counterparts, and it was radio that carried the main burden of arousing the country as international crisis deepened in the late 1930s, and in the war period itself.

After World War II, radio was able to reassert briefly its dominance as a mass entertainment medium. But its time was drawing to a close. Through the war, glowing color advertisements had promised to expectant consumers the wonders of the new medium that combined the sound of radio with the motion picture. Radio, as it had grown in the 1930s and 1940s, would suddenly be outstripped by its cousin, television (Barnouw, 1968).

TELEVISION: THE LAST MASS MEDIUM?

Almost from the time that wireless transmission became possible, there existed the possibility that technology could develop the means of sending not only sounds but images. By 1919, Vladimir Zworykin, working for RCA, obtained permission from his employer to push ahead with the experiments that led to modern television. Yet the first commercially useful picture transmissions took place not by wireless but by wire, when news services began to transmit still photographs via a rather slow scanning apparatus. This technique came into general use in newspapers in 1935, with the creation of Associated Press Wirephoto. Later, wireless transmission of news photos also was available.

The possibilities of television—or some of them at least—had long been foreseen. Cartoons in the 1920s prophesied the broadcasting of sports events and entertainment. Demonstration broadcasts started in the 1930s, and the war merely deferred what had come to seem inevitable—that television was destined to become the dominant mass medium.

Halting and primitive though early television seems in retrospect, in actuality the medium found its format and its national audience with unprecedented speed. At the end of World War II, in 1945, there were a half dozen experimental stations and a few thousand sets in operation. In a decade, more than 400 stations went on the air, all but filling the available channels in metropolitan areas. Moreover, by 1955 four-fifths of the households in urbanized areas had television sets, and that figure soon rose beyond 90 percent. By 1955, more than 30 million sets had been sold, and they were moving out of the stores at a rate of 7 million a year.

Just as quickly, television made its impression on advertisers. In 1950, only one advertising dollar of every thirty went to television; seven years later the proportion was one dollar out of eight. The chief sufferer was radio—especially network radio, which all but vanished as a source of evening programming.

Truly, television was radio's heir, and not only in the obvious form of advertising dollars. The entertainment format of television—programs appearing weekly at a given time, comedy or drama series offering endless activities of fixed characters, daily soap operas—is largely a transplant from radio. Similarly, television news remained tied to the roundup format originated in radio. There has been some evolution in a quarter century that emphasizes the particular qualities of television: Television shows Hollywood's recycled films rather than offering the pale dramatized versions that once were heard on radio. Moreover, television has been able to move toward longer programs, and its coverage of special events—such as congressional hearings—has a fascination for audiences never exercised by radio.

More important, much of television has remained under the same corporate control as radio. National television, rather than opening the way to a host of new entrepreneurs, as did newspapers, magazines, and radio in their pioneer days, remained studded with such familiar entities as NBC, CBS, and the American Broadcasting Company, broken off from NBC in 1943 in a federal antitrust ruling. These companies have remained owners of channels in the largest cities, and have determined as well the content and type of the most widely seen programs, not only over their own facilities but through resale to stations in the United States and abroad.)

Against the possible drawbacks of such concentrated control can be placed the advantages of strength—particularly the ability of the networks to marshal overwhelming resources to cover news events of national importance. Indeed, since the 1950s Americans can be said to have experienced their history through television: the ventures into space that culminated in broadcasts from the moon, the assassinations of a president, his brother, and a black leader; the Vietnam war, seen nightly for a decade; politics as viewed in the national conventions or in such episodes as the Kefauver hearings of 1951 and the Watergate hearings of 1973 and 1974. In this aspect of its work, television has been unrivaled and the public has come increasingly to depend on it for this service (Barnouw, 1970).

THE MULTIMEDIA ERA

In its swift acceptance and its continuing popularity, television represents a culmination of the Graphic Revolution that started with the innovations of Hearst, Pulitzer, and Scripps. Each stage of media evolution has been marked, roughly speaking, by these characteristics:

1. The development of a new technique or combination of techniques for presenting material more directly, more simply, more cheaply.

2. A popularization of material—from prose to headline, to spoken word, to photograph, to moving picture, to spoken word combined with moving picture. Each successively demanded a bit less of the consumer and attracted a broader audience.

3. An expanding economic base that provided for the necessary expenditure, whether that expenditure was made by advertisers, consumer purchases, or consumer investment in such equipment as broadcast receivers.

4. What might be called an increasing privatization of consumption—the dramatically enlarged capacity of the individual household to acquire mass-media products without joining a crowd to do so.

5. A layering of one medium atop its predecessors, sometimes altering the character of the older media but never extinguishing them entirely.

At the moment, there appears to be no new mass medium on the horizon, and it is difficult to imagine what that medium might be. Cable television, certainly an innovation, is hardly new in the character of communication it offers the consumer, but is rather a variant on over-the-air television. Cable, returning broadcasting in part to wire transmission, has the potential of offering higher quality and greater variety than broadcast television. But thus far cable television systems have remained small and, many of them, unprofitable. By comparison with "free" over-the-air broadcasting, consumers find the cable fees high.

Unless cable finds new means for rapid expansion, or a new medium appears, the expansion phase of the Age of Mass Media may be near its end. Newspapers, magazines, radio, and television may all be approaching their limits in acquiring new audiences; their statistics have attained remarkable stability in recent years. Now the mass media face an era in which they are no longer a novelty, and may meet increasing resistance, or at least inertia, in their audiences. Survival in this new era may prove as great a challenge as was pioneering in the old.

HOW THE ECONOMY ABSORBED THE MEDIA

The arrival of new media over the last hundred years and their swift acceptance by the American public have meant a willingness to pay. Even when newspapers and magazines are sold cheap and radio and television are ostensibly free, there must nevertheless be a sizable investment to make these great engines run. The investment rises all the more steeply when—as in fact happened—each new medium tends to become a supplement rather than a successor to its forerunners. A nation that paid only for newspapers, magazines, and books a century ago has come to pay not only for greater quantities of printed matter but for film, radio and television stations and receivers, and a bewildering variety of sound-reproducing equipment.

In contrast with societies where media enterprises are governmental, mass media in the United States have derived their support largely from private expenditure. There has been a degree of government help (such as favorable postal rates) or even government investment (as in public television). But business and the consuming public have between them largely determined how much would be spent on media. Not surprisingly, this investment has increased mightily over the years: From a low point in the Great Depression, 1933, the total spent by consumers and advertisers on the major forms of mass media doubled by 1943, doubled again by 1949, and doubled yet again by 1959. In the four decades following 1929, the total investment rose from $6.16 billion a year to $34.77 billion.

Yet by themselves these figures mean little, for nearly every type of goods or service in the American economy expanded in the same period. Where did the larger expenditure on the media come from? Did Americans stop buying other things to buy their magazines and radio sets? Were Americans putting an ever-larger share of their resources into the media?

The best indications are, surprisingly, that there was no such striking increase in that share. When total expenditures for all media are viewed as a share of the gross national product—that is, the total estimated output of the entire economy—they show great stability over the years. Between the end of World War II and 1970, the percentage of the gross national product devoted to media expenditures never fell below 3.92 percent and never rose beyond 4.38 percent. The overall trend, in fact, has been a gentle decline in the percentage.

Charles E. Scripps (a descendant of E.W.) has suggested from such phenomena an hypothesis of constancy, which he has stated as follows:

> in spite of the increasing complexity of mass communications, with the advent of new media, the pattern of economic support has been relatively constant, and more closely related to the general economy than to the various changes and trends taking place in the mass media field itself. . . . The consistency evident in the pattern of economic support for the mass media . . . suggests that mass communications have become a staple of consumption in our society much like food, clothing and shelter. (quoted in McCombs, 1972b:5)

This hypothesis suggests that new media have come into existence in two ways: first, that the economy has expanded enough to make room for them; second, that there has been unnoted displacement of older media. It is possible to think of spending for the media as a pie of ever-growing size; older media may get slices that represent a smaller proportion of the whole, but at the same time the pie gets big enough to give them a helping as large as before. In the years since broadcast reception started to come into the home, there has been indeed a considerable reslicing of the pie, especially in the way that consumers have spent their money.

The picture drawn by leading investigators of the constancy hypothesis is roughly as follows: Since 1929, consumer spending for printed materials has been stable (when considered as a proportion of total consumer spending for the media); there has been a mild long-term trend toward spending a greater share for books, as opposed to newspapers and magazines. But the situation in the sight-and-sound media has been much more fluid: Motion picture admissions, which constituted a little over a quarter of consumer expenditures at the end of the 1920s, rose to a peak of more than 40 percent in the years of World War II and then began a drop that continued for 20 years, until theaters were receiving only about six percent of the total. At the same time, expenditures for radio and television receivers and phonograph records and equipment rose from less than one dollar in four to bearly half of all consumer spending for the media. The obvious conclusion is that people stopped going to the movies and stayed home to watch television—not a profound conclusion, but one that suggests that television was a greater threat to the allied medium of film than to the contrasting print media.

Where does this long-term trend lead us? Many critics see an end to the first age of mass media. For one thing, one notes, "homes are now a clutter of TV and radio sets, stereos, newspapers, magazines, and other artifacts of mass communication" (McCombs, 1972b). He suggests that the ability of individual households to consume more (or to give more time to) these artifacts is near its limit, and that consumer spending for the media may be diverted into other recreational channels.

Moreover, the kind of home media reception made technically possible by cable, computers, and other new "information machines" may not prove possible economically. The so-called "wired-nation" concept—the hookup of cable systems to numbers of homes comparable to those reached by older media systems—would be enormously costly, far beyond the scale of spending the economy has permitted for mass media. Only enormous economic growth, or the utter collapse of older media, or the production of new services of great importance to consumers and advertisers could bring about the development of such a system. The obstacles to change thus are substantial.

CONCENTRATIONS OF POWER

Besides the shifting of spending from one medium to another, other long-term economic processes have affected the media. Possibly the most important is what could be called the movement from fragmentation to integration—the tendency of larger economic units to absorb smaller ones, the tendency of similar economic units to join forces, the tendency of a producer to seek control over the entire production process, and the tendency, more recently, of economic units to seek stability through diversity. It is not really possible to say that the mass media have demonstrated these tendencies any more than other parts of the economy, but so fragmented were media enterprises at the start that the movement has been striking.

Four types of concentration have been apparent in the media:

1. Cross-control: the ownership of more than one type of medium in a given locality—for example, the ownership of a radio station by a local newspaper publisher.

2. Multiple control: the ownership of more than one unit of a medium—for example, ownership of a group of newspapers in various localities.

3. Conglomerate control: the ownership of media by companies with a variety of other interests—for example, ownership of a television station by an insurance company. The process also works in the other direction: Companies starting with media interests can become conglomerates by branching into other fields.

4. Oligopolic control: for want of a better term, this one (meaning control by a few) is offered to describe domination by a handful of larger units of a phase of media operations—for example, the control of television entertainment programming by the major networks (Johnson and Hoak, 1970).

Thus, the types. How important are they in describing the current structure of mass media in the United States?

Cross-control. This phenomenon exists to a degree in most of the larger cities and many smaller ones. A Federal Communications Commission survey found that in 72 communities the only local newspaper also owned the only broadcasting station; in roughly 180 more places daily newspapers controlled a station, but not the only one. In addition, broadcasters who own television stations customarily have radio outlets in the same market.

Multiple control. The trend toward creating chains has been most striking among newspapers; in broadcasting, it has been controlled somewhat by the FCC. Before World War I, more than 95 percent of the daily newspapers were unaffiliated with groups, but by 1971 more than half were under chain ownership. In the same period, the number of groups had increased from 13 to 155, while the total number of newspapers had decreased. Among television stations, only one in five of commercial VHF (channels 2–13) outlets were singly, independently owned as of 1970; the rest were either affiliated with groups of stations or owned by newspapers. In radio, multiple owners controlled about 75 percent of the AM and FM stations in the nation's 50 largest cities. Similar arrangements are visible as well in cable television systems.

Conglomerate control. This form of concentration is harder to measure than others, but simple observation confirms that this type of organization is increasingly characteristic of all the larger units in the mass media. Hardly any major company now relies on any single form of communication enterprise. The so-called television networks—CBS, NBC (through its parent, RCA), and ABC—are actually conglomerates with increasingly diverse interests. Some of these interests stem from their broadcasting expertise, such as program syndication, station ownership, and electronic manufacturing and research. But they have moved into such other fields as book and magazine publishing, sponsorship of vocational schools, toymaking, and housing development. For a time, one network owned the New York Yankees baseball team.

Companies that started out printing magazines or newspapers have also diversified. A common step has been for publishers to obtain a share of control of paper companies, thus assuring themselves of a supply of their basic raw material. But they also have steadily broadened the range of products. Time Inc., which started with a single magazine, branched into others, and then into book publishing and broadcasting. The New York Times Company still puts out a newspaper, but it also publishes other dailies, operates magazines and a book company, and offers such secondary media services as microfilming.

Oligopolic control. This phenomenon is perhaps rarer than the others in the media. It is certain, in any case, that the situation among the media is far different from that in, say, the automobile industry, where for years, three or four companies controlled most of the American market. Instead, it could be said that the media landscape reveals patches of oligopoly—in the aforesaid networks; in the dominance of wire news by The Associated Press and United Press International (although they have been challenged in recent years by services offered by individual newspapers); and in the long-lasting concentration of more than half of all national magazine advertising among a few mass-circulation publications at the top.

Put simply, all this means that in an increasingly complicated economy, the economic organization of the mass media has followed that of other enterprises in becoming larger and more complex. Thus, the dangers of concentration of control resemble those in any monopoly of consumer staples—the possibility of price or quality manipulation, the limitation of consumer choice. These possibilities are most strikingly illustrated in the country's major cities, where the former multiplicity of newspapers has been succeeded by a narrower and narrower selection, limited in most by the mid-1970s to not more than one morning and one evening newspaper, often under the same ownership.

There is a deeply rooted American suspicion of monopoly (a good deal of it justified), memorialized in a sequence of antitrust legislation dating from the 1880s. The suspicion may be especially sharp in the case of monopolies of information, for they go against the grain of the diversity implied in Jefferson's axiom that "error of opinion may be tolerated where reason is left free to combat it." Among a majority of press critics, there is an assumption that the old days of competition among newspapers produced benefits for the public that the present monopolies fail to provide. Moreover, they evidence the not unreasonable fear that single, unchallenged sources of information have the power to mislead, or even to lie.

Yet in practice a condition of pure monopoly—in either economics or information—is almost never attained by a medium. Other media, as well as media with regional or national scope, tend to move into any local information vacuum. Moreover, even if, say, a newspaper is a quasi-monopoly in its domination of local news and advertising, public pressure can be a corrective. Monopoly publishers tend to be forced into common-carrier roles. That term may remind one of a bus or train; the analogy is not too remote. A bus or train is supposed to carry all passengers who pay and maintain reasonable decorum; in media terms a common carrier is a passive vessel of communication that accepts all material offered. Telephone and tele-graph are the classic common carriers of communication. Newspa-pers and broadcasting stations taking on common-carrier functions tend to use most information coming in from all segments and fac-tions of the community without imposing censorship or a political point of view. V. O. Key, the late political scientist, described this function pungently:

> The monopolization of local circulation areas makes it prudent to turn out a product whose content antagonizes few readers. Some monopolistic owners develop common-carrier conceptions of their role, justified in terms both of fairness and of the strategy of maintenance of monopoly . . . . (Key, 1961:392)

Clearly, news media operated on a common-carrier principle offer both benefits and drawbacks for their publics: What is lost in coher-ence and intelligence may be made up in balance and ease of access.

On the still more positive side, concentration can be said to have made possible many information benefits that might otherwise not have been offered to the public. The size of the larger media corpo-rations, such as the big newspapers, the wire services, the networks, and news magazines, has meant the organization of resources and the collection and dissemination of news on a scale never before attained. Moreover, enlargement through diversification has brought into the traditionally perilous media field a stability that permits bet-ter-planned use of talent and money. Finally, the media have been able to supersede to a degree an attitude of defensive backwardness toward social change that may have been a reflection of their eco-nomic insecurity.

Whatever the merits of concentration, there is little sign that mea-sures now contemplated will halt or deflect it. Federal regulation has had a mild impact on broadcast properties; the only federal legisla-tion of recent years dealing with newspapers in fact encouraged con-centration, rather than resisting it. Although media monopoly has been the subject of increasingly intense debate in recent years, some of concentration's most determined opponents have already conced-ed that many larger units are beyond the powers of the American system to break up or even to regulate effectively.

The mass media of the United States have grown with the country's advancing technology, long-term affluence, and increasing urbanism. The first true mass medium, capable of reaching all seg-ments of a populace, was the urban daily newspaper, spawned late in the nineteenth century by such innovators as Hearst, Pulitzer, and

Scripps. Other variations and forms of mass media developed rapidly thereafter—the popular magazine, brought into being at the turn of the century by Curtis, Munsey, McClure, and others; pictorial journalism, which flourished in the tabloid journalism of the 1920s and the magazines of the 1930s; film, which captured a mass theater audience by the 1920s; radio, which prospered in the 1930s and 1940s; and finally, television, the most widely used mass medium of the past two decades.

With their growth, the various forms of the mass media have taken on increasingly the forms of big business—most recently, in the creation of broad-based communications conglomerates—and the problems of big business such as the danger of monopoly. Although new variants of older forms, such as cable television, have become available, no distinctly new medium is now on the horizon. Nor does it appear that further media development will be rapid, for both the expenditure of consumer time and the rate of spending permitted by the economy have approached their limits. Thus, the media may be approaching an age of maturity following a period of development that lasted roughly a century.

The American media are a product of our history. Media systems in other countries have, of course, developed differently, responding to different conditions and needs. The following chapter will survey briefly some of these other types of systems and compare them with ours.

MASS MEDIA: A CHRONOLOGY

1883   Joseph Pulitzer purchased the New York *World*.
        First major newspaper syndicate founded by Irving Bacheller.
1886   Mergenthaler Linotype available to newspapers—also high-speed presses, wood-pulp paper.
1889   American Newspaper Publishers Association, first national trade association in field, founded.
1893   Frank Munsey and S.S. McClure introduced the 10-cent popular magazine.
1894   First extensive use of halftone process for printing news photographs.
1895   William Randolph Hearst bought the New York *Morning Journal*.

1900 The Associated Press (AP) organized in its modern form to supply wire news to member newspapers.

1907 E.W. Scripps founded United Press (UP) to compete with AP.

1908 First university school of journalism founded at Missouri.

1909 Peak number of daily newspapers in the United States—2600.

1910 Hearst founded International News Service (INS) as rival to AP and UP.

1914 Audit Bureau of Circulation founded to monitor newspaper circulation claims on behalf of advertisers.

1919 Radio Corporation of America founded by General Electric, Westinghouse, and American Telephone and Telegraph.

Joseph Medill Patterson started the New York *Daily News,* which became the country's largest newspaper.

1922 First radio commercial broadcast on WEAF, New York.

Reader's Digest founded by De Witt and Lila Wallace.

American Society of Newspaper Editors, first national professional newspaper group, founded.

1923 *Time,* first major news magazine, founded by Briton Hadden and Henry R. Luce.

1924 First radio transmission of photographs.

1926 National Broadcasting Company organized by David Sarnoff.

1927 Columbia Broadcasting System organized under William S. Paley.

Federal Radio Act placed broadcasters under regulation.

1928 *Amos 'n' Andy* attracted mass audience to radio.

1933 Syndication of *The Lone Ranger* led to founding of third network, Mutual Broadcasting System.

American Newspaper Guild, reporter-editor union, founded.

1934 Communications Act established the Federal Communications Commission (FCC).

1936 *Life,* popular photo magazine, founded by Luce.

1939 Pocket Books began mass marketing of paperbacks.

RCA started regular television broadcasting with programs from the New York World's Fair.

1940 Founding of *Newsday,* most successful of new suburban papers.

1941 FCC authorized commercial FM broadcasting.

1943 American Broadcasting Company formed when NBC sold its Blue Network by government order.

1945   Supreme Court ruled that AP's membership practices were in restraint of trade; all media entitled to purchase AP service.

1950   First community-antenna television system, Lansford, Pa.

1951   First coast-to-coast television hookup, for Japanese peace conference, San Francisco.

1956   Three Crowell-Collier magazines cease publication.

1957   National Educational Television established—start of publicly supported TV.

1958   Merger of UP and INS created United Press International.

1966   Closing of *World Journal Tribune* brought to end an era of New York City newspaper mergers.

1969   *Saturday Evening Post* ceased publication; Curtis Publishing Company dismantled and removed from family control.

1970   Newspaper Preservation Act exempted certain newspaper combinations from antitrust enforcement.

1971   *Look* magazine ceased publication.

1972   *Life* magazine ceased publication.

FURTHER READING

Historical treatment of the mass media as an entity, as opposed to consideration of individual media forms, is not extensive. The most widely used textbook in the field is Edwin Emery, *The Press and America* (3d ed., Prentice-Hall; 1972), but it concentrates on journalism rather than other media developments. John Tebbel, *The Media in America* (Crowell, 1974), synthesizes early media history, but devotes only a fifth of its space to the twentieth century. Among surveys of individual media, Frank Luther Mott's *American Journalism* (3d ed., Macmillan; 1962), remains the most valuable source for the history of newspapers; Alfred McClung Lee's *The Daily Newspaper in America* (Macmillan, 1937) still stands alone as a comprehensive account of the newspaper *system* of communication. Also of lasting value is Theodore Peterson's *Magazines in the Twentieth Century* (2d ed., University of Illinois Press; 1964), which can be used in conjunction with Mott's older *History of American Magazines* (5 vols.; various publishers, 1930–1968). Erik Barnouw's encyclopedic *History of Broadcasting in the United States,* issued in three separately titled volumes (Oxford University Press, 1966–1970) has been published in a one-volume condensation, *Tube of Plenty* (Oxford University Press, 1975).

Outstanding works devoted to particular aspects of media history include Daniel Boorstin's provocative *The Image* (Atheneum, 1962); William Stott's *Documentary Expression and Thirties America* (Oxford University Press, 1973), which considers a critical period in media development; Dan Lacy's *Freedom and Communications* (2d ed., University of Illinois Press, 1965), which discusses the social wellsprings of media growth; and Fritz Machlup, *The Production and Distribution of Knowledge in the United States* (Princeton University Press, 1962), which considers the media in a larger economic system.

Ronald T. Farrar and John D. Stevens, eds., *Mass Media and the National Experience* (Harper & Row, 1971) is a pioneering effort in collecting essays of media historians; among these, most notable is Willam E. Ames and Dwight L. Teeter, "Politics, Economics, and the Mass Media" (pp. 38–63). New work in media history is presented and reviewed in the quarterly *Journalism History,* founded in 1974 and published at California State University, Northridge, California.

CHAPTER TWO
Contrasting Media Systems

One of the ways of learning about our own mass-media system is to study it in the comparative, or international, perspective. Not only can we find out how it resembles or differs from other systems, but we can gain insight into how various types of mass-media systems function in different societies, and thus perhaps arrive at judgments on how well our system serves us. Moreover, by examining the performance and social setting of the world's media systems, we can perhaps learn better to communicate with other peoples.

Such study is not necessarily simple. Any American who tries to get a general picture of the world's media systems is likely to encounter difficulties on three counts:

First, we know far more about our own media than we do about foreign media. As a result, we tend to ask misdirected questions about media performance in a country—for instance, what is the role or future of public television in Japan—when we still do not have such basic facts as whether Japan even has a counterpart to our PTV.

Second, many of our concepts of mass communication do not always fit cases abroad. Take a simple and common assumption such as the following:

> The important component of any definition of mass communications is modern technology. To have *mass* communication, a message must be amplified or reproduced many thousands of times. This requires printing presses, newsprint, radio and television transmitters and receivers, and cinema projectors and theaters. (Hachten, 1971: xv)

To apply this concept to China or the Soviet Union—indeed a majority of the countries in the world—is to ignore the nature of their media systems. For instance, China's "mass communication system" does not depend heavily on modern technology; it utilizes, shrewdly and systematically, such simple channels as blackboards, wall newspapers, hand-written *tatzepao* or "big-character posters," street corner shows, "revolutionary story-tellers," *hsueh hsi* or study

43

meetings, small group discussions, and plain person-to-person conversation. In the Soviet Union,

> the newspapers are supplemented by a network of hundreds of thousands of mimeographed and "wall newspapers," put out in a single handwritten or typed copy on the bulletin boards of factories, farms, and housing developments. . . . It is characteristic of Soviet policy that these wall newspapers are not haphazard or uncontrolled phenomena, but are rather considered as integral parts of the total press apparatus, with regular part-time editors and "correspondents," all closely supervised by the local Party organizations. (Inkeles, 1968:278)

Another Soviet example:

Harrison E. Salisbury of the *New York Times* was walking down a narrow Moscow street one day when he spotted a big crowd watching a large portrait of Stalin in front of an art store. Salisbury couldn't understand all the fuss, because nothing was more common in those days than portraits of Stalin. Finally, a Russian said to him: "Look at Stalin's hair. It's gray!" Salisbury was still puzzled, because he knew Stalin's hair had been gray for some years. "But don't you see?" the Russian explained, "This is the first time his hair has been shown gray in an official portrait. It has a meaning. It means that Stalin is growing old. It is the first step to prepare us for a change . . ." (Salisbury, 1965:25–26).

It is of course hard for Americans, who rarely pay much attention to official portraits of their presidents in post offices and federal buildings, to believe that Russian citizens would rush to see a portrait of Stalin in an art store to get an important political message. Nevertheless, this is a form of political communication in the Soviet Union.

Third, and this is perhaps hard to believe, we do not know nearly as much about our national communication system and our national communication policy as we should. To be sure, research on communication policy has become a national concern, but this is a rather recent development. "Ten years ago," a leading communication scholar reported in 1974, "few communications practitioners thought in terms of any overall communications policy, and few communications researchers would have recognized policy research as an established category" (Pool, 1974:33). Until very recently American students of communication were concerned mainly with different parts or aspects of mass communication—communicators, channels, content, audience, effects, control—rather than with the whole system. The temptation is to compare the situation with the old parable of blind men and the elephant. But American students of communications are not really so "blind"; they see the elephant, but they tend to concentrate on one function or another, rather than on all the uses of the whole animal. Now it is no longer even enough to study the elephant, but its *gestalt* and the environment as well. And we should also try to get to know some other kinds of elephants in other lands.

HOW DO WE STUDY OTHER MEDIA SYSTEMS?

Let us start by agreeing that every country has the media system it has earned. The structure of a system is dictated by politics and economics and, to a certain extent, shaped by geographical, linguistic, and cultural forces. There are as many media systems as there are countries. Our first task therefore is to find a way to classify them.

There is no shortage of media system typologies. They range from the simplistic up. Most of them are based on: (1) political systems, ideologies, or styles (democratic vs. authoritarian; Western vs. Soviet; capitalistic vs. communist; closed vs. open societies) and (2) types and degrees of control of media (state-operated, public corporation, public interest partnership, or private enterprise). Other elements distinguishing media systems include modernization (traditional, transitional, and modern); development (developed and developing or underdeveloped or LDC—less developed countries); finance (public or private, advertising practices, license fees, taxes, government subsidies); geography (European, American, Canadian, Asian, African, Soviet Union, Latin American); types of programming (educational, cultural, commercial, political, entertainment); and types of audience (elite vs. mass; high-brow, middle-brow, low-brow).

One of the best known media system typologies is the one developed by Siebert, Peterson, and Schramm (1963). The typology consists of four major theories: (1) authoritarian, (2) libertarian, (3) soviet-communist, and (4) social responsibility. Their work is what one may call the intellectual history of mass communication. There are, first, two lines of development—authoritarian and libertarian—and within each of these there is an older and a new form. Authoritarianism took a spectacular new form in the soviet-communist concept; from libertarianism comes the social responsibility theory.

Modern communication, as they see it, was born into an authoritarian society. Western Europe was under authoritarian governments when printing came into existence, and there was already a tradition of authoritarian thought. These governments kept the new medium under strict control. From political and social revolutions during the seventeenth and eighteenth centuries·emerged the libertarian theory, built on the philosophy of the Enlightenment belief in the innate rights of mankind and in the ability of the people, given a fair chance, to rationally distinguish truth from error. More than a century later a new type of mass-media system developed in the Soviet Union and was later emulated in most communist countries. It is a form of authoritarianism which is based on the theories of Marx, Lenin, and their successors, and which sees mass media—indeed all vehicles of human expression—as instruments of propaganda and organization. This is a radically different form of authoritarianism.

Similarly, libertarianism has taken a new direction in the United States and Britain and a few other countries. Schramm explains and traces the development of the social responsibility theory in this way:

> By the late nineteenth and twentieth centuries, this unlimited libertarianism had been modified in practice. Psychology cast doubt on the ability of "rational man" to sort out truth from error, given the ability of one side to say more and say it better. Concentration of ownership in the media raised the question of whether a truly free "marketplace of ideas" existed and whether all viewpoints, popular or unpopular, would be represented. Film and broadcast media, because they were supposed to have a heavy influence on morals and beliefs, and because channels had to be allocated to avoid interference, invited a higher degree of control by official bodies. Consequently, in the twentieth century the media were asked to assume more responsibility for their own performance than merely to present their own ideas and observations freely and government undertook, even in the most libertarian societies, more acts of control. (Schramm, 1973:154)

Another widely used classification discusses communication systems in three categories: those of democracies, communist states, and developing nations (Davison, 1965).

There are even simpler schemes. For instance, one analysis sees only two kinds of media systems today: those that are "subordinate" to government and those that are "non-subordinate" to government (Terrou and Solal, 1951).

One of the problems with such typologies is that they cannot always take into account the more subtle and distinctive differences within a group of systems. It is not always easy to fit a country into one of the theories or groups. For instance, many countries are both communist and developing. Developing countries are sometimes divided into two subgroups: the Third World of needy countries and the Fourth World of the newly rich oil nations. Moreover, countries change and so do their media systems.

Here we propose to view the world's media systems along three dimensions: (1) the degree to which a media system satisfies individual needs vs. social needs, (2) the degree of government vs. private control, and (3) the degree of sophistication and diffusion.

THE INDIVIDUALISM-COLLECTIVISM CONTINUUM

A sensible way to understand a social system is to start by looking at the basic assumptions or premises which it holds about the nature of man, the nature of society, and the relation of the individual to society and the state. Of course, no country is exactly as prescribed in its constitution or as claimed by its ideologues. But such premises, principles, and values constitute the basis on which a society is built. What goes in and comes out of a communication system reflects these conceptions of man and society.

Two major and fundamentally different concepts of man and of his relation to society seem to be more useful than others in distinguishing one system from another. One is individualism, which places the individual above the group. The other is collectivism, which places the group above the individual.

We are not suggesting an either-or conceptualization. No country is completely individualistic or collectivistic. A principal task of ruling groups in collectivistic societies is to cope with individualism. On the other hand, a country that avows individualism may find a degree of collectivism unavoidable. In that sense, all countries are somewhat schizophrenic.

If we arrange all the communication systems in the world on this individualism-collectivism continuum, we see roughly three groups: (a) at the individualism end are the major Western industrialized nations plus Australia and Japan, with the United States as the extreme case; (b) at the collectivism end are all the communist countries, with China as the extreme case; (c) between are what are commonly called developing countries.

The avowed American concept of the human being is that he or she is an individual, and that the goal of the society is to preserve and enhance the dignity of the individual. The assent of the individual is the standard of political legitimacy. The individual has rights that are protected by the constitution, which presumes a populace that is basically rational, responsible, and self-directed. The individual exists of course in a social network, but, theoretically at least, can move in and out of subcollectivities without the permission of the government or approval of a peer group. In the American open class system, the individual has no title, legal safeguard, or political identity that assures him a certain position in society or protects him from skidding into an inferior social position, or from rising to a higher one. From individual striving—so goes the doctrine—emerges the general good.

In the Maoist concept of humankind and society, the man or woman is not viewed primarily as an individual, nor is there a philosophy of individualism. On the contrary, the entire nation is taught to eradicate it through the familiar Maoist formula of "struggle-criticism-transformation," which constitutes an important part of the Chinese communist communication system.

Mao views a single human being as a member of collectivities at various levels—as a member of a class, the masses, the people. "Who are the people?" Mao asked in 1949 shortly before the People's Republic of China was proclaimed. His answer: "At the present stage in China, there are the working class, the peasantry, the urban petty bourgeoisie and national bourgeoisie." The "masses" are members of these classes.

One of the most important Maoist teachings is the principle of "serving the people." "Our point of departure," Mao has said, "is to serve the people whole-heartedly and never for a moment divorce ourselves from the masses, to proceed in all cases from the interests of the people and not from one's self-interest or from the interests of a small group, and to identify our responsibility to the people with our responsibility to the leading organs of the Party" (Mao Tse-Tung, 1967:95). This is not just idle sentimental Mao-talk. It is part of a serious Maoist design, which makes massive and shrewd uses of persuasive communications, to establish in China a totally new value system or incentive system. In almost all societies, one works hard, supposedly for some personal reason—to be rich, to be famous, to be powerful. But in Mao's China, one is taught to work hard to "serve the people"—not to find fulfillment in individual accomplishments but to concentrate on the common good and collective goals.

One of the most important Chinese slogans—and an important task of the entire communication system in China—is "to destroy selfishness and establish collectivism" (*po szu li kung*) and many and long campaigns have been carried out under this title. To Mao, revolutionary development is not just a complete change of the structure of social institutions but also a total transformation of the cultural ethos. It is, of course, not a new notion that one should be selfless and concentrate on the public good. This is taught in every country and by all major religions. But to make purging a nation of egoism and selfishness the focus of a continuing campaign with the conviction that it can in fact happen is something distinctively Maoist.

The American model, in short, tends to accept society as it is and people as they are. It views people as having the ability to reason and to know self-interest, and thus sees the need to give people maximum opportunity for the exercise of reason and pursuit of self-interest. It is fundamental to this model that the assumed rationality is possible only on the basis of a free flow of information and ideas. The assumption is that out of a multiplicity of voices, some false and some sound, the public ultimately can be trusted "to digest the whole, to discard that not in the public interest, and to accept that which serves the need of the individual and of the society of which he is a part" (Siebert et al., 1963: 51).

The Maoist model does not accept society as it is; it opposes conditions as they are. It does not accept people as they are; it sees them as a potential in the transformation of a "poor and blank" country into a modern and industrialized nation. The basic Maoist theory is that a prerequisite for the building of a new communist state is the cultivation or creation of a new communist man and woman. "People can change the land, technique, output and village," says a familiar Maoist teaching, "because they have changed their thinking." This implies the use of a powerful system of persuasive and coercive communication to alter attitudes and thought and to mobilize and manipulate the energy of the masses.

The American doctrine of individualism has produced a commercial and private-enterprise communication system that is probably as free from government control as any other system in the world. Under the Maoist code, by contrast, there exists a communication system which serves a communist ideology to produce what Benjamin Schwartz calls "the emphasis on the individual's total self-abnegation and total immersion in the collectivities as ultimate goods" (B. Schwartz, 1965:11).

GOVERNMENT VS. PRIVATE CONTROL

The pattern of ownership or degree of control is another criterion commonly used to distinguish media systems. We could think again in terms of a continuum and divide the world's media systems into three groups along it: (1) those under strict government control; (2) those under mixed government, public, and private control; and (3) those under predominantly private control. Again we see the communist countries at one end of this continuum, with China as the extreme case. We see the industrial countries in the West, Australia, and Japan at the other end, with the United States as the extreme case. Most of the rest fall in the middle somewhere.

Even in the same part of the spectrum there can be considerable variation, as can be seen by examining control of broadcasting among industrialized nations. No other major broadcasting system in the world is as commercial and private as the American, even with government licensing. The British Broadcasting Corporation (BBC) is a nonprofit corporate body set up by a royal charter; it is run by a board of governors that has complete theoretical freedom with its programs, but the board is appointed by the Queen in Council (that is, by the party in power). Britain's Independent Television Authority (ITA) was created in 1954 to provide commercial programs. The Authority controls the amount and content of television commercials (limited to an average of not more than six minutes per hour). Radiodiffusion-Television Francaise in France is a public organization under the joint supervision of the Minister of Information and the Minister of Finance and Economic Affairs, who keep a close watch if not control over political broadcasts. The Nihon Hoso Kyokai (NHK) of Japan is a public juridical "person" largely free from government control but regulated by a government agency. German broadcasting is under chartered corporations in the *Laender,* or states; these are neither private companies nor government agencies but public bodies operating free of government controls. The Canadian broadcasting system consists of both public and private station operations financed through commercial advertising and public funds. In Sweden, television functions as a private company under the direction of a board of eleven members; the chairman of the board and five other members are government appointees.

Chinese and Soviet newspapers offer a basis for a comparison at the other end of the spectrum. One major contrast is in advertising policy. Not surprisingly, there is no place for advertising in the Chinese Communist press. The six-page January 1, 1973, issue of the *People's Daily,* which is the largest (most Chinese newspapers are four pages) and the most important publication in the country, did not have a single advertisement. The closest thing to that was an announcement on page 5—a box announcing a new newsreel welcoming the visit of the Queen of Iran. Similarly, the January 30, 1973, issue of the same paper—both issues randomly chosen—had no advertising beyond an announcement of a newsreel about the visit of the president of Zaire. Perhaps the only "business office" type of information one gets from the newspaper is the price of the newspaper itself: 5¢ an issue or $1.50 a month (in Chinese currency).

The *People's Daily* was not always like this. It carried advertising—or at least announcements that appeared in the form of advertisements—during the early days of the People's Republic. There was advertising even in the 1960s. The February 18, 1961, issue of the paper, for instance, devoted one-fourth of page 4 to products of the

Friendship Pharmaceutical Plant in Tientsin. The same issue even carried a telephone number for the advertising department of the paper.

The story of newspapers in the Soviet Union is different. In the mid-1960s a delegation from the American Newspaper Publishers Association visited the Soviet Union and came back with quite a bit to say about advertising in the Soviet press. One delegate reported:

> Advertising is coming into the Soviet Union newspaper scene at a fast rate. Directors of newspapers are looking forward to advertising to bring in an important part of the increased revenue. They will need more revenue for expansion in the future, to meet rising costs, and to increase the standard of living for their employees. At the present time only 2 to 3% of the total newspaper revenue comes from advertising. However, this percentage of advertising varies from newspaper to newspaper. (McCormack et al., 1967:16)

The same American publisher reported that the *Evening Moscow* had the largest advertising income of any newspaper in the nation, that 25 percent of its total revenue was derived from advertising sales, and that, at the time of his visit, the paper had a three-month backlog of ad orders waiting to be run in the newspaper.

This American visitor went on to say that "the Communist Party has decided that advertising properly used can contribute to the Soviet Union economy," that "advertising with a sales message was no longer looked on with the disfavor that it had been in former years," and that "the Party points out that ads in the right taste and the current use can aid distribution of products and contribute to the good of all workers"—a conclusion that Peking would scorn (McCormack et al., 1967:17).

The Japanese media system is an example of mixed public and private ownership and control. Japan's newspapers and magazines are mainly private enterprises. But the relative importance of public and private broadcasting is about the reverse of the situation in the United States. The Japanese equivalent of the American ABC, CBS, and NBC is a single publicly owned national broadcasting network, NHK (Nihon Hoso Kyokei). It is financed by subscription fees. Japan has as well a large number of commercial broadcasting stations but they are not equal to NHK in importance and influence. NHK operates two separate radio networks, two national television networks, and a national experimental FM radio network. It is the world's largest public television network, with a staff of more than 30,000, including 1000 reporters.

Ninety-nine percent of Japan's TV set owners dutifully and diligently pay NHK a fee. Hidetoshi Kato, one of Japan's leading communication scholars, explains their total acquiescence this way:

Our people have been used to paying for broadcasting from the beginning, so everyone has accepted the concept that broadcasting and telecasting are something to be bought, like gas and electricity. There is no legal punishment if you don't pay your fee. There are thousands who don't pay; but the NHK collectors return month after month to persuade them to pay, and finally they get most of these holdouts. (Krisher, 1972:24)

NHK's president is appointed by the prime minister, and the network theoretically is supervised by the postal minister, but it maintains considerable independence since its income flows directly from the people. "Any attempt by the government," as an American correspondent puts it, "to blackmail NHK into a point of view through financial pressure would surely arouse the public."

As of January, 1975, Japan had 53 privately owned commercial radio companies with 180 stations, and 88 commercial television companies with 1776 stations, with key stations, notably in Tokyo, controlled by the four major national newspapers—*Asahi, Mainichi, Yomiuri,* and *Nihon Keizai.*

Japan's commercial television still trails far behind NHK in popularity. One explanation is that the Japanese public has grown up with and remained loyal to public television and holds a somewhat condescending view toward the commercial product.

The media of a country are not invariably owned or controlled by its own government or citizens. There are systems in some countries that depend on patronage from foreign and domestic interests. One finds such a system in Lebanon. In an article entitled "Press for Rent" a professor of mass communication at the American University of Beirut starts with this scene:

Toward the end of his term of office, the former President of Lebanon, Charles Helu, received the then newly-elected members of the Lebanese Press Union. After formal introduction, Helu jokingly but with a mild tone of seriousness, addressed the Council members, saying: "Now that I have met you in your official capacity, may I learn what foreign countries your papers unofficially represent? . . . Welcome to your second country, Lebanon."

Later, in a magazine interview, Helu explained: "We don't have a "Lebanese press," rather we have a "press in Lebanon." (Dajani, 1975:165)

Helu's statement to the Lebanese journalists was not new. A few years earlier, the late President of Egypt, Gamal Abdel Nasser, told a group of visiting Lebanese journalists: "You have freedom of the press but lack a free press" (Dajani, 1975:165).

The Lebanese professor quotes a journalist, Ibrahim Selameh, who goes even further:

The press which is published in Lebanon represents all the countries and states of this world—including Puerto Rico, Nicaragua, and Zambia—but not Lebanon. . . . The press in Lebanon is not at all free; rather it is mortgaged and in debt to those—Arabs or Tartars—who possess money and can afford to rent it. Naturally, it is impossible for the rented press to violate the rent contract. . . . The press in Lebanon is rented to capital in all its mobile forms, nationalities, and levels, and it is, in the final analysis, bound, not free. . . . And so our journalists look at the world through the context of bonds and contracts and not through radio stations, wire services and facts. The Lebanese press writes for its subsidizers and not for its readers. (Dajani, 1975:167)

Subsidies to the Lebanese press come in various ways. One form is for the patron government or agency to rent the publication completely for a yearly or monthly figure. The patron then pays all the costs of production as well as the staff during the contract period. Another form of subsidy is for payments to be made to promote certain programs or causes. Other methods include gifts of equipment or paper, or subsidization through advertising budgets.

The Lebanese situation is not an isolated case; it is perhaps extreme but certainly not unique. This is what happens to small developing countries that cannot support their publications with government subsidies, circulation revenues, or advertising and therefore accept financial assistance from outside sources. Even in larger nations some media may be under foreign control. Canadians, for example, are highly sensitive to United States influence on parts of their communication system.

If we consider advertising a form of subsidy, then there is ample evidence of foreign influence on the media systems of many countries. For instance, if all American and Japanese companies were to cancel their advertisements in Asian newspapers, the impact would be felt immediately in half a dozen nations. Nor are foreign government and corporation advertisements inconsiderable in the American press.

The impact of multinational corporations, many of them controlled by United States interests, on mass media in developing countries is a question which has attracted the increasing interest of communication researchers and development specialists. To some writers, one of the most important sources of power for the multinationals in developing countries is their control over communications. According to this view, the corporations gain a competitive edge by using the mass media to shape the tastes, goals, and values of workers, suppliers, government officials, and consumers in countries where they are doing business (Barnet and Muller, 1974). Some researchers go even further and maintain that the national, regional, local, and tribal heritages of the Afro-Asian and Latin American have-not countries are "beginning to be menaced with extinction by the expansion of modern electronic communications, television in particular, emanating from a few power centers in the industrialized world" (Schiller, 1969:109).

Foreign financial interests have substantial media holdings in the United States, too. One newspaper chain in the United States, the Thomson Newspapers, is part of a larger, British-based group of mass media enterprises with properties throughout the world. The 1975 edition of the *Editor & Publisher International Year Book* (p. 357) lists the papers in Lord Thomson's chain. There are more than 40, including mainly small and medium-sized dailies in 25 states:

THOMSON NEWSPAPERS—Dothan (Ala.) Eagle; Douglas (Ariz.) Dispatch; Fayetteville (Ark.) Northwest Arkansas Times; Eureka (Calif.) Times-Standard; Oxnard (Calif.) Press-Courier; West Covina (Calif.) San Gabriel Valley Daily Tribune; Ansonia (Conn.) Evening Sentinel; Key West (Fla.) Citizen; Punta Gorda (Fla.) Herald-News; Dalton (Ga.) Daily Citizen-News; Valdosta (Ga.) Daily Times; New Albany (Ind.) Tribune; Ledger & Tribune; Council Bluffs (Iowa) Nonpareil; Leavenworth (Kan.) Times; Lafayette (La.) Daily Advertiser; Salisbury (Md.) Daily Times; Fitchburg (Mass.) Daily Sentinel and Leominster Enterprise; Taunton (Mass.) Daily Gazette; Adrian (Mich.) Daily Telegram; Albert Lea (Minn.) Evening Tribune; Austin (Minn.) Daily Herald; Laurel (Miss.) Leader-Call; Portsmouth (N.H.) Herald; Herkimer (N.Y.) Evening Telegram; Newburgh (N.Y.) Evening News; Oswego (N.Y.) Palladium-Times; Rocky Mount (N.C.) Evening Telegram; Canton (Ohio) Repository; Coshocton (Ohio) Tribune; East Liverpool (Ohio) Evening Review; Greenville (Ohio) Daily Advocate; Lancaster (Ohio) Eagle-Gazette;

Marion (Ohio) Star; Portsmouth (Ohio) Times; Salem (Ohio) News; Steubenville (Ohio) Herald-Star; Zanesville (Ohio) Times Recorder; Greenville (Pa.) Record-Argus; Hanover (Pa.) Evening Sun; Kittanning (Pa.) Leader-Times; Meadville (Pa.) Tribune; Monessen (Pa.) Valley Independent; Mitchell (S.D.) Republic; Petersburg (Va.) Progress-Index; Fairmount (W.Va.) Times-West Virginian; Weirton (W. Va.) Daily Times; Fond du Lac (Wis.) Reporter; Mantowoc (Wis.) Herald-Times Reporter

In countries where media are privately owned, knowledge about the formal ownership or control of a newspaper or broadcasting enterprise does not necessarily enable one to infer very much about its policy. Owners or patrons from outside a country may pay little attention to what is published or broadcast, and may be interested mainly in profits, or they may seek to dictate content. The same is true in countries where the media are publicly owned: Some are quite independent while others are forced to follow government guidelines. And even government-controlled media are sometimes subject to extensive foreign influence. Press and broadcasting policies in some countries of Eastern Europe have, in the past at least, followed the lead provided by Moscow. A great many patterns of ownership and control of media systems are possible. How well they serve their respective societies depends not so much on their formal structure as on how they function in practice.

DEGREE OF SOPHISTICATION AND DIFFUSION

We hear a good deal about the widening gap between have and have-not nations. For the past four years, according to a *New York Times* report (September 28, 1975), the per-capita income of the one billion people in the 30 poorest countries—already at subsistence levels—has declined further, while the industrial nations have held their own.

We do not observe a similar trend in the world's media systems, for there has been growth in the developing countries, and the growth is, in some cases, impressive. On the other hand, the industrial nations have not stood still, and the gap between mass media in developed countries and mass media in developing countries is still wide—and possibly widening as well. Just how wide is the gap? And what does it mean? Consider first the cases of Japan and India. The scholar Hidetoshi Kato has said that Japan has a "super-mass" media system. A few statistics will support his statement. Japan's "big three" in the newspaper industry—*Asahi Shimbun, Mainichi Shimbun,* and *Yomiuri Shimbun*—each has a circulation of between 7 to 8 million, morning and evening editions included. This is more than triple the circulation of the New York *Daily News,* the largest U. S. newspaper.

Japan and England have the highest number of copies of newspapers for each 1000 population in the world, nearly double the rate of circulation in the United States. Table 1 shows the newspaper circulation figures of nine countries as of the early 1970s:

Table 1
NEWSPAPER CIRCULATION IN SELECTED COUNTRIES

Country	Circulation	Copies per 1000 population
Japan	57,820,000	528
England	29,557,000	528
Soviet Union	84,953,000	347
West Germany	19,701,000	319
U.S.A.	62,510,000	297
France	12,160,000	237
Poland	7,553,000	226
Italy	7,267,000	133
India	9,096,000	16

The Japanese are big consumers of mass communications. An NHK survey in 1973 showed that the average Japanese spent 44 minutes a day reading newspapers and 54 minutes reading all printed matter, including newspapers, and three hours and 23 minutes watching television (*The Japanese Press, 1975*).

Every household in Japan has at least one radio and one TV set and every Japanese has easy access to the broadcasting media, especially to NHK. So, when an NHK audience rating says that a program attracted 43 percent, it means literally 43 percent of the whole Japanese population. Since the population of Japan, according to the recent census, was a little over 110 million, 43 percent means approximately 50 million people. There have been very few American radio or TV programs which have attracted 50 million people simultaneously. But a program with 50 million audience is common in Japan.

Even a casual observer of the Japanese communication system can tell that it is efficient and vigorously utilized. The usual explanations are Japanese successes in science, technology, and education. Another important factor should be noted: the homogeneity of the population. In a world filled with racial tension and ethnic problems, here is a society where there is almost no racial conflict. It has no language problems. Everyone reads, writes, and speaks Japanese. "Japanese people," as Kato puts it, "are intellectually homogeneous."

The homogeneity of the population makes it easier for Japan to have a centralized and national system of mass communication. For example, Japan has no need to divide its newspapers into "mass newspapers" for the masses and "quality newspapers" for the elite, as do the British. *Asahi Shimbun* is called "the newspaper of the mass elite." Japan has "national newspapers" with nation-wide circulation; "bloc newspapers" with circulations spanning several prefectures; and "prefectural newspapers" circulated within a province.

As of January, 1975, there were 112 daily newspaper members of the Nihon Shimbun Kyokai (Japanese Newspapers Publishers and Editors Association). Of the 112, 91 were general newspapers, 18 were sports newspapers, and three were English-language newspapers. The total circulation of the 112 dailies in October, 1974, was 40,006,000, and the figure would be 59,100,000 if the morning and evening editions were counted separately.

Newspaper circulation in Japan has reached a point of saturation and the competition among the national newspapers is fierce. The Japanese Newspaper Publishers and Editors Association reported:

> In the process of the intense competition that has developed in the race to reach the 7,000,000 level, one of the three nationals lost so many subscribers when it raised its subscription rate in July, 1974, it ended its first half business terms for 1974 in November with a deficit of 3,000 million yen (U. S. $10 million). As a result, the entire board of directors, in a move rarely seen in Japan's newspaper world, resigned en masse. (*The Japanese Press, 1975*:15)

In contrast with Japan, India reveals many of the media problems of less-developed nations. The reach of mass media in India, as S. C. Dube,[1] one of India's most respected communication scholars, puts

---

[1] The information given in this section is based mainly on the works of S. C. Dube of the Indian Institute of Advanced Study in Simla, India, particularly his articles: "Communication, Innovation and Planned Change in India," in Daniel Lerner and Wilbur Schramm (Eds.), *Communication and Change in Developing Countries* (Honolulu: East-West Center Press, 1967) and "Communication and Change in Developing Countries: A Review of Last Ten Years," in Wilbur Schramm and Daniel Lerner (Eds.), *Communication and Change: The Past Ten Years—and the Next* (Honolulu: University Press of Hawaii, forthcoming).

it, is still limited. Some of the English-language newspapers enjoy national and even international reputations and as of 1971 had ample-sounding circulation figures: *Indian Express*, 462,009; *Times of India*, 262,302; *The Hindu*, 201,357; *Statesman*, 193,522; *Hindustan Times*, 149,566. These publications do not reach down into the villages and their readers are drawn from the small English-speaking minority.

India's most important medium of mass communication is radio. As a result of the so-called "transistor revolution," radio is no longer a novelty in the countryside. According to figures gathered by Dube, in 1973 the total number of licensed radio receivers was 14,033,919. In 1963, the figure was only a little more than a quarter of that. But over two-thirds of India's radio sets are concentrated in urban areas. In 1974, All India Radio had 45 full-fledged radio stations, 25 auxiliary stations, and 5 auxiliary studio centers covering 67.5 percent of India's territory and 80.3 percent of its population.

Television, according to Dube, is still in the experimental stage. It has only four centers for originating and transmitting programs and one relay center. TV can cover only 2.7 percent of the area and 4.7 percent of the population, and the number of licensed TV sets was only 163,446 on December 31, 1973.

Dube foresees only slow expansion of the mass media in India. He believes that for a decade or so newsprint is likely to be in short supply, and that this is bound to inhibit the growth of newspapers. To build more powerful radio transmitters would be expensive and would require scarce foreign exchange. Despite these difficulties, he says, substantial expansion of the radio network is planned, but the time available for specialized broadcasts that cater to the needs and interests of different sections of the country may still be inadequate. TV will gradually cover all the metropolitan centers, but, except for the areas served by SITE (Satellite Instructional Television Experiment), there is little likelihood of its reaching more than 10 percent of the villages in the next twenty years. He concludes that the only feasible option for India is to make the most effective use of what resources are available.

In 1961 UNESCO set a minimum goal for mass communications in the developing countries. The UNESCO yardstick was that "every country should aim to provide for every 100 of its inhabitants at least ten copies of daily newspapers, five radio receivers, two cinema seats and two television receivers" (UNESCO, 1961:35). Many countries, India among them, are still unable to attain even these modest goals. In UNESCO's *World Communications* (1964) it was estimated that some 2,000 million persons living in more than 100 countries and representing 70 percent of the world population, still lacked adequate communication facilities.

A French journalist, "after a nonscientific evaluation of figures provided by UNESCO," devised an "index" that takes into account newsprint consumption, postal traffic, the number of TV sets, radios, and telephones. He took France as base 100, and found:

the United States in the lead with 320, or almost double the second place country, Sweden, with 175. Then come most of the Northern European countries and Japan with a rating of 135. France at 100 is followed by two industrialized Communist countries, Czechoslovakia and USSR, both under 80. Italy and Southern Europe are 75, Israel 58, Mexico 40, and Greece 30. At the bottom are poor countries, such as Egypt 25, Brazil 22, Morocco 10 and India barely 3. (Servan-Schreiber, 1974:243–44)

As noted earlier, there has been considerable media growth in developing countries in recent years. Wilbur Schramm has looked at the pattern of media growth from 1963 to 1973 in ten selected countries.[2] His findings are shown in Table 2.

Schramm calls the last ten years (1963–1973) the "decade of the transistor." His study shows that more than 100 million of the approximately 153 million radios in the three great developing regions—Africa, Asia (excluding Japan and the Asian USSR), and Latin America—were added between 1963 and 1973 (Schramm, forthcoming).

Table 3, also from the forthcoming Schramm study, compares media development from 1963 to 1973 in different continents.

Taking all the figures together, Schramm estimates that the total media distribution in Asia, Africa, and Latin America is somewhere in the neighborhood of

153 million radios
27 million television receivers
63 million copies of daily newspaper circulation
17 million cinema seats

Clearly, changes of importance have been taking place in the availability of communication media in the developing countries. The growth is particularly notable in Asia. Asia had 17 million radios in 1963; ten years later it had 75 million. Newspaper circulation rose from 14 to 25 million.

There are other reasons for hope. Satellites hold much promise. A communication satellite can be a sudden and giant step forward in creating a modern communication system. India, for instance, has

[2] Wilbur Schramm, "Ten Years of Communication Development in the Developing Regions," a paper delivered at East West Communication Institute Conference on Communication and Change in January, 1975, Honolulu. The paper is to be published in Wilbur Schramm and Daniel Lerner (Eds.), *Communication and Change: The Past Ten Years—and the Next* (Honolulu: University Press of Hawaii, forthcoming). Professor Schramm reports that 1973 figures are from unpublished UNESCO survey data, obtained through the kindness of E. Lloyd Sommerlad, Director of Mass Communication Planning and Research for UNESCO, Paris; 1963 figures are from *UNESCO Statistical Yearbook*.

Table 2

MEDIA GROWTH IN DEVELOPING COUNTRIES: NUMBER PER 1000 PEOPLE

		Radio receivers	TV receivers	Daily newspapers (copies)	Cinema seats
India	1963	8	—	13	7
	1973	21	0.1	16	5
Iran	1963	68	5	12	7
	1973	230	33	25	9
Philippines	1963	40	2	20	26
	1973	42	11	17	—
Kenya	1963	23	1	9	1
	1973	64	2	10	1
Nigeria	1963	11	0.1	10	2
	1973	23	1	6	0.7
Senegal	1963	45	—	6	10
	1973	67	0.3	5	12
Saudi	1963	12	3	—	12
Arabia	1973	31	19	7	—
Ecuador	1963	106	—	52	—
	1973	261	23	43	18
Mexico	1963	169	28	115	—
	1973	266	57	110	28
Peru	1963	182	—	85	—
	1973	138	28	118	—

been making plans for experimental satellite television broadcasts to remote areas. Indonesia, Iran, and Brazil are all making similar plans. The developments may be spectacular. Schramm has suggested that the next ten years may well become the "decade of the satellite."

On the other hand, the developing countries have a long way to go. Look again at Schramm's figures. These two-thirds of the world's

Table 3
MEDIA GROWTH IN THREE CONTINENTS: NUMBERS IN 1000S

		Radio receivers	TV receivers	Daily newspapers (copies)	Cinema seats
Africa	1963	6,020	329	3,319	1,105
	1973	14,038	1,510	4,387	1,223
	Ratio 1973/1963	2.33	4.59	1.32	1.11
Asia	1963	17,059	868	14,028	5,193
	1973	74,931	6,969	24,896	5,519
	Ratio 1973/1963	4.39	8.07	1.77	1.06
Latin America	1963	22,482	4,756	15,730	7,101
	1973	50,306	18,896	23,551	5,627
	Ratio 1973/1963	2.24	3.97	1.50	0.79

people still have no more than one-fifth of the world's radios. The United States alone has about twice as many radio receivers as all the developing countries together. The two-thirds of the world's people have about a fifth of the world's newspaper circulation, not much more than Japan alone. They have less than one-tenth of the world's television receivers.

THE STRANGE CASE OF CHINA

We turn now for another look at the mass communication system in China. This is perhaps the least comprehensible of all systems for Westerners. We have placed it at the opposite extreme end of our individualism/collectivism continuum; we also see it as an extreme case of government control. It is not a system that is blessed with modern and sophisticated communication facilities. But it is an unusually effective system of persuasive and coercive communication which makes use of all available vehicles to influence attitudes and behavior. It is the most pronounced case of "otherness" on which we need perspective.

We do well to try to understand the Chinese media system in Chinese communist or, more specifically, Maoist terms. For the thought of Mao governs every system and policy in China. A. Doak Barnett sees it this way:

The ideological revolution being pursued by the Chinese Communists involves much more . . . than merely formal indoctrination in the basic tenets of the major Communist prophets—dialectical materialism, class struggle, and all the rest. It also demands a continuing effort to change many of the most fundamental traditional values and attitudes of the Chinese people.

The ideas of harmony, compromise, adjustment, and stability, which have been so important in China in the past, are anathema to the Communists. In their place, the new regime is trying to induce the Chinese people, especially the younger generation, to accept a very different set of values and attitudes, emphasizing struggle, change, progress, and innovation. "Work, study, and struggle"—these, above all, are the basic requirements for the good life in the Chinese Communists' scheme of things. These, together with other essentials such as iron discipline, self-sacrifice, acute class-consciousness, intense patriotism, heightened political awareness, and a strong collectivist outlook—plus, of course, technical skill—are the prerequisites for the "new Socialist man" who is required to achieve their utopian blueprint of a future Communist society. (Barnett, 1965:37–38)

A major part of this blueprint is a program of mass persuasion that is new not only in the history of China but also in the history of communication. It is basically a process of socialization that affects the minds of the entire Chinese population—a process of socialization on which all other processes of socialization in China are based.

In 1956 when the People's Republic of China was only eight years old, a French correspondent had this to say:

The head of a good Chinese citizen today functions like a sort of radio receiving set. Somewhere in Peiping buzzes the great transmitting station which broadcasts the right thought and the words to be repeated. Millions of heads faithfully pick them up, and millions of mouths repeat them like loud-speakers. (Guillain, 1957:137)

This is a system which utilizes virtually every possible means of communication to reach the Chinese mind. It includes, for example, all schools and all forms of education. A headline of an almost full-page story in the *Kuang Ming Jih Pao* (*Enlightenment Daily*, Peking, May 11, 1975) reads: "Schools must become an instrument of the dictatorship of the proletariat." The system includes also every form of "criticism" and every means of "struggle" and "reform." This is such an enormous and complex system of communication that it is difficult to scale it down to size or to describe it in simple terms. Only a few of its special characteristics can be examined.

The Organization

At the moment, two publications serve as key links in the entire Chinese communication system. One is *Jen Min Jih Pao (People's Daily)*. The other is *Hung Chi (Red Flag)*, a magazine. Both are organs of the Central Committee of the Chinese Communist Party.

What is published in the two publications is reprinted and quoted in newspapers and other publications at different levels. Their reports are carried by the People's Broadcasting Station in Peking, and picked up by stations in the provinces and other cities; these stations in turn send the word further down through the radio broadcasting network, which makes the messages available to listeners through radio sets and wired loudspeakers that are available in schools, mess halls, communes, and other public gathering places. The messages from *People's Daily* and *Red Flag* are printed as pamphlets or booklets that are made available for study groups or other special groups.

This may sound as though everything one reads or hears in China is dictated by the authorities in Peking. It does not quite work that way. The messages from *People's Daily* and *Red Flag*, unless they concern party directives or official orders, are not repeated verbatim. In transmitting a message from Peking, the local newspapers, radio stations, wall newspapers, and other channels normally "integrate" the message with the local situation. The purpose is not, as an American journalist might describe it, to add some local color to the story; it is to relate it to the local situation and, more important, to set the stage for local propaganda and agitation activities.

People's Daily and *Red Flag* constitute required reading for all cadres (party and government officials) and for those seeking to climb through the hierarchy. The party newspaper is published in Peking and several major cities. *The Economist* (November 18, 1972) reported that six cities print from a matrix produced in Peking and delivered by airplane, while three—Canton, Chengtu, and Urumchi—receive copy by facsimile transmission.

To a certain extent, the relation between the two party publications and local communication systems—both mass media and interpersonal channels—is something like that between the theme and the variations in music. *People's Daily* and *Red Flag*, and the People's Broadcasting Station in Peking, provide a way for all cadres and the people to hear policy: They announce, guide, and support mass campaigns which go on forever throughout the country; they recognize and commend local successes.

Another key link in the Chinese communication system is the New China News Agency (NCNA). It collects and disseminates news at home and abroad. It was once described by Lu Ting-i, director of the party's department of propaganda who was purged during the Cultural Revolution in the 1960s, as "the Party's eyes and tongue." It has a virtual monopoly over news in China. It also performs another important function: to keep party authorities, cadres, and trusted individuals informed of events in the world. This is done through a publication called *Tsan kao Hsiao Hsi* or *For Your Information* (the literal translation is *Reference Information*). This is considered "classified material." Very little is known about this publication, although many visitors to China have seen it. It is a four-page printed tabloid and contains news items which are taken from foreign news agencies and press reports but which do not appear in the Chinese communist press. Many of these items deal with sensitive issues, and some are critical of the party and the government. One issue of the publication in June, 1973, that was available in Hong Kong, apparently having been smuggled out, carried news dispatches of TASS, AP, AFP, UPI, and, perhaps surprisingly, the United States Information Agency. It also carried an item taken from the *Congressional Record*.

Television does not yet play a very important role in the country, simply because not many receivers are available, and very little is known about this medium in China. According to the *Japan Times* (February 3, 1971) there were about 100,000 to 200,000 television receivers in China at that time.

Hsueh Hsi or Study

One of the most important features of the Chinese communication system is *Hsueh Hsi* or study. It is something distinctly Maoist, and it has become a fixture. Everyone in China belongs to something; everyone in China studies. This is no ordinary study. It is not a simple matter of reading a few books. It is a regular weekly affair—about two hours or longer—organized to study, as Mao once prescribed, "the theory of Marx, Engels, Lenin and Stalin, the history of our nation, and the circumstances and trends of the present movement." Much attention is devoted to the study of the Thought of Mao Tse-tung.

Interpersonal Communication

The Chinese communication system does not depend heavily on new communication technology; it makes extensive use of interpersonal communication—face-to-face conversation, discussion, group meetings, campaigns.

The main channel for organizing, guiding, and informing this interpersonal communication is the *kan pu* or cadres. They are highly disciplined, politicized, and resourceful party and government workers who carry communication both up and down, to and from top leadership, and horizontally in the village, neighborhood, commune, or factory. They are politically educated to see the "big picture" or the "horizon" as the party sees it; they are trained in the work of propaganda and agitation; they have authority to get things organized and done at the local level. They are propagandists.

Moreover, cadres and people are encouraged to be "creative" and "imaginative" in the use of local resources to push forward the policies and tasks of the party. And these often involve the use of traditional media and various forms of interpersonal channels. In the recent anti-Confucius and anti-Lin Piao movement, for instance, the party branch of a primary school in Peking "organized all teachers and students to study Marxism-Leninism, Thought of Chairman Mao, and to use the Marxist standpoint and method to compose . . . more than 1,000 new songs . . . to effectively deepen, widen and continue the anti-Confucius and anti-Lin movement" (*Kuang Ming Jih Pao, Enlightenment Daily*, Peking, August 24, 1974). A "revolutionary story-teller" in Chinghustao, a city in North China, tells how, for more than 13 years he has used the simple technique of story-telling during after-work hours to assist the ideological work of the party (*People's Daily*, Peking, July 18, 1975).

Mass Movements
The never-ending parade of mass movements in China is by now well known. Tasks vary; tactics change. One movement always follows another with only the briefest interruption. It is through these movements that the Chinese Communist Party seeks to mobilize and manipulate the energy and enthusiasm of the masses for party tasks. It is in the service of developing the consciousness of the masses that the Party has sought to exploit every potential of communications.

Unity of Communication
The Chinese have used rather unusual methods to establish or reestablish important links of social communication in China. Mao has defined the working class as the leading class in China and the peasantry as its principal ally. One of the most important political tasks in the nation is to teach the population to learn from the peasants and the workers. The party does not rely on mass media alone to tackle this vital political task. It simply sends bureaucrats, scholars, students, and "white collar" workers to spend some months at a time working and living with peasants and workers. This is the Chinese way to establish communication links between groups and persons who otherwise would have only generalized knowledge of each other. This was a notion which Chairman Mao expounded on May 7, 1966. As a result, there are hundreds of "May 7 Schools" or camps established throughout China to carry out this process of reeducation.

Use of Communication

We now turn to a news story reported by the New China News Agency to illustrate how many parts of this communication system were put into use in a commune in the anti-Confucius and anti-Lin Piao mass movement in China.

The entire front page of the August 4, 1974, issue of the *Kuang Ming Jih Pao* (*Enlightenment Daily*) in Peking is devoted to this NCNA story. It is a report of how a village has under the local party leadership learned "to occupy the ideological and cultural front for the Proletariat," and how it has accomplished "ten new things during the anti-Confucius and anti-Lin Piao Movement. The "ten new things" as described by the NCNA correspondent:

1. "Establish a political evening school that is well received by the masses." This is a description of how the evening school has involved more than 250 people (nearly half the population) to study three times every week.

2. "Cultivate ideological workers among poor and middle peasants." The story reports how the political evening school has produced 58 ideological workers and how members in the commune, once illiterates, can now take notes of "60,000 to 70,000 characters" and produce "forcefull and critical poetry and writings."

3. "Poor and middle peasants go on stage to talk about history." This is a description of how poor and middle peasants use Mao's writings—particularly his "On Practice"—and various Chinese historical materials to criticize teachings of Confucius and Mencius and to use history to prove how "man, not heaven, determines."

4. "Production of revolutionary model plays." This is a description of how 220 out of 250 people, who can engage in labor, work in the village, participate in the production of revolutionary model plays and writing and singing of songs in the field, on playgrounds, in the mills, and at meetings.

5. "Establishment of an After-Work Art and Literary Propaganda Team."

6. "Development of activities in the production of poetry and songs by the masses."

7. "Opening of a new library."

8. "Telling of revolutionary stories."

9. "Development of athletic activities."

10. "Change of old habits and old customs and establishment of new styles." The story reports how 12 betrothed girls decided to return dowries, which are considered old and feudalistic customs deriving from the teachings of Confucius and Mencius.

DISTRIBUTION MECHANISMS

We turn finally to a set of problems that is obviously important but often neglected in the study of alternative media systems. They are problems of delivery and distribution of information. They involve institutions (such as post offices and labor unions) and facilities (such as telephones and telegraphs) which we assume to be important but dimly understand. They are critical problems in the emerging field of communication policy research, although they have yet to capture wide and serious attention of the public.

In many countries, mostly developing nations, the problem of delivery and distribution is one of finding or opening new channels to allow the flow of information. In other countries, mostly developed nations, the problem is one of dealing with questions created by a convergence of political, economic, and, most importantly, technological developments.

Take the case of Brazil. For understandable reasons, the military government seems to be more interested in producing information directly than opening new channels to allow the flow of information. Telecommunication is a field that has developed rapidly in recent years, perhaps largely because of its strategic and military importance. But the basic problems of the communication system in Brazil remain unchanged. Alberto Dines, a prominent Brazilian journalist, speaking at the Columbia University Graduate School of Journalism in 1974, examined some of the basic chronic problems in Brazil.

One is the postal service. The Brazilian mail is still unable to reach all parts of this huge country. Even in those regions covered by the post office the service is unreliable and irregular. Besides that, the concept of inviolability of mail does not exist. Violations of mail and parcels are common, in some cases just for robbery, in others for political reasons. Dines gives one example to illustrate the lack of a distribution system to allow the flow of printed information:

Recently one Federal agency, which was making a very interesting effort to fight adult illiteracy, planned to issue a weekly or monthly newspaper, written in a simple way, with big letters and heavily illustrated, to be distributed to those who already completed their literacy programs but were still unable to pay for copies of regular newspapers and magazines. The agency had the necessary funds, but the project did not go forward because of the lack of a proper distribution outfit. How to reach those people scattered all over Brazil? The agency had their names and the places where they lived. But how to reach them?

At this time I was the managing editor of *Jornal do Brasil,* and we proposed that distribution should be made by using the only channel available: the delivery network of companies that produce bottled gas for cooking. This network is highly efficient, reaching its customers regularly, and could be used for other purposes. Our idea was approved.

Let us turn to the case of a developed country and look at the problem of delivery and distribution from a somewhat different angle. The country is France. This is how a French journalist sees the problem of newspaper circulation:

> In France, the distribution structure and the not very prosperous situation of the press stems for the most part from the outrageous monopoly held by the Nouvelles Messageries de la Presse Parisienne (NMPP) and the newsstand dealers. . . . These powerful lobbies (the NMPP and the vendors) have united to effectively block any innovation which might inconvenience them. In this way, three developments that could have put the French press on a really sound footing and prevented the current "press crisis" were nipped in the bud: subscriptions for magazines, direct delivery of dailies to customers, and large-scale distribution of Sunday papers. The first two are an absolute condition for large circulation. It is obvious that having to go to the newsstand every time you want to buy a publication— as the distribution monopoly forces readers to do in France—is an obstacle to increased circulation. By refusing to distribute papers on Sunday, the monopoly has deprived the French press of a weekly boost, which in the United States as well as Great Britain, insures heavy sales and profits. (Servan-Schreiber, 1974:249–50)

As this quotation suggests, the media system in France has its own individual style and flavor. Even though France is a Western industrialized democracy, like the United States, its system differs from ours in several important respects. The same is true of Great Britain, West Germany, and other industrialized democracies of the West.

We have seen how mass communications in the different nations of the world vary along three crucial dimensions. Some are oriented primarily toward serving the needs of individuals; others emphasize collective goals. Some are almost entirely in private hands; others are controlled or operated by a government or a single political party. Some are sophisticated and reach almost every member of a society; others make use of simpler technologies and are less pervasive.

All these characteristics—function, control, and degree of complexity—affect the content of the media. Naturally, since the United States is at one extreme end of the continuum in all three respects, the content of its mass communication system differs markedly from the content of media in China, which is at the other extreme in two of the three respects. Other factors that are peculiar to each society enter in, too. Some of these will be considered in the following chapter, which focuses on the news content of the American press.

FURTHER READING

Two overviews, both somewhat dated, are useful in gaining a picture of media systems throughout the world. A classic that deals with the principal philosophies underlying national systems of mass communication is *Four Theories of the Press*, by Fred Siebert, Theodore Peterson, and Wilbur Schramm (University of Illinois Press, 1963). W. Phillips Davison's *International Political Communication* (Praeger, 1965) devotes three chapters to mass media in industrialized democracies, communist states, and developing countries, respectively.

The forthcoming volume, *Communication and Change: The Past Ten Years—and the Next,* edited by Wilbur Schramm and Daniel Lerner (University Press of Hawaii), is a mine of information about media in developing countries. This should be available in 1976. In the meantime, Wilbur Schramm's *Mass Media and National Development* (Stanford University Press and UNESCO, 1964) provides an excellent summary. See also Lucian W. Pye's *Communications and Political Development* (Princeton University Press, 1963). For further information on media in the Soviet Union, see Mark W. Hopkins' *Mass Media in the Soviet Union* (Pegasus, 1970) and Alex Inkeles' *Public Opinion in Soviet Russia* (Harvard University Press, 1951); and for background on communications in present-day China see Frederick T. C. Yu, *Mass Persuasion in Communist China* (Praeger, 1964). This book gives a number of graphic illustrations of propaganda and education campaigns.

Strangely, there are few summary treatments of mass media in Western democracies and Japan. *The Power to Inform,* by Jean-Louis Servan-Schreiber (McGraw Hill, 1974), includes a great deal of information on communications in democracies; and *Television: A World View,* by Wilson P. Dizard (Syracuse University Press, 1966) compares television systems in different countries, including the United States, Western Europe, and Japan. A slightly more up-to-date account is Walter B. Emery's *National and International Systems of Broadcasting* (Michigan State University Press, 1969). For the most part, however, one must consult the literature on individual nations.

CHAPTER THREE
Media Sociology

HOW CONTENT IS SHAPED

Media sociology seeks to explain why the content of mass communications is as it is. Why do different newspapers present different versions of the same event? Or why do several television networks select many of the same stories for presentation on a given evening? Naturally, the reasons differ from country to country. This chapter will be devoted primarily to the situation in the United States, although some observations will apply to mass communications in other industrialized democracies as well.

There are some simple explanations for the content of American media, but they don't really explain very much. One of the most common of these is that the newspaper publisher or broadcasting station owner includes the news he wants to include and leaves out the rest. Or he may slant a story in a particular way to suit his own political or economic interests. A closely related theory is that the commercial media are money-making, business enterprises, and that their content is dictated by the business class in its own interest. Some of the adherents of this point of view maintain that those who are in power use the press and broadcasting to mold the minds of the masses, to manipulate them so that they will remain passive and not cause any trouble (Schiller, 1973).

The theory that the publisher or owner determines the content of the mass media had some merit in the days when newspapers were numerous and small—when one man did much of the newsgathering and editing, and perhaps even set the type himself. Benjamin Franklin, as publisher of the *Pennsylvania Gazette,* probably could include or exclude just about any item. Even in the era of mass journalism a Pulitzer or a Hearst could put the stamp of his own personality on a whole news organization. There are still a few newspapers in the United States that are extensions of the personality of the publisher. One of the largest of these is the Manchester (New Hampshire) *Union-Leader*, which reflects faithfully the convictions of its conservative publisher, William Loeb. There are also some smaller newspapers and some radio stations that carry on the tradition of egocentric journalism. But when it comes to most of the larger mass media one can explain little of the content by reference to the personality or economic interests of the owner. The owner does have considerable power, as we shall see, but it is limited by a number of other factors that, collectively, are usually more important in determining what is printed or broadcast.

Another simple explanation is that journalists determine content, for, to all appearances, they decide what to write and how to write it. Some of those who favor this theory charge that professional newsmen are increasingly recruited from liberal or radical groups that support an "adversary culture." Journalists therefore give the public news that reflects unfavorably on existing institutions, and the media provide a forum for "radicals" and "troublemakers" (Efron, 1971). It is certainly true that journalists and editors exercise great influence on editorial content but they, like the publishers and owners, are also circumscribed by other forces that limit what they can or cannot do.

A third approach would have it that the audience is the dominant factor in the determination of media content. If people like what is offered, a newspaper or broadcast enterprise will succeed; if it does not serve the public adequately, it will fail:

> Our media system operates on the premise that the audience is the customer and those who own and use the system are salesmen. . . . By constantly being polled, the audience determines the type of programming that is offered by television and radio. (Newspapers and magazines learn of consumer desires by their circulation figures.) (Seiden, 1974:5)

Commenting on some of these simple explanations of media content, a student of the press wrote recently:

> Whatever the merits of each of these views, they share a common perspective. They all treat news as if it were the product of a single value-maximizing individual. . . . They all agree "Who pays the piper calls the tune." They disagree mainly about who the piper is and who pays him, and what their tastes in music are. (Sigal, 1973:4)

Empirical studies of media organizations and news events have identified a number of factors, in addition to journalists, audiences, and ownership, that influence content. A detailed analysis of the way the London press and television covered a demonstration opposing the war in Vietnam on October 27, 1968, illustrates the effect of some of these factors. The British Broadcasting Corporation, which has the policy of relying on its news professionals to judge the newsworthiness of a particular event, decided to cover the demonstration in its regular news broadcasts. The Independent Television Network, whose policy emphasizes making full use of television's capability of showing news in the making, carried the event "live" as it was occurring. One of the London dailies had a substantial amount of space in which to report the demonstration, so it carried early reports as well as later ones. Another paper had much less space available, so it used mainly later reports of violence. Some news organizations had more reporters available than others, some had early deadlines and some later deadlines, and their newsrooms were differently organized. Each of these factors influenced what was reported. All the media focused on the question of whether there would be violence and on what little violence did take place, but the pictures they gave of the demonstration varied substantially (Halloran, Elliott, and Murdock, 1970).

Another detailed analysis, this one of the editorial processes at the *Washington Post* and the *New York Times*, noted the importance of established news gathering routines, the impact of bureaucratic struggles within the two news organizations, and the degree to which sources of news could influence what was published. Whether one story rather than another would appear on the front page, or would be carried at all, depended in part on whether it came through a news channel that was regularly monitored, on the persuasiveness of the editor who handled it, and on the relationship between the reporter and the source providing the information (Sigal, 1973).

Thus, in order to explain either why the content of two or more media is similar or why it varies strikingly, one must take a number of different factors into account. For convenience, these may be divided into two groups: environmental factors, exterior to the medium itself; and internal factors, including organizational structure and personnel.

ENVIRONMENTAL INFLUENCES

If one compares the mass media in the United States with those in a developing country, the importance of the political and economic environment immediately becomes apparent. Some countries are too poor to support elaborate mass communication systems: They have difficulty importing paper for newspapers and magazines and technical equipment for television. Private capital is usually very limited, and for this reason as well as for political reasons the government may run television and radio itself, and may even publish some newspapers. In many countries, the media are mainly or entirely government controlled; in others, the government exercises great influence on content through censorship or through indirect pressures such as allocation of newsprint or licensing of journalists.

The Political Setting

Differences in the political environment cause differences in media content even in such similar industrialized democracies as Great Britain and the United States. English libel laws, for instance, are more stringent than those in America and prevent British media from carrying news about individuals that would be published as a matter of course on the other side of the Atlantic. Similarly, British media are strictly limited in what they can say about a matter that is a subject of a legal proceeding. When a widely used tranquilizer (thalidomide) was alleged to have caused numerous deformities among new-born infants, the British press was able to write relatively little about this because a case against the drug's manufacturer was in the courts. While American reporters have sometimes been excluded from legal proceedings by the presiding judge, and some publications have been threatened with contempt of court charges, American media have much more latitude to comment on cases before the courts. On the other hand, the British Broadcasting Corporation, since it is supported by fees collected by the government from radio and television set owners, is free to present programs that American networks would hesitate to broadcast because of fears of low audience ratings and consequent loss of advertising revenue.

The characteristics of the United States that most affect media content are that it is wealthy, it relies on private enterprise to provide most goods and services, and it has a strong guarantee of freedom of the press built into the First Amendment to the Constitution. The United States therefore can afford a full range of the mass media; most of these are private, profit-making enterprises; and they are largely free from government interference as far as their content is concerned.

Nevertheless, federal, state, and local governments do exercise some influence on media content. Broadcasting stations must be licensed by the Federal Communications Commission (FCC), which is charged under the law with ensuring that they operate in "the public interest, convenience, and necessity." If a station fails to comply, its license may not be renewed. Actually, very few licenses have ever been withdrawn, but the possibility makes broadcasters more cautious. The FCC has issued some regulations affecting content. The most controversial of these, the "fairness doctrine," requires that broadcasters maintain a balance in discussion of contested issues and that any person attacked over the air be given time to reply. In addition, an equal-time statute requires parity in time offered all candidates for a given political office. The effect of both of these provisions has been to reduce discussion, for broadcasters dislike to yield air time for free replies or for the succession of minor party candidates that might fall under the equal-time edict.

Print media are affected by governmental regulations and practices less directly. Many publications are dependent on the mails for distribution, and changes in postage rates may make the difference for them between survival and failure. A reporter who has written a story about a matter that becomes the subject of a court case may be subpoenaed as a witness and given the choice of revealing his sources or going to jail. Some states now have "shield" laws, which enable a reporter to protect the sources of a story. But others do not. Some journalists have gone to jail for refusing to reveal their sources. And the threat of a subpoena may make reporters more cautious about what they write.

Unofficial government pressures may also be important. Print as well as broadcast media depend on government agencies for access to information, and officials who wish to bring pressure on them may cut off these sources. Or, officials may offer favors to selected media—for example, reporters from one publication may be given exclusive interviews or access to newsworthy information. During the Vietnam War, when the government was unhappy about the stories being written by correspondents stationed in Vietnam, arrangements were made for other reporters to be flown over for brief tours.

On the whole, however, the political and economic environment in the United States is more hospitable to the mass media than it is in most other parts of the world. The social environment is too. American journalists enjoy a somewhat higher social status than their colleagues in many other countries. They are more respected and cannot so easily be refused interviews or brushed off with a few general statements. It is accepted that people in public life should be willing to answer questions from the press; failure to do so is usually interpreted as discourtesy, deviousness, or worse.

The News Infrastructure

In addition to the political and economic climate, there are more specific aspects of a society that influence media content. One of the most important of these is the extent to which news and entertainment materials are easily available. Most newspapers and broadcasting organizations create relatively little of their content themselves; instead, they select it from a variety of sources that provide it in finished or semifinished form. These sources are sometimes referred to collectively as the infrastructure of the press. Some societies have rather little in the way of a press infrastructure; others have a rich one. When a newspaper or television station is started in a developing country, one of the first problems it faces is how to fill a broadcast day or how to fill its columns. By contrast, most media in industrialized countries are deluged with material they can use; their problem is how to select from among the wealth of possibilities.

As far as news is concerned, the most important part of the press infrastructure consists of the wire services. Daily newspapers in the United States subscribe to the Associated Press, the United Press International, or both. Many subscribe also to the British-based Reuters service and some to the French-based Agence France Presse or the Soviet TASS. It is possible for newspapers to rely completely on one of these services, or a combination of them, for all their national and international news. Technology has made it possible for wire service news to be set in type automatically at the local newspaper plant, so that it appears in the paper untouched by human hand at the local level. Large and distinguished papers have their own networks of correspondents, but even they use some wire service materials in their columns and rely on the wire services to alert them to important stories.

Television and radio also rely heavily on the wire services. The networks have their own correspondents, but these correspondents are relatively few. A major network may have only two or three camera crews to cover all of Asia. Small broadcasting enterprises rely on wire services for national and international news almost completely. Many radio stations of modest size use what is called the "rip and read" technique: A newsman tears off sections from the wire service printout as it comes over the ticker and then reads from these when the time for news bulletins comes. Others use standard prepackaged news summaries prepared by the wire services.

A substantial number of news services are available to media that are willing to pay for them. The *Washington Post* and *Los Angeles Times* offer such a service. So do the *New York Times*, Copley Press, the Knight-Ridder Newspapers, the *Chicago Sun-Times*, and others. These services do not always compete directly with the wire services but may offer supplementary material and interpretation on important stories that their own correspondents have covered.

Features, entertainment, and opinion materials, all can be bought. If you are publishing a small newspaper, you can obtain editorials all ready to print, which you can claim as your own, garden columns, political columns, medical columns, bridge columns, astrology columns, and of course comic strips. The cost depends on your circulation, but a garden column, for instance, might cost a small paper only $12 a week—far less than it would have to pay someone to write it. A recent issue of *Editor & Publisher* lists more than 350 syndicated services, from Adventure Feature Syndicate to Women's News Service.

If you are a broadcaster, similar prepackaged materials are available. Just buy the film or tape and run it. Stations affiliated with networks can make use of the voluminous news, public affairs, and entertainment materials offered by the network. Independents can subscribe to such agencies as Visnews (a London-based news film enterprise), and can buy old motion picture films and television features very cheaply.

But the materials that can be purchased are only the tip of the iceberg. News releases and "handouts" are of almost equal importance. Journalists traditionally profess to distrust such handouts; nevertheless, nearly all newspeople admit that they could not function as well without news releases. There just aren't enough reporters to gather all the information necessary and write all stories first-hand. For instance, as of 1970, the *Washington Post* had a staff of 30 to cover all national news—to report on the activities of hundreds of federal agencies, business enterprises, labor unions, universities, and thousands of voluntary organizations—churches, civic groups, fraternal organizations, and so on. It has been estimated that about one third of newspaper news content is based on press releases (Cutlip, 1962).

When properly used, the handout can be a valuable adjunct to news gathering. Naturally, no organization is going to publicize unfavorable information about itself. But a journalist soon learns which agencies and organizations provide accurate materials, and which handouts should be viewed with suspicion. Furthermore, in many cases the journalist does not use the handout as it is written by the public information or public relations officials. Rather, he or she will make one or two telephone calls to check the facts and will sometimes conduct a number of interviews with persons named in the release or with others who might know about the story. The handout thus provides the basis for a news report that may include further information and reflect a different point of view.

Small radio stations and weekly newspapers are particularly dependent on the handout. They may have only two or three reporters to gather and write all the local news they carry. The only way they can provide coverage of the community is if other people bring the news to them.

This arrangement has important implications for democracy. If you and your friends decide to back a particular candidate for local office, or if you want to organize a money-raising event for some environmental cause, you cannot expect that the local press will automatically give attention to what you are doing. More newsworthy stories may claim the attention of the handful of reporters available. But if you write a news release and distribute copies to the local press and radio, the editors may decide that it is interesting enough to use. Or they may send a reporter to talk with you. The press thus becomes not only a newsgatherer but also a judge of what activities are important enough to deserve space in the paper or time on the air. If the press consistently refuses to use your releases, and if you are convinced that what you have to say is important to the community, then you may have a justified basis for complaint. Perhaps the local paper is biased politically or is dominated by a business concern. Such cases do occur, although fortunately they are rare.

If your story is excluded from the local press you are not completely defenseless. Sometimes you can persuade another paper or radio station to use the story, thereby causing embarrassment to the one you first approached. Or, you might be able to persuade an official to make a statement incorporating the substance of your story. Very few local media will refuse to carry a statement from a prominent official.

So much news is based on releases from interested parties and on routine events that can be controlled by the news source—such as press conferences—that some students of the press have concluded that most mass media content merely reflects what those in power would like to reveal. Only accidents and scandals, they argue, provide insight into what really is going on, since these cannot be foreseen (Molotch and Lester, 1974). There is some truth in this, insofar as each institution can exercise control over information that it releases itself. But many different interests are engaged in prepackaging news and staging news events, and they represent different, frequently competing, points of view. An industry may issue a release stating its side of a story, only to have a consumer group send out a release that gives quite a different impression.

If the mass media use materials reflecting only one point of view, then there is cause for alarm. But this is not usually the case. Indeed, one researcher concludes that the press has an institutional bias in favor of new attitudes, opinions, and behaviors, which gives it a "constant potential for social subversion'" (Roshco, 1975:125). In some cases, it has been found the press gives more attention to "antiestablishment" groups than to those that represent vested interests. During the first ten months of 1970, for example, the mass media in Minneapolis carried more stories on Students for a Democratic Society than on the American Legion; and a total of 202 stories on "minority" groups as opposed to 112 on "established" groups (Fedler, 1973). On the other hand, a study of press coverage of the massive oil spill off Santa Barbara, California, in 1969, found that the national press gave far more attention to news generated by the oil companies and the federal government than to the views and activities of local officials and conservationist groups—although the local press provided more even coverage (Molotch and Lester, 1975). Imbalanced coverage *may* represent media bias, but it may also mean, among other things, that some groups are not providing the press with information, or are not staging newsworthy events.

Another part of the press infrastructure consists of *other* media. If you watch reporters or editors at work, you will find that they spend a lot of time reading other publications, or possibly monitoring radio and television, as well as the wire services. They want to know if they have missed any big stories and to find leads that they can develop into stories themselves. Nearly all journalists reporting on national and international affairs at the *Washington Post* read the *New York Times*, while their opposite numbers in New York are reading the *Post*. Journalists who specialize in covering science will (or should) read a large number of scientific periodicals; those who cover religion will read religious publications, and so on.

Other media are particularly important for foreign correspondents. If you are reporting from Moscow for an American newspaper or broadcasting network, a lot of your time will be devoted to reading the Soviet press, listening to the radio, and viewing television. You will also interview officials at the American embassy, those at other embassies, and Soviet officials to whom you can gain access. But your time is limited, and you have to decide which story to focus on. One of the best ways to do this is by monitoring the Soviet media. The same would be true if you were stationed in Western Europe and were responsible for covering news in several countries. Your decision as to where to travel and how to spend your time would be heavily influenced by what was published in the press of these countries.

Try to imagine how difficult it would be to run a newspaper or broadcasting station in a country where the press infrastructure was poorly developed! You might obtain international news from one of the big wire services, if you could afford it, but there might be only a

rudimentary service providing national news. The government probably would supply you with official statements, but might not have
public information officials to write press releases in a popular style.
And few handouts from other sources would be available. Other
publications, if they existed, would suffer from similar difficulties
and could provide you with few additional stories and leads. You
might be reduced to monitoring the radio, both medium wave and
short wave, to obtain what national and international news you
could, and to importing cheap entertainment and feature material to
fill your available space or time. Indeed, one of the criticisms made
of the United States in other countries is that it provides cheap entertainment materials that dominate the local media and subvert indige-
nous cultures. One of the problems of developing countries is how
to build an adequate infrastructure for their mass media.

Personnel and Audiences

Personnel is another category of resources that a society must be able
to provide if its media are to operate efficiently—especially managerial, editorial, and technical personnel. Again, the United States suf-
fers from no shortage in any of these specialties. As of 1974, the
Gallup Poll reported that one in every hundred college students had
the intention of entering some branch of journalism, and in that year
more than 50,000 students were enrolled in schools or departments
of journalism throughout the country. Most of these students probably intended to devote themselves to the editorial side of journalism,
or to public relations and other parts of the press infrastructure, but
education for managerial and technical positions in the media is also
comparatively well developed in the United States.

By contrast, many countries have no facilities for journalism education and few for learning on the job. Both individual nations from the
industrialized world and international organizations have attempted
to assist in training the necessary specialized personnel, but severe
shortages persist. The United States Information Agency has provided educational assistance to both editorial and technical employees
of media in developing countries; the United Nations Educational,
Scientific and Cultural Organization has helped to establish journalism schools in various parts of the world; and the International Press
Institute has conducted seminars for managerial personnel in Asia,
Africa, and elsewhere. But a large proportion of those who operate
the media in developing countries have had to go abroad for training. Thousands have attended journalism schools in the United States
and other industrialized nations. For example, in 1974 Iran sent 33 of

its National Iranian Radio and Television employees to Michigan State University for one term of intensive study. At the same time, Iran was engaged in founding an Academy of Communication Arts, but it was not expected to be ready to open its doors until 1978. The quality of the personnel that a society can provide for journalism, and the training available to this personnel, has a direct effect on the content of that society's mass media as well as on the quality of the media services.

Finally, there must be an audience for the media, and the level of education, tastes, and needs of this audience will naturally affect the content and structure of mass communications. The fact that radio is the dominant medium in many parts of the world is due in part to low levels of literacy: not enough people are able to read to support an extensive network of newspapers and magazines. Countries with numerous local languages have a problem even with radio. In which languages should one broadcast? If mass-circulation printed materials are produced, they must be simply written and rely heavily on illustrations.

American society provides a basis for a highly diversified media network. There are mass audiences for television programs and national magazines, elite audiences for some newspapers and regional audiences for others, and specialized audiences for radio, motion pictures, recordings, and for the incredible diversity of magazine publications. Content is structured for each of these audiences—and many others. If a mass medium fails in the United States, it is rarely because there is no audience for it. The failure is more likely to be due to the fact that competitors offer content that more nearly satisfies the needs of this audience, or that the audience is fragmented among competing media, or that advertisers don't think it important to reach the audience in question. When the mass-circulation magazines, *Life*, *Look*, and the *Saturday Evening Post*, died, each still had millions of subscribers. Their failure was due not to lack of audience interest but to insufficient advertising.

MANAGEMENT AND ORGANIZATION

Owners and managers of today's mass media make numerous decisions that affect media content. Most often, we don't know what factors enter into these decisions; certainly each decision is likely to be somewhat different from the next. But it would seem likely that the personality of the decision-maker, pressures from inside the media organization, and pressures from outside would all be important in most cases.

Ownership of a media enterprise can usually be determined, but management is difficult to define. In a small newspaper, an editor may make decisions as to what the reporters should do, but also serve as a reporter himself. In a television network, an executive producer will give instructions to other editorial personnel, but will also take a hand in writing copy or selecting films. Here we will be concerned mainly with managers in fairly large organizations whose decisions affect the structure of the organization and gross allocations of personnel and budget.

What sort of people are the media managers? In an effort to find out, Columbia University's Bureau of Applied Social Research recently interviewed 65 people who were randomly selected from the top echelons of the largest daily newspapers and national magazines, and the three broadcasting networks. This sample included publishers, editors, network news executives, news commentators, and leading columnists. Nearly all of them were married white males with a college education, and slightly over half were born in the Northeastern United States, but otherwise they were quite diverse. Surprisingly, only eight percent identified themselves as Republicans; 36 percent were Democrats; and the majority called themselves political independents or stated no political preference. When their opinions on major social and political issues were compared with those of elites from other sectors of society (business, labor, civil servants, politicians, voluntary associations, and so forth) it was found that they tended to be more liberal on most questions than leaders of the other groups included in the study, except for liberal organizations, minority organizations, and intellectuals (Barton, 1974–75;Weiss, 1974).

The small number of Republicans is surprising, since a large proportion of the sample came from newspapers, and the bulk of the American press has ordinarily backed Republican presidential candidates (Bagdikian, 1972). It would seem probable that, when it came to endorsement of a presidential candidate, the owners stepped in and overruled the opinions of the editor and other top staff members. Indeed, this has been publicly acknowledged in some cases, where the owner or publisher has personally signed an endorsement, while the editor has made his dissenting views known.

It is popularly believed that owners and top management are primarily concerned with making money. This is undoubtedly true in some cases, especially in corporations where the board of directors represents investors who have little interest in the enterprise beyond the financial returns. Nevertheless, those who have studied newspaper, magazine, and and broadcasting enterprises at close hand have rarely found that money-making is the sole consideration in a decision by management. There is also, for instance, the image of the enterprise and what critics will say (Bogart, 1974). In the case of newspapers, many of which are family properties or are controlled by one family, an element of pride in the paper enters in. A British editor has noted that several newspapers in England were continued by their owners and managers even after they had ceased to be profitable. The *Observer*, for one, has been preserved by periodic subventions from family funds (Wintour, 1972). A researcher who conducted a detailed study of the *Washington Post* and the *New York Times* concluded that the profit motive alone was not sufficient to explain management decisions: Profits were important, but tradition, craftsmanship, and other values played a role (Sigal, 1973).

Some management decisions about personnel and budget obviously affect media content directly. If a newspaper has no foreign or national correspondents then it must contract for wire services or other sources for foreign news. Increasing the size of the local reporting staff will make many more stories about local politics possible. Decisions about how much money to spend for columnists and comic strips—and which ones to buy—are likely to affect the basic impression that a paper makes on its readers. In broadcasting organizations the amount of money budgeted for special events, as well as for regular news coverage, plays a role in determining what can and cannot be covered. The major networks started drawing up their budgets for covering the landing of the first astronauts on the moon several years before the landing took place. The quality of weekend news on most television stations is affected by the unavailability of sufficient reporters and camera crews.

Organizational decisions made by management affect content more indirectly but nonetheless basically. Management must decide what the principal subunits of the media organization will be, and what each one will do. This often determines which reporter covers a given story, and how much space or time it receives. The metropolitan, national, and foreign news desks of the *New York Times*, for instance, may compete with each other for the right to handle a story. How much space the story deserves and where it will be placed may cause further conflicts. The Washington Bureau of the *New York Times* and also the *Sunday Times* enjoy a large measure of autonomy, with the result that stories filed from Washington or published on Sunday may be handled differently from stories written in New York and published in the weekday editions. When two subdivisions of an enterprise become embroiled in controversy, the publisher or network president may be called upon to arbitrate.

Pressures on Management

Owners and managers are subject to pressure from many quarters, including government, advertisers, the business community, special interest groups, their own employees, the competition, and the public in general. The extent to which decisions are actually influenced by these pressures naturally differs from medium to medium and from case to case. The larger and stronger media have shown themselves highly resistant to government pressures, even when these are intense. When, for instance, President Kennedy asked *New York Times* publisher Arthur Sulzberger to transfer David Halberstam out of Saigon, the publisher declined to do so. Indeed, the *Times* went so far as to cancel a two-week vacation for which Halberstam was due, in order to avoid giving the impression that it was acquiescing to governmental pressures (Sigal, 1973). Public attacks on the television networks by Vice President Agnew, who accused them of biasing news against the administration, appear to have affected network policies little.

Smaller and weaker media have more difficulty in resisting governmental pressures, although many of them do. A small-town weekly paper may be heavily dependent on official advertising from the county or township government—for instance, publication of local ordinances or announcements of zoning decisions. A word from an official to a publisher to the effect that advertising might have to be transferred to another paper could be enough to influence the publisher's decisions. On the other hand, there are instances in which small newspapers and radio stations have persisted in exposing corruption in local government even in the face of extensive harrassment.

The situation with regard to pressures from commercial advertisers and the business community is similar: Large media usually can withstand them, but smaller publications and broadcasters may find resistance more difficult. A study of the airing of controversial public affairs programs by television stations (for example, programs on racial segregation) found that the more prosperous stations, especially those affiliated with networks, aired such programs in spite of local objections. The financially weaker independent stations were less likely to carry them (Wolf, 1972). The same researcher sought to compile lists of cases in which advertisers had been successful in influencing program content directly. He found a few, but the number of cases is not impressive. Of course, there probably are further instances of such successful intervention that never become known. Advertisers on television influence content when they refuse to sponsor programs that they—or pressure groups to which they are responsive—find objectionable. A network will sometimes have to present the program without sponsorship as a costly public service.

A more subtle form of influence results from the circumstance that newspaper and television executives are often members of the same social circles as other members of the business community, especially in smaller cities and towns. They may belong to the same country clubs and go to many of the same cocktail parties. How much is the media manager influenced by casual conversations on the golf course? Nobody knows. But, however great these informal influences may be, they may be at least partially offset by the membership of most publishers and station owners in trade groups, such as the American Newspaper Publishers Association, the American Society of Newspaper Editors, or the National Association of Broadcasters. An executive must be able to live with his or her decisions not only as far as the local business community is concerned but also when he or she meets with opposite numbers from other media.

Special interest groups have often been able to influence management decisions with respect to matters that concern them. Commercial television, in particular, since it must draw its huge audience from all segments of society, has been eager not to give offense to any group within this audience. Ethnic groups, including black Americans and Americans of Italian descent, have been successful in reducing the extent to which television programs have treated members of these groups in a stereotyped manner. Homosexual groups, using such techniques as sit-ins at broadcasting offices as well as more conventional means, have been influential in persuading networks to deal seriously with the subject of homosexuality and not to ridicule or malign homosexual characters who appear in entertainment programs.

Media managers are frequently influenced by their own staffs. Questions relating to organization and budget are of constant concern in negotiations with a unionized staff. Decisions on personnel may be affected by pressure from ranking employees. For instance, the publisher of the *New York Times* reversed his decision to appoint a new head for the newspaper's Washington Bureau following representations by several well-known journalists (Sigal, 1973). A British editor has reported instances in which printers refused to set copy for stories with which they disagreed (Wintour, 1972). Such incidents have occurred in the United States as well, usually directed at radical publications. A more subtle influence may occur when a publisher or television executive adopts the opinions of his own editorial writer (Bogart, 1974).

What the competition is doing is another important influence on management decisions. Network programming decisions, for instance, are conditioned by knowledge of the programs that other networks are scheduling for the same time period. Should one compete directly by carrying a program that will appeal to the same audience, or should one aim for a different audience? Decisions of newspaper management about whether to include a special section for residents of a given suburb will depend in part on whether another paper is already serving that suburb. And the decision of one medium to carry a controversial story, for example, one that the government alleges will endanger national security, may rest on whether other media have already carried the story or are known to be about to do so.

As the reference to national security suggests, the decisions of media managers are affected by their conception of the public interest. The *New York Times* held up a story on the CIA-backed invasion of Cuba in 1961, management having concluded that publication might compromise the whole undertaking. Home-town newspapers often like to speak well of the community and its leaders, and are reluctant to "rock the boat" (Breed, 1958). They may withhold news about collusion between local government and business, stories that reflect unfavorably on local churches, or behavior that might question such basic values as the "work ethic." One reporter told a researcher who was studying categories of news that were avoided that his city's community chest quota had not been reached for several years, but that neither he nor any other reporter had mentioned this in print.

The interests of private persons, too, are often taken into account in policies governing publication. Most media will not carry the names of rape victims, or of minors who are accused of crimes; in some states, such anonymity is prescribed by law. They may also withhold information if they believe that a story might expose an innocent individual to personal danger.

The extent to which managerial decisions are influenced by a desire to give the public what it wants varies from case to case. Conceptions of public taste and interests certainly enter into decisions about both entertainment and news programming on commercial television, in view of the direct relationship of audience size to income, but even here there are variations from organization to organization. Some stations have hired consultants to advise them on how their news programs may be restructured to attract larger audiences.

The result in many cases has been to turn the news program into an entertainment show emphasizing sex, scandal, and chit-chat at the expense of more serious issues (Shosteck, 1973–74). Other stations have held to more conventional news formats.

Conceptions of what the public wants tend to play a lesser role in the decisions of newspaper managements. Some papers sponsor periodic public opinion polls to learn about the reactions of their readers, but it is remarkable how few do this. Nevertheless, newspaper managements frequently seek to "dress up the front page" with more pictures or a new typographical design, or encourage a livelier style of writing, in an effort to retain and build circulation. The publisher of a medium-sized newspaper told one of the authors recently that he would like to see more international news in his paper, but that his editor believed the readers would not stand for this. Management decisions thus tend to reflect an interplay of influences, one of which may be dominant in one case and another in the next. They may affect content directly, indirectly, or scarcely at all.

The extent to which management intervenes in the work of editorial employees also varies from organization to organization and from case to case. As has been noted above, a publisher may sometimes kill an individual story or insist that a given editorial be written. Sometimes the personal preferences of high-ranking editors can affect even fairly minor matters. A former editor of the *Providence Journal* hated dogs, and the only time he permitted a photograph of a dog to appear in the paper was when one killed a small child (Bagdikian, 1974). And for many years a Sunday editor of the *New York Times* insisted that the term "red" should not be used to describe communists in the Sunday edition of the paper. This caused some difficulty for headline writers, who like short words. Ordinarily, however, management restricts itself to larger questions, leaving decisions on day-to-day content to employees farther down in the organization.

Management's influence on content may be exercised in more subtle ways. Several researchers have concluded that, even when those higher up in a newspaper or broadcasting organization are careful not to intervene in day-to-day decisions about content, reporters and editors soon learn what the management's preferences are and handle their stories in such a way as to please their superiors (Bogart, 1974; Breed, 1955). This is the key to security and advancement. Another researcher has found that journalists tend to seek employment by news organizations with whose policies they already agree (Sigelman, 1973).

But the extent of these subtle influences, and the degree to which they affect all employees, are difficult to determine. One can find numerous instances in which reporters have successfully circumvented the preferences of those higher up (Tuchman, 1972). And the fact that newspapers that are members of the same chain may support different presidential candidates, or that morning and afternoon papers under the same ownership may have different editorial policies, also suggests that other forces in addition to the influence of management are at work (Bagdikian, 1974; Bogart, 1974).

PRACTICES AND PRINCIPLES OF JOURNALISM

Most decisions about the day-to-day content of the media are made by reporters and editors. Because they are the ones who usually determine which items will be admitted to the columns of a newspaper or magazine, or will be aired by a broadcasting station, they are sometimes referred to as "gatekeepers" (Gieber, 1964; White, 1950). The individual reporter may determine to a large extent what subject he or she will write about and then attempt to "sell" the idea to an editor. Even if a subject is assigned, the reporter decides what aspects will be covered, and how the story will be written or filmed. Editors then decide whether the story will be used, in whole or in part, and whether it should be rewritten or severely edited. One editor may approve a story, only to have another one higher in the chain of command kill it.

Foreign news supplied by the wire services goes through the longest gatekeeping chain. An item may be written by a "stringer" in Bavaria (who is the first gatekeeper) and sent to an editor in Frankfurt. This editor must then decide whether to kill it, rewrite it, or transmit it further. If the item survives the Frankfurt office, it will go to London, where another editor must make the same decisions. The London office may transmit the item to New York, where it may die or may be transmitted to subscribing newspapers and broadcasting stations. Editors within these news organizations must then decide whether to use it. Not surprisingly, the chances are that the item from Bavaria will never reach an audience in the United States unless it is sensational or of exceeding importance.

How do these gatekeepers make their decisions? First, they are individuals like the rest of us, with their own interests, ideas, and preferences. In addition, they have their own subjective definitions of what is news or what will appeal to the audiences they have in mind. Finally, they are exposed to pressures from many of the same sources that influence management decisions, and in addition are likely to be affected by the sources from whom they obtain information, their fellow reporters and editors, other journalists, and the commonly recognized standards of journalism.

The extent to which the decisions of gatekeepers are influenced by their individual interests is suggested by an experiment reported by an Associated Press executive at a recent meeting of journalists at Stanford University. Ten telegraph editors, most of whom had been police or city hall reporters prior to being put in charge of incoming wire copy, were invited to visit a number of Latin American countries, their expenses paid by a foundation grant. Following their return, the amount of news from Latin America carried in their newspapers increased by 75 percent. Less dramatic examples of the influence of journalists' interests can be seen in newspaper offices (and to a smaller extent in television newsrooms) every day. One reporter is known for a preference for stories about the supernatural; another may have developed an expertise in race relations. Public relations personnel, before they send an information release to a news organization, frequently try to find out which staff member is most likely to be interested in it. If it is sent to this person, the chances are better that it will be picked up and used.

American journalists tend to be somewhat more liberal than conservative. In a 1967 survey of foreign correspondents, about 60 percent expressed a preference for the Democratic party (30 percent identified themselves as "Liberal Democrats), 20 percent preferred the Republican party, and nearly all the rest considered themselves independents or declined to state a political preference (Bogart, 1968). A 1971 survey of a cross-section of editorial personnel in the American mass media, conducted by the National Opinion Research Center of the University of Chicago under the sponsorship of the John and Mary R. Markle Foundation, found a quite similar distribution. About 40 percent of the journalists queried classified themselves as left of the political center, another 40 percent saw themselves as middle of the road, and the remaining 20 percent put themselves right of center. Journalists in the Middle Atlantic and New England states tend to be more liberal than others. (Data from this survey will be analyzed in Johnstone, Slawski, and Bowman, forthcoming.) It is generally agreed that personal political preferences influence a journalist's work, but the extent of the influence has not been documented.

What Is "News"?

Whatever a reporter's or editor's individual preferences, he or she will attempt to judge each story by its newsworthiness. Is it news, and if so, how important is it? Journalists frequently have difficulty defining what they mean by "news," indeed they may be irritated if you ask them for a definition. But after even a brief period of experience they all have a "news sense." When asked by a social scientist why he chose one item rather than another for inclusion in the evening news, a television journalist replied that "it grabs me" or "it doesn't grab me." He knew immediately which stories were worthy, from his point of view, of being included, even though he couldn't explain why (Warner, 1968). What is even more remarkable is that there is a high degree of agreement among journalists as to what is news. They seem to judge stories subjectively, but obviously have some objective standard against which each story is measured.

Just what is this standard? Social scientists have devoted considerable effort to determining what it is that makes a story newsworthy. One analysis of items included in radio news broadcasts concluded that five factors were particularly important. If an item had all five it was very likely to be used; but it might still be used if it had fewer of the factors but to a higher degree. The five factors were:

High Impact It should make a difference to the news audience. A story about inflation or a new tax probably would have high impact.

Conflict This may be physical conflict, but is more likely to be a difference of opinion.

Known Principal A story about a prominent personality is more likely to be news than the same story about an unknown.

Proximity The event should be close in either a geographical or a psychological sense. A fire downtown is a proximate event, but a far-away airplane crash in which someone from the same city is killed may be close psychologically.

Timeliness This implies not only recency, but that the item is relevant to the concerns of the moment.

Of the five factors, conflict, known principal, and timeliness seemed to be the most important (Buckalew, 1974).

Other researchers have suggested additional characteristics that make for newsworthiness. One of these is the length of time it takes an event to occur. Something that occurs suddenly, like an earthquake, is more likely to be reported than a gradual development, like the spread of a desert into farmlands, even though the latter may be more destructive. Thus the move of millions of black Americans from the farms of the South to the cities of the North in the decades following World War I was scarcely noted by the press, even though it was one of the most massive migrations in human history. Another characteristic is that an event should fit in with the mental image of what one expects. For example, an incident regarding a snake charmer or an exotic religious cult in a developing country is more likely to be reported than the construction of a modern dam or bridge there (Galtung and Ruge, 1970).

If the characteristics of what is defined as news sometimes seem to be strange or irrational we should not blame the journalists—at least not exclusively. A social scientist has pointed out that what is visible and what is important is defined by society as a whole, and the journalist should not be criticized for adhering to standards that the rest of us also use. At one time, poor and black minorities in American society were regarded as invisible, and consequently there were few stories about them unless they engaged in criminal behavior against a middle-class person. (Crimes committed by one poor or black person against another were ordinarily not reported.) As social structure changes, the characteristics of news content change also (Roshco, 1975).

That an event is defined as news does not necessarily mean that it will be reported; there is always more news than can be used. Furthermore, a given event can be reported in many different ways; journalists have to make innumerable decisions about which details to include and which to exclude. This applies to editors as well as reporters. A story of 800 words may be cut to 50 in order to fit it into the available space, or a three-minute film sequence may be cut to 45 seconds.

Pressures on Journalists

A variety of influences play on journalists as they decide which stories to use and how to handle them. One would think that their perceptions of audience interests and their expectations of probable audience reactions would play a major role. This is sometimes the case. When researchers interviewed a number of reporters and editors and asked them whether they had been thinking about their readers as they worked on a story, it turned out that many of them had. One expected the readers to be angry and to disagree. Another, who had just finished a story on the conviction of a public housing official said he thought the story would be of interest to the thousands of people who live in housing projects. These mental images had at least some effect on the way the story was handled (Pool and Schulman, 1959). Journalists who write for very specialized audiences, in particular, seem to think of their readers as they write. A European newsman, who reported on diplomatic events for an elite newspaper, said that when he wrote a story he often thought of a particular group of officials in another country—he wanted to make his own country's policy clear to them (Davison, 1975).

But on the whole it is remarkable how little journalists think about their audiences, and how little they know about the people who will read or see their work. A researcher who interviewed the editors and producers responsible for television network news broadcasts reported that there seemed to be considerable doubt as to what the audience really wanted and also a feeling that it was improper to play up to the audience too much (Warner, 1968). One television newsman said he sometimes had the feeling nobody was watching. When a cross-section of American journalists were asked whether it was "very important" to concentrate on news of interest to the widest possible public, only about one-third said that it was (Johnstone, Slawski, and Bowman, 1972–73).

In any case, journalists are not much better than anyone else when it comes to predicting audience tastes. A group of newspaper managing editors was asked to predict which of a large group of articles would appeal most to the public, and their answers were then compared with those of a random sample. It was found that the editors had done only slightly better than would be expected under the laws of chance (Bogart 1968–69). And a group of television news directors estimated that more than four out of five members of their audiences would prefer male announcers, while most members of their audiences told researchers that they didn't care whether the announcers were male or female (Stone, 1973–74).

Nevertheless, it is remarkable how close journalists and the public come to agreeing which are the most important *categories* of news. If one compares the issues defined as "most important" by respondents to the Gallup Poll and those on which *Time, Newsweek,* and *U.S. News* published the most stories, the similarity is very great (Funkhouser, 1973). A study in Knoxville, Tennessee, which compared the judgment of three editors of the *Knoxville News-Sentinel* with that of a sample of subscribers, also showed a high degree of agreement as to which issues were of greatest importance (Garrison, 1973). Both of these studies may be reflecting a tendency of the public to rank as important those issues they read about in the press or learn about from broadcast news.

News sources may exercise a more important influence on the way stories are handled than do perceptions of audience interest. Much of the news that journalists obtain depends on the cooperativeness of their sources. This is true not only with respect to exclusive information obtained from high level government officials, but also for stories about crime, science, and many other subjects. The identity of sources must sometimes be protected, some information must be withheld, and stories must be written in such a way that the source will be cooperative the next time. Several studies of Washington correspondents have emphasized the closeness of relationships between reporters and government officials. This does not necessarily mean that journalists soft-pedal information that is unfavorable to the government, but it does mean that they must take the source into consideration when writing the story (Nimmo, 1964; Rosten, 1937).

Special interest groups and advertisers seek to influence reporters and editors just as they try to influence management. Their success in doing so differs from one news organization to the next and from one subject to another. Some trade associations offer prizes to journalists writing the "best" story in the area with which the trade association is concerned. Other interest groups invite journalists to lavish parties and pay their expenses on junkets. In general, influence of this type plays a lesser role in political news than in news about sports, fashion, or commercial products.

But by far the strongest influences on the way a journalist conducts his work come from inside his own news organization and from the pressure exercised by the norms of the profession.

A former reporter for a large daily has described how life in a news organization can be made happy or miserable by a success or failure in having a story published in a prominent position. If one's story makes the front page, or the first page of the second section (known as the "split page") the result is likely to be a good assignment next time. There are also the more intangible rewards of a byline and the esteem of one's colleagues. But if the story is severely cut and tucked away on an inside page, or is not published at all, the penalty may be severe: One could be assigned to writing obituaries or to covering stories of secondary importance (Darnton, 1975). Since a story has no chance of being published unless it meets the approval of an editor higher up the line—perhaps the national editor or the foreign editor—these individuals are really the ones for whom the reporter writes. He or she may think about the audience and may take precautions not to alienate a good source, but the preferences of the editor matter even more.

Television reporters have an added incentive for providing editors and producers with material that the latter are likely to find newsworthy and deserving of a spot on the evening news show. Many stations pay an additional fee, on top of the regular salary, to each reporter whose story is used on the air.

The way in which personal interests may combine with the preferences of editors higher up in the organization is illustrated by the remarks of a former radio reporter. She recalled that one of her problems was lack of time to develop all the stories for which she had good leads. Most of her work was done on the telephone, but there weren't enough hours in the day to make all the calls that would be desirable:

One factor (in deciding which calls to make) was my interest in talking with the newsmaker. If he or she was a famous person I would make a special effort to get him/her on the telephone. There was the reinforcement effect of talking with a "celebrity," plus the added reinforcement of having the news director congratulate me on getting such an important person on tape.

As the quotation above illustrates, the inclinations of reporters and the preferences of editors usually are congruent: Both are likely to have the same mental image of the "ideal story." Consequently, it is rare that a reporter has to ask himself what it is that the editor would like to have. Rather, the reporter pursues an ideal established by the community of journalists as a whole, knowing that the closer he can come to this the more likely the story is to be used.

One indication of the similarity of judgment between reporters and editors, or between groups of journalists that are working together on, for example, a network newscast, is that they do not need to talk with each other very much. Conversations are brief. A few words usually suffice to convey an opinion, since all are fairly well acquainted with what the others think and how they will react to any given story (Warner, 1968).

The similarity of news judgment among different groups of journalists is shown dramatically by the extent to which the evening news shows of the three TV networks resemble each other. Repeated studies have found that most of the same stories are used by at least two of the networks, and many are used by all three, even though these stories come from different reporters and are selected from a mountain of possibilities. One researcher, studying a two-week period in 1971, found that 70 percent of the stories on weekday newscasts were used by two networks, while all three networks carried 58 percent of the stories (Lemert, 1974). Two other researchers, using a sample of newscasts from 1973, emerged with almost the same figures (Fowler and Showalter, 1974).

You might suspect that this striking similarity in news judgment results from each network finding out what the others are going to do and making its decisions accordingly—much as they do in the case of entertainment materials. But this is not the case. News broadcasts are made up on such a tight time schedule that little communication among networks would be possible, even if it were attempted. Many decisions are made at the last minute. Here is a description given by one participant-observer who studied network news policies:

> The atmosphere is hectic. It is 20 minutes before air time. The graphics man comes in quickly to show the Executive Producer the final graphics for the program. The show is still 45 seconds too short. Two stories are chosen from the wires, and a writer is called in and told to write the stories, each 45 seconds long. Three additional stories, 40, 25, and 50 seconds each, are prepared as insurance, for insertion into the program should it run too long or too short. There is still no word on the Chaplin footage, and the decision is made to use the prepared story with the old film footage for the first broadcast and to keep the second half of the second broadcast open. (Batscha, 1975:209)

Even though most journalists use similar standards in judging news, this still leaves plenty of room for diversity of treatment caused by editorial policy, audience preferences, technological factors, and other influences. Thus, two media may present the same story but give it different emphasis and treatment. During the Vietnam War it was found, for instance, that "hawk" newspapers gave smaller estimates of the number of persons attending antiwar demonstrations than did "dove" newspapers (Mann, 1974). But they all reported the demonstrations. Media that attempt to reach different audiences, or that have differing amounts of time or space available for the presentation of news, show much less overlap in subjects covered than do the the three networks—all of which appeal to substantially the same audience and have about the same amount of news time available (Sasser and Russell, 1972).

Most journalists share a common set of standards with regard to their professional performance, but they subscribe to individual journalistic standards with differing degrees of intensity. Newspeople usually agree that a journalist should investigate claims and statements made by the government, should get information to the public as quickly as possible, and should concentrate on news that is of interest to the widest possible public. But journalists differ as to how important each of these guidelines is. In a study based on a national cross-section of newspeople, researchers found that 78 percent of the respondents rated the first statement as "extremely important" (investigate government statements); 56 percent felt that speed was of equal importance, but only 39 percent considered that appealing to the widest possible public was "extremely important" (Johnstone, Slawski, and Bowman, 1972–73).

The effect of widely shared standards and practices among journalists is not to eliminate the influence of other factors but to moderate them. This is difficult to prove conclusively, but a number of experimental studies suggest that it is the case. One researcher tried to determine whether stories written by student journalists with favorable attitudes toward a news source would contain more favorable facts about this person than the stories written by reporters with unfavorable attitudes. They did not. The journalistic role, with its norm of impartiality, had apparently led all the reporters to write with relative impartiality (Drew, 1973). Another experimenter asked two groups of editors in Oklahoma and California to rate 48 news stories according to how likely they would be to use these stories in their papers. One group was composed of editors who were classified as "high authoritarians" on the basis of their responses to a psychological test; the other group was composed of "low authoritarians." There were some differences in the news decisions made by the two groups, but the similarities in their evaluations of the stories were more impressive than the differences. The influence of shared news values appeared to be far greater than the influence of personality (Snipes, 1974).

Journalistic norms of "objectivity" and "balance" explain in part why the mass media are so often attacked both from the left and the right. The efforts of journalists to be fair and impartial lead to stories that rarely reflect faithfully the view of any one interest group (Hall, 1974). Naturally, the press is more often accused of prejudice than praised for fairness. Nevertheless, some observers have been impressed by the efforts of individual reporters, at least, to be fair. A former aide to both President Eisenhower and President Nixon has said that although he was interviewed by the press hundreds of times he could recall only two instances in which he felt the reporter was biased and was attempting to prove a point regardless of the facts he might uncover (Hess, 1974). Some students of mass communications have seen efforts to be objective as a "strategic ritual" that is used by journalists to cover up their biases (Tuchman, 1972). Cases of bias can be found, but there is no question that the common standards of journalism—including the ideal of "objectivity"—exercise powerful influence on the practices of individual journalists.

How do these standards and practices develop? Some reporters, who are trained in schools or departments of journalism, absorb them during the educational process; but close association with other journalists after being employed by the mass media is even more important. As we have seen, what colleagues and editors think is highly relevant to reporters. In addition, most journalists devote close attention to what other journalists are doing; they read newspapers and magazines extensively and keep in close touch with television and radio. This pattern of attention encourages the development of a common conception of what the news is and how it should be handled. Indeed, news is sometimes defined as what is in the news media.

The strength of associations within the world of journalism enables the individual reporter to resist outside pressures to a greater extent than otherwise would be possible. It can also lead to phenomena that critics of the press have viewed with uneasiness. One of these is what has been called the "wolf pack" psychology. When one event has been defined within the community of journalists as "the big story" there is a tendency for all media to devote major attention to it. Sometimes the event is indeed an important one, and deserves all the attention it receives. But sometimes a lurid crime or a juicy scandal is "the big story." Then the public may be deprived of information about matters that are of greater significance.

When, in September, 1975, an unsuccessful attempt was made on President Ford's life, this event dominated the mass media, occupying a large portion of the available space and time for news. One journalist speculated about the information that might have been given more prominent treatment if the assassination attempt had not occurred. Among the news that was ignored that day, or almost ignored, was President Ford's program to give the United States self-sufficiency in energy resources, Secretary of State Kissinger's proposals for a new approach to peace in the Middle East, and numerous important local stories—including one on sanitation problems in New York City and a teachers' strike in Boston (Brown, 1975). There usually are hundreds of reporters present at the launching of a major space mission. Are so many really necessary? Couldn't a handful of wire service reporters do the job?

The established practices of journalism make it easier for skilled manipulators to influence news content. Senator Joseph McCarthy was able to dominate the front pages and airwaves with his charges of communists in government even though he never produced satisfactory evidence to back up his charges. Nevertheless, these charges satisfied the formal criteria for news, and the mass media felt obliged to give them prominent treatment. That is, the standards of journalism permitted reporters to relay the charges without determining their accuracy. Political groups of all shades and press consultants of all prices routinely take advantage of the tendency of journalists to react in a predictable manner to sensational accusations.

Nevertheless, on balance, the group norms of journalism offer reasonable assurance to a society that it will be informed of many events and ideas that are of significance to it. They dilute the power of owners, managers, and special interests. And if they can be exploited by manipulators, at least manipulators of all points of view have fairly even chances of access to the press. As one student of the mass media has concluded: "A press that values its autonomy and objectivity will offer outlets to well-documented advocacy, even when it runs counter to prevailing social values. Such advocacy will come from outside sources or from the press's own ranks." (Roshco, 1975:125)

The news content of American print and broadcast media can be explained primarily in terms of influences exerted by the social environment, the decision of owners and managers, and the norms of journalism.

American society shapes the character of the media system as a whole. It is a wealthy one. People can afford to buy television receivers, radios, magazines, and newspapers. The American government can exert various pressures on the media, but the extent of its influence is limited by the guarantee of press freedom in the constitution. There is a well-developed infrastructure for news, including wire services, feature services, public information releases of many kinds, and specialized media. Trained journalists are available, and the American audience is, on the whole, a literate one with tastes for many subjects.

Owners and managers also exert important influences on news content, but their freedom to mold the media is limited by the social environment, on the one hand, and the norms and practices of journalism on the other. Decisions of media managers with regard to budgets, assignments, and organizational structure have far-reaching implications for what is printed or broadcast. The structure of a news organization in itself often determines what stories are carried and how they are presented.

Of all the influences on media content, the norms and practices of journalism are the most immediate. Most journalists share a common conception of news—that which deals with prominent individuals or groups, involves conflict or change, and is of immediate relevance to the audience. Most journalists try to deal objectively and fairly with the news. They also try to interest their audiences, but like members of all professions they are more concerned with what their colleagues and immediate superiors will think about their work than they are about the reactions of the public. This is why the norms and practices of journalism are so significant in the shaping of news content.

FURTHER READING

A number of anthologies offer excellent selections on various aspects of media sociology. The volume edited by Jeremy Turnstall (*Media Sociology: A Reader*, University of Illinois Press, 1970) includes an article on "Decision-Making in Network TV News" by Malcolm Warner and a thoughtful discussion of the characteristics of news by Johan Galtung and Mari Holmboe Ruge—"The Structure of Foreign News." Another useful anthology, *Sociology of Mass Communications*, is edited by Denis McQuail (Penguin Books, Harmondsworth, England, 1972). Two chapters in *Mass Communication Research*, edited by W. Phillips Davison and Frederick T.C. Yu, offer convenient summaries of the role of journalists and the role of management, respectively, in the formation of media content. These are the chapters by Ben H. Bagdikian, "Professional Personnel and Organizational Structure in the Mass Media," and Leo Bogart, "The Management of Mass Media."

An outstanding monograph, reporting case studies of the *New York Times* and the *Washington Post*, is *Reporters and Officials* by Leon V. Sigal (Lexington Books, 1973). More popular descriptions of newspeople at work are found in Timothy Crouse, *The Boys on the Bus* (Random House, 1973) and Edward J. Epstein, *News from Nowhere* (Random House, 1973). Those who are interested in a sociological approach to the phenomenon of news will find it in *Newsmaking* by Bernard Roshco (University of Chicago Press, 1975).

EFFECTS

Part Two

What happens when you see an advertisement in a magazine?

Many effects are possible. You might yawn and turn the page; you might read the ad and either remember or forget what you read; you might make a mental note to buy the product next time you have the opportunity; or you might discuss the ad with a friend or relative.

Nobody could predict what your reaction to that advertisement would be, or what you would do as a result of seeing it, without knowing quite a lot about you: what other information sources you had available, whether you needed the product being advertised, whether you usually liked to read advertisements or just skipped them, and so on. And what happens to you as a result of being exposed to hundreds of advertisements nearly every day? Do you learn to disregard them, do you become cynical about advertising claims, or do you live be-yond your income? Again, the answer is "it depends. . . ."

Predicting the effects of other kinds of communications—television drama, newspaper stories, or radio talk shows—is equally difficult. Since each person is different, an almost infinite variety of reactions is possible. Nevertheless, we can make intelligent guesses about what will happen as a result of one or more communications if we can find answers to a series of questions:

What other communications on the same subject are available?

What kinds of people are exposed to the communications? What information, habits, and attitudes do they already have? What groups do they belong to? What do their friends and relatives think?

How can these people use the information? Will it make them feel better, or help them do something they want to do?

These questions are frequently interrelated. The answer to one may depend on the answer to another. For example, let's assume that the magazine advertisement you see is for a compact car. Perhaps you are interested in cars and have friends who are also interested and like to work on them. If this is the case, you probably read quite a lot about cars and may even subscribe to a specialized automotive magazine. But there may be something new in the advertisement—a new price, or information about recently developed optional equipment.

So what are the effects of the advertisement? The first effect is that it claims your attention; you read it. You may also remember some of the things it says; it increases the amount of information you have. You may use some of this information in talking with your friends; it provides material for conversation. Probably, since you know a lot about cars already and have many other sources of information, it won't change your attitude about the car being advertised. You may already have made up your mind about the kind you like best. On the other hand, if the ad really tells you something you didn't know before, you might go down to a showroom and look at the car; the ad would affect your behavior.

Communications can have effects on groups and organizations, as well as on individuals. Political parties, for instance, often react to press reports about what other political groups are saying and doing. They may also be influenced by reported reactions of other people to their own statements and activities. In addition, political parties issue news releases and buy advertising space to help raise money, to recruit supporters, or to get out the vote. The fact that mass media are available thus affects what these parties do.

Business organizations, government agencies, educational institutions, even social groups also make use of information from mass communications and rely on the media to carry their messages to a wider public. Some could not function without the mass media; others would function differently. Indeed, the kind of communication system we have helps to determine the shape of our society, just as the way our society is organized has a lot to do with the way the mass media function. If one changes the other changes, too. This is why controversies about the way mass media should be organized and conducted are so important. If government controlled all the media, opposition parties would find it difficult to survive. If minority groups in the population are not treated fairly by the media they are likely to be dissatisfied. Areas that are not adequately served by newspapers and broadcasting stations may stagnate economically.

The following three chapters will discuss in more detail the questions that have been raised above. The first chapter describes the channels of information that are available to us. The second deals with psychological and social factors that condition our responses to communications of all kinds. The third examines some of the uses of mass communications that are made by individuals and by organizations. Knowledge about other channels of communication, the psychological and social characteristics of audiences, and the uses of information will help to explain why the mass media have certain effects—or why they sometimes have no effect. But we rarely can provide complete explanations or make exact predictions. Many aspects of communications will have to be studied more intensively before better explanations and predictions are possible. Communication is so complex that it may never become an exact science, but by examining your own experience, and by observing what goes on around you, you can add to the total stock of our knowledge about it.

One other caution to keep in mind is that while it is convenient to speak about the effects of communication, it may be misleading. For communication is like water or air; it is found everywhere that human society exists. We are not likely to ask: "What are the effects of water?" Instead, we would want to investigate how water is used by the human organism, how it affects agriculture, how it can help to generate electricity, etc.

Similarly, what we are really concerned with in this section is the part played by the mass media in the lives of individuals and in the functioning of our society. How do communications help to satisfy your own wants and needs, and those of others? How do they contribute to political life, economic life, and cultural life? And how could they contribute more to the satisfaction of both individual and social needs? These are the important questions.

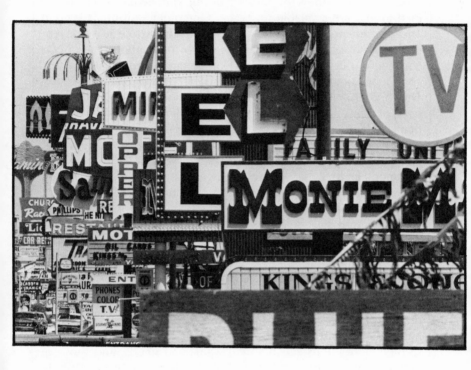

CHAPTER FOUR
Communication Channels

WHAT INFORMATION IS AVAILABLE?

A group of 41 Columbia University students recently tried to list all the communication channels to which they had been exposed during a period from Wednesday at 4:00 P.M. to Thursday at 4:00 P.M. They also recorded the approximate time that was devoted to each channel. Surprisingly, the total time that was spent in communication activities averaged 15 hours and 13 minutes, out of 24 hours, distributed as follows:

Television	1 hour, 03 minutes
Newspapers	53 minutes
Radio	1 hour, 18 minutes
Magazines and journals	30 minutes
Books	2 hours 29 minutes
Recordings	15 minutes
Motion pictures	03 minutes
Billboards, posters, handbills	19 minutes
Personal conversation (less than 5 minutes)	2 hours 24 minutes
Personal conversation (more than 5 minutes)	2 hours 05 minutes
Group discussions (3 or more involved)	1 hour 21 minutes
Lectures	2 hours 20 minutes
Other (reading personal mail, junk mail, labels, etc.)	13 minutes

Of course, this group was not typical of all students, and students are very different from other population groups, so this experiment does not tell us much about the behavior of the average person.

Students read more books than most other people, they attend more lectures, they watch television less, and so on.

Nevertheless, their listing brings out several important points. One is that it is very difficult to recall—even for a period as short as 24 hours—all the communication channels to which one is exposed. Several of the participants in the experiment mentioned later some communications that they had not remembered at the time they made their lists. A few had forgotten to report reading car-cards in the bus or subway; others neglected to mention that they had over-heard conversations in which they had not participated; one had had an exchange with a policeman, which he had not considered either a conversation or a discussion.

It is even more difficult to remember and to classify communications that do not involve words—either written or spoken. But these can be very important. If you see an automobile accident this may tell you more than if you read about it in the newspaper. Watching first-hand a skilled worker expertly perform a task or an accomplished athlete demonstrate physical coordination may mean more than viewing the same scenes on television. If someone shakes his fist at you, or shrugs his shoulders, that too is a communication. Propagandists and public relations specialists often arrange events that have a symbolic significance: For instance, a political candidate may ostentatiously eat a piece of pizza in an Italian neighborhood. This is often called "propaganda of the deed," or, in terms of the 1960s, "street theater."

The listing above reminds us also that exposure to communications can occur at the same time as other activities, and that one may be exposed simultaneously to two or more channels. Some people like to listen to the radio while reading; others are involved in conversation while viewing television; and most of us engage in communication activity while travelling.

Most important, however, is the reminder that person-to-person conversation is the single most important communication channel for most of us. It not only takes up a great deal of our time, but it affects the way we perceive communications received through other channels. Indeed, the main point to be made in this chapter is that we cannot understand the impact of the mass media unless we take person-to-person communication into account. The mass media affect each other, too—what we read in the newspaper may influence our attitudes about what we see on television, and vice versa—but the most important conditioning influence is likely to be what we hear from other people, or what we say to them.

A dramatic illustration of the power of person-to-person conversation was noted by the Iowa Poll (conducted by the *Des Moines Register and Tribune*) a few years ago. Two candidates for a state office were actively campaigning, filling the press and airwaves with their appeals. At the same time, the Iowa Poll was conducting periodic surveys to determine the public support for each. For several weeks, the proportions of voters favoring each candidate remained fairly stable. But then, suddenly, one went way down in the poll.

In trying to find a reason for his decline in popularity, the researchers examined attitudes toward the candidate among voters from various regions of the state, among various age groups, and among males and females. They found that sex appeared to be the decisive variable: Support among women had remained about the same as before, but had declined sharply among men. Then, in the survey conducted shortly thereafter, the proportion of women favoring this candidate declined to about the same proportion as among male voters.

Further questioning of respondents provided an explanation. A scurrilous story about the candidate's personal life had begun to circulate shortly before his decline in the polls. At first, because the story concerned sex, it was passed around only among men. But then, apparently, some men told their wives and the story began to circulate among women as well. This word of mouth communication, interacting with the campaign material publicized by the mass media, had influenced a large proportion of the voters.

One should not conclude from this illustration that word of mouth communication necessarily influences people more than information from the mass media. Sometimes it does and sometimes it doesn't. If you hear a rumor, you may want to check on its accuracy by consulting a newspaper or some other established news source. For instance, a study in Canada found that one-third of those who heard about the surprise marriage of Prime Minister Pierre Eliot Trudeau from another person checked this report by referring to the press, radio, or television. By contrast, only about one in ten of those who learned of the marriage first from one of the mass media checked on it through other sources (Fathi, 1973). Or, to take a different kind of example, you are more likely to have confidence in a chemical or mathematical formula if you find it in a text than if you hear it from a friend—unless your friend happens to be an expert chemist or mathematician. One researcher, who was studying the ways communities handle controversial issues, concluded that the media were quite useful in disasters such as floods, when people want to know what to do, but were less useful in community disputes when people want to know what to think (Coleman, 1957).

It is difficult to generalize. As the above examples indicate, different people react to information received through any given channel in different ways. A lot depends on the subject being treated, on the attitudes of the individual, and whether or not the source is a trusted one. The important thing is that we have many communication channels available to us and that information from one source is frequently complemented—or contradicted—by information from other sources.

Nevertheless, each channel does have certain capabilities. Some types of information are transmitted better through one than another. Some enjoy more confidence than others. Some reach one segment of the population better; others are more likely to reach other segments. If you want to inform people, or to persuade them, it is important to choose the right channels.

When you communicate with a person face to face, that person can hear your words, can watch your gestures, or may even feel the pressure of your hand. If you are wearing perfume or have used shaving lotion the sense of smell, also, may be involved. On the other hand, if you are talking with a person by telephone, the whole burden of communicating is borne by your voice. If you write a letter, then the words on the paper must carry most of the meaning.

Furthermore, when you speak directly to a person you can observe how he or she reacts. Even in a fairly large meeting you can usually tell whether people understand what you are saying and whether they approve or not. A telephone conversation does not allow you to see the expression of the person on the other end of the line; still, this person has the opportunity of responding to you immediately and you may be able to infer something from pauses, grunts, or sighs. But if you appear on television, speak on the radio, or write an article for a magazine, it is unlikely that you will ever know very much about the response of your audience. Many people may have turned off their receivers or skipped the article. In addition, channels differ in what could be called retrievability. If you write a letter or an article those whom you are addressing can preserve your words if they wish. They cannot do this if you speak over the telephone or from a broadcasting station unless they have recording facilities. And, ordinarily, a person-to-person conversation is not preserved at all.

Thus, the various channels of communication differ markedly: in the senses that are involved (hearing, seeing, smelling, touching—even tasting); in the number of people that can be reached; in the degree to which you can perceive their reactions; in the extent to which they can choose to attend to your message or not; and in the way the communication can be preserved for future use—whether in a film archive, as a newspaper clipping, on the tape of a recorder, or not at all.

Because different channels are able to convey different shades of meaning, those who attend an official hearing or debate and those who later read the verbatim transcript of what was said may receive quite different impressions. This is often the case with congressional hearings. For many years, Congressman John Rooney of Brooklyn was Chairman of the House subcommittee that had to pass on the appropriations of the Department of State and the U.S. Information Agency. Those who read the transcripts of these hearings were often impressed by the sharpness of Congressman Rooney's remarks. He seemed to delight in humiliating the high government officials who appeared before him. What the transcripts did not show, however, was that Mr. Rooney's sometimes abrasive words were often accompanied with an exaggerated wink, a broad grin, or a humorous gesture. The impression he made on those in the hearing room was quite different from the one the written record of his words conveyed.

Some students have concluded that when people are conversing face to face more than half the meaning is transmitted by nonverbal communication. The expression of the face can modify or supplement the impact of words. How people stand or sit tells us something about their attitudes toward others who are present as well as about their own self-assurance. For instance, if a person slouches in his chair while talking with someone of higher status this is usually interpreted as an expression of disrespect. Clothing, too, can convey meaning. Even the distance that we stand from another person while talking with him is a form of communication (Harrison, 1973). Some emotional states are expressed better by gestures and actions than by words, as suggested in the adage:

When in trouble, when in doubt,
Flap your arms and rush about.

The ways of communicating without words are learned by children as they grow up, just as spoken languages are learned, so that nonverbal communication differs from culture to culture. When you converse with a Latin American, he is likely to think that you are standing too far away from him, and that this indicates coldness or suspicion. But, it may seem to you that he is standing too close, and thus being over-familiar. The meaning of distance differs in the two cultures (Hall, 1959).

Since television and film can transmit nonverbal signs, as well as language, one might conclude that their content is richer than print. It is; but this does not necessarily mean that we learn more from television and film than from the print media. For one thing, we have more control over the latter; we can read at our own pace and go back and read again if we do not understand the first time. For another, we tend to concentrate our attention more when reading.

Numerous studies, going back almost to the time talking motion pictures (or "talkies") were first introduced, have explored the relative advantages of print and film in communicating information. In one recent study, the experimenter filmed scenes of a number of married couples discussing their plans for a summer vacation. She then prepared four information sources: videotape with sound (the way you would see it on your television set); videotape without sound; the sound track alone; and a typed transcript of what the actors in the film said to each other. Then she exposed matched groups of observers to each of these information sources and asked them afterward to describe the people they had observed (the actors) in as much detail as possible.

She found, as you would expect, that the videotape with sound conveyed more information than sound track by itself or the videotape without sound. But even the pictures alone conveyed most of the information about the emotional characteristics of the actors— what kinds of people they were. The written transcript, on the other hand, was particularly good at providing factual information and information about characteristics other than emotional—for example, how logical the actors were. Of course, additional variables were involved, too. Some observers were keener than others in picking up information from visual cues; some tended to read the transcript more carefully than others. In addition, some of the couples who were filmed conveyed more of their meaning by gestures and glances; some relied more on the spoken word (Gartner, 1972).

There are, of course, important differences *within* channels. A film may be skillfully made, and transmit meaning clearly, or it may be poorly made and confusing. A book or article may be well written or garbled. Some people speak more clearly than others. Techniques have been developed for determining how easy or difficult written and spoken material is, and attempts have been made to study the "language" of film. One of the best known of the techniques for analyzing written materials is the "Flesch Scale," which is based on number of words per sentence and number of syllables per word. A researcher who applied this analytic technique to a random sample of stories carried by the Associated Press and United Press International on a randomly chosen date, February 11, 1972, found that nearly 95 percent of the AP material and two-thirds of the material supplied by UPI was within the reading ability of the average high school graduate. The rest of the material was more difficult, and was better suited to college-educated readers. Thus, there may be appreciable differences even in communications that are intended for very similar publics (Hoskins, 1973).

There are even greater differences within channels when the communications are intended for different audiences. Technically, a large urban daily and an underground weekly are both newspapers, but there is little similarity in content. There are often wide differences in programming between commercial television stations and public television. A magazine may be designed to reach a small audience of several thousand scientists or a mass audience of millions.

In spite of the major differences within channels it is useful to recognize that each one does some things best and other things less well. Some can reach large numbers of people, others are particularly good at reaching certain population groups, still others are well adapted to communicating specialized information, and so on.

AUDIENCE SIZE

Television is commonly believed to have the largest audience of any mass medium in the United States. Nearly all American homes (about 96 percent) have TV receivers, and about a third of them have more than one receiver. In the average home a set is on over six hours per day, and the average individual watches more than three hours. The amount of viewing differs by season, however. On nearly every night of a winter month, about 65 percent of all homes have a TV set on, no matter what programs are being televised, but this figure declines substantially during the summer when daylight lasts longer and the weather is better in most of the country.

Commercial television attracts most of this huge audience, but in a 1970 survey 20 percent of the respondents said that they watched educational television (or public television) at least once a week. More might have watched if they had been able to, but at that time only about half of TV homes could receive a public television signal (Bower, 1973).

The total audience for daily newspapers is of almost equal size. A national survey in 1969 found that 78 percent of Americans 18 years or older said they read a newspaper on an average weekday. One third of the respondents claimed to read two or more papers each day. Another survey, at about the same time, found an even larger proportion of adults (90 percent) who said they were newspaper readers (Rivers, 1973).[1]

[1] Differences in percentages are often caused by different question wordings. For instance, if you asked "Do you *regularly* read a newspaper," you would probably find fewer people saying "yes" than if you asked "Do you usually read a newspaper?"

Radio is the third medium that blankets the American public. Researchers have not paid so much attention to the radio audience in recent years, so fewer figures are available, but a study by the National Broadcasting Company in 1965 showed that about 92 million people were being reached by radio each day. By contrast, only about 81 million a day were being reached by television in 1972 (Schramm and Alexander, 1973). But people spend more time with TV. A recent study in New York found that the average person over 18 spent 2 hours and 59 minutes a day listening to radio and 3 hours and 15 minutes viewing television.

Less is known about the size of the national audience for other mass media—magazines, books, motion pictures, recordings, billboards, direct mail, and so on. We do know that almost everybody reads *some* magazines. In a national survey conducted in 1974, only nine percent of the respondents said they had not looked at any magazine during the past month (and four percent couldn't remember or didn't answer). Of the rest, 22 percent said they had looked at one or two, and 65 percent said they had looked at three or more. Indeed, 17 percent claimed to have read 10 or more magazines during the past month.

Books, too, reach a huge audience. On any given day, about one-third of adult Americans spend from 15 minutes to an hour reading a book (excluding comic books). Religious literature, and especially the Bible, occupies the attention of nearly a quarter of these readers.

We know the number of admissions to motion picture theatres—about one billion during 1974—but since some people attend many times and others almost never do it's difficult to arrive at a single figure for the size of the motion picture audience. Two-thirds of admissions are accounted for by persons under 25 years of age.

The same is true of recordings. Sales of phonograph records and tapes amounted to about two billion dollars in 1973, but it's probable that a relatively small proportion of the population spent most of this money. Furthermore, we don't know how often the recordings are played.

Nearly everyone is exposed to billboards or to advertising sent through the mails, but different people give different degrees of attention to these messages.

The sizes of audiences for all media are likely to differ according to the hour of the day, the day of the week, the season of the year, and the geographic area of residence. For example, between 7 and 8 o'clock in the morning, only about 8 percent of the homes in the United States are likely to have TV sets on, but around a third of all adults will be listening to the radio. The situation in the evening is reversed: many more people are viewing television then. A lot of those who read a newspaper weekdays and Sundays don't bother to read one on Saturdays.

AUDIENCE CHARACTERISTICS

It is usually important to know what kinds of people are being reached by a given medium, as well as how many. Some of the variables commonly used in the analysis of audience data are age, education, sex, race, and socioeconomic status (SES) or income. Some of these variables are related to each other. For instance, people over 65 are likely to have lower incomes than those in the 35–65 year groups. People with more education are likely to have higher incomes than those with less education, and so on.

Other variables, too, are sometimes related to media use. One of these is personality. Would you, for instance, think that women who described themselves as having many friends and being well liked would watch more or less television than women who did not think of themselves this way? You might reason that a person who had a lot of friends would spend more time visiting with them and therefore wouldn't have so much time to watch TV. If so, you would be wrong. At least, a survey conducted by the *Los Angeles Times* in 1970 found that women who rated themselves as "sociable" were more likely to be heavy viewers of TV (five or more hours the previous day) than to be light viewers (no viewing at all the previous day). Light viewers, it turned out, were more oriented toward doing things, and described themselves as engaging in physical activities requiring lots of energy (Gutman, 1973).

TV viewing seems to be related to the life cycle. Young children are heavy viewers, while teenagers watch less than any other age group. Then viewing goes back up for those between 20 and 29, only to decline between 30 and 49. From age 50 on, television use is likely to be heavy again (Bower, 1973). One can speculate about the reasons for these viewing patterns. Young children have time to watch—and they do. Teenagers are involved in more activities outside the house, but when they marry they are more likely to stay home weekends and evenings. After the children arrive (for the 30 to 49 age group) there is less time for TV, but this changes after 50. There is no proof that this speculation is correct; it just seems probable.

The amount of television viewing varies also according to sex, education, race, and income. Women watch more than men; those with less than a college education more than the college educated; blacks more than whites; and lower-income groups more than higher-income groups. Indeed, family income seems to affect the amount of viewing even by young children: 6 to 11 year olds in households with less than $5000 annual income watch about 30 hours per week, as opposed to about 24 hours per week in households with incomes over $10,000.

Some researchers have suggested that these variables are not as important as they look, and maintain that the amount of time spent watching TV depends largely on how much time one spends at home. Thus, women watch more than men because more women than men are at home during the day; those with less income and education are not likely to have such demanding jobs or so many social engagements as the better educated and more affluent; retired people don't have to go to work; and so on. This explanation would seem to apply also to children in low-income households: They are less likely than other children to engage in organized after-school activities, since these often cost something or require transportation.

The theory that time spent with television depends mainly on opportunity, rather than on age, sex, race, education, or other variables, is supported by the observation that all these groups spend about the same number of hours viewing during evenings and weekends. These are times when nearly everyone can watch, regardless of whether they are employed or go to school. As far as evening and weekend viewing are concerned, there is no difference between men and women, and the better educated watch about as much as the less educated. Race, age, and a few other variables still make a difference, but not a big enough difference to be very interesting (Bower, 1973).

Nevertheless, the fact remains that some population groups *do* have more time to watch TV than others; therefore, the TV audience tends to be disproportionately composed of older people, women, blacks, and those with less income and education.

Another important characteristic of the TV audience is that it is composed very largely of people watching in groups. Indeed, three-quarters of a sample of teenagers in a midwestern town told researchers that they "rarely" watched television alone. And the evening audience is composed heavily of family groups. This means that many people talk with each other while the television set is on. They may discuss the programs, or they may talk about other things and pay little attention to what is on the tube (Chaffee, 1972).

Newspapers, magazines, books, and other print materials, by contrast, are usually consumed by people who are alone or who prefer to read rather than to talk with those around them. Those who commute to their jobs by public transportation are especially likely to be heavy consumers of print.

As with television, age, education, sex, race, and socioeconomic status are related to newspaper reading. In 1969, for instance, it was found that 82 percent of those in the 35 to 64 year age group were regular readers of newspapers, while only 73 percent in the 18 to 24 year age group were (Rivers, 1973). Later surveys show that the picture is much the same today. Men are somewhat more likely to read a newspaper on weekdays than are women, but on Sundays there doesn't seem to be any significant difference. Better-educated people read newspapers more than less-educated, whites more than blacks, and those with higher incomes more than those with lower incomes. In a recent survey, 70 percent of adults in families with less than $7500 income said they usually read a paper weekdays; while 85 percent of those with a family income of $15,000 or more were regular weekday readers.

Only 11 percent of American adults say that they rarely or never read a newspaper, but this proportion varies in different areas of the country. There have been a number of studies of nonreaders, who are usually poor people with little education who live in rural areas (Penrose et al., 1974).

An important characteristic of newspaper readers is that they are significantly more involved with their local communities than are nonreaders. They are more likely to belong to local organizations, to attend public meetings, and to have lived in the same community for three years or more (Rarick, 1973; Schweitzer, 1974).

A small number of newspapers and magazines reach a large proportion of "VIPs" in the United States. In a study made in 1971 and 1972, a sample of 545 top leaders from business, politics, labor, civic organizations, and the mass media were interviewed and asked about their reading habits. Well over half of those who were interviewed were readers of the New York Times; almost as many read the Wall Street Journal. Those who were in high political positions, as well as labor leaders and mass media executives, were likely to read the Washington Post. When asked to mention their favorite columnist, the respondents overwhelmingly chose James Reston. Tom Wicker was the next most frequently mentioned.

The members of this sample of influentials were also queried about their magazine reading habits. Significantly, no one magazine emerged as a clear choice for all groups. Business and labor leaders most frequently mentioned Business Week, with Time second; political leaders chose U.S. News and World Report, then Newsweek; in the case of leaders of civic organizations there was a tie between the *New York Times Magazine* and *Newsweek*. Other magazines mentioned fairly frequently by members of all groups included *Fortune, New Yorker, Reader's Digest, Saturday Review, Harper's, Foreign Affairs*, and the *New Republic* (Weiss, 1974).

In general, patterns of magazine readership follow those for newspapers, except that young adults under 30 seem to read somewhat more than those who are older. Men, the more educated, and the more affluent are heavier magazine readers. The greatest difference is by education: Those with less than a high school diploma say they read an average of 2.8 magazines each month; those who have been to college say they read an average of 5.5.

ABILITY OF THE MEDIA TO TRANSMIT INFORMATION

If you ask which medium conveys information best, then you should ask two more questions: Information about what? And to whom is the information supposed to go?

People increasingly say that they usually get most of the news about what's going on in the world from television. When the Roper Organization asked a national cross-section about this in 1974, 65 percent replied "television" and only 47 percent said "newspapers." (The percentages add up to more than 100 because some people mentioned two media—for example, "newspapers *and* television.") Table 1 shows the trend during the past 15 years (Roper, 1975).

Table 1
PRINCIPAL SOURCE OF INFORMATION ABOUT WHAT'S GOING ON IN THE WORLD TODAY

	1959	1963	1967	1971	1974
Television	51%	55%	64%	60%	65%
Newspapers	57	53	55	48	47
Radio	34	29	28	23	21
Magazines	8	6	7	5	4
Other people	4	4	4	4	4
Don't know/ no answer	1	3	2	1	*

Until 1974, respondents with a college education chose newspapers in preference to television, but in that year the two media were chosen with about equal frequency: 56 percent of the college educated said "television" and 55 percent "newspapers."

Of course, when one asks for sources of information about "what is going on in the world today," this is a very broad question. That is why it is desirable to specify more precisely what aspect of the news. When queried about national or statewide politics, more people say that they get most of their news from television than from the press, but if they are asked about local elections or local issues they are more likely to mention newspapers than television. (In 1974, 41 percent said "newspapers" and 30 percent "television.") It is also interesting to note that "other people" are mentioned fairly often as the best way to become acquainted with candidates running in local elections—by 14 percent in 1974. In Table 1, in response to the more general question, only 4 percent mentioned "other people."

When it comes to information about science and health, people are more likely to turn to the print media than to radio or television. A rather old national survey (1957) found that 41 percent of the respondents mentioned newspapers as their primary source of science news, as opposed to 27 percent who mentioned TV and 25 percent who said "magazines." For those who had at least some college, magazines were the favorite source, being mentioned by 44 percent. These results are confirmed in general by more recent studies (Wade and Schramm, 1969; White, 1969–70). Similarly, people report print media as their major sources of information about health and medicine, with reliance on newspapers and magazines increasing as the education level increases. Thus, 70 percent of college graduates who knew about polio vaccine reported print media as their major sources of information, as opposed to 37 percent who mentioned broadcast media. Among high school graduates, 57 percent relied on print and 46 percent on broadcast sources.

It seems safe to conclude that people look to different media for information about different subjects. Books are good sources for many types of specialized information—how to grow tomatoes, for instance, or what happened at the battle of Bunker Hill. Magazines may provide either specialized or rather general information, depending largely on the type of magazine. Radio is convenient for learning about such things as the weather and traffic conditions. Television entertainment programs are full of information and misinformation about the way people lived on the American frontier and how detectives spend their time.

It is also clear that different types of people place primary reliance on different channels. In general, the more highly educated people are, the more they rely on print media for information.

How much do people remember of what they read or see or hear?

And is material from one medium remembered better than from another? Again, the answer seems to depend on the kind of information being presented and the attentiveness of the people one is talking about. A recent experiment in Canada, using hypothetical news stories as its subject matter, found that a little more was remembered from print sources than from either radio or television. But the differences were very small. The subjects forgot 77 percent of the material presented on television and 73 percent of what they read in newspapers (Wilson, 1974). Other studies have found that people learn slightly more from television or that there is no appreciable difference among media in their ability to impart information.

The fact remains, however, that most people watch television with a rather low level of attention, and when they listen to the radio they usually are doing something else at the same time. A study in the San Francisco Bay area, conducted for the National Association of Broadcasters, found that almost half of a random sample who watched the evening news show on television couldn't mention a single news item from the show when they were telephoned later that same evening. Indeed, some researchers have concluded that when people say they get most of their news from television what they really are saying is that they don't get much news at all (M.J. Robinson, 1974). On the other hand, people do seem to derive most of their impressions about the personalities of political candidates—their honesty, intelligence, warmth, and so on—from seeing them on television (Kraus, 1962).

In short, the question about which of the mass media is best at imparting information doesn't make much sense unless one specifies what sort of information and to what audience. All media have certain strengths and weaknesses. A television news story is seldom longer than 300 words, while a newspaper story may run to 1000 words, and magazine articles or books may be almost any length. You probably can read three times as fast as a radio announcer speaks, but on the other hand you can listen to the radio while driving. A more relevant question is which channel is more effective in doing a particular kind of job or, even better, what mix of channels is most effective.

PERSON-TO-PERSON COMMUNICATION

Almost everything we learn from mass media channels is affected in one way or another by what other people say to us or what we say to them. We may pay attention to a newspaper story or TV program because we know our friends are likely to be interested in it and we want to be able to discuss it with them. Our attention may be distracted by others when we are reading, listening, or viewing. Whether or not we believe a particular report may depend on what we have heard about the report or its source from other people. Most of us spend a large proportion of our waking hours in person-to-person communication. And once we express an opinion about something we have heard or read we tend to hold this opinion more strongly. Our attitudes are affected by what we say to other people as well as by what they say to us.

Most person-to-person communication takes place in groups consisting of two people (known to social scientists as "dyads") or in slightly larger groups. Researchers who have studied small groups find that communication in each group usually conforms to a particular pattern: Some members talk more than others; some are more likely to take the initiative in making proposals; some usually express support or approval of ideas advanced by others; some characteristically don't agree with anything; and so on. Once one has become acquainted with the pattern of communication in a particular group, it is possible to predict fairly accurately how the members of this group will stand or sit in relation to each other and the kind of remarks each is likely to make (Bales, 1950). Even a "common language" may develop. Certain expressions take on a meaning—sometimes a humorous one—that is known only to members of the group.

But person-to-person communication does not necessarily remain bottled up in small groups. Social scientists at the Massachusetts Institute of Technology have estimated that each person "knows" from 500 to 2000 other people. That is, these are people one recognizes, can call by name, and at least occasionally communicates with. In an experiment with a small group of volunteers, it was found that during 100 days each person had social contacts with from 72 to 685 others. If we assume that a person has a total of 1000 acquaintances, then friends of friends of friends would number one billion. Therefore, it is likely that there would be not more than two "intermediaries" between any two people in the United States (Pool, 1973a).

It is important to stress that this is true in theory only, since in practice your friends may have about the same friends you do; most of those in a particular social "universe" may belong to the same ethnic group, the same church, or the same geographical community. People don't communicate at random, but through social networks, and for the most part they communicate with other people who are like themselves. Nevertheless, there is enough overlap between various social universes so that ideas and messages do circulate by mail or by word-of-mouth among tremendous numbers of people.

The way very diverse individuals are linked together by acquaintance networks is illustrated by an experiment conducted in widely separated geographical regions of the United States. A number of people in different localities were given pamphlets and asked to forward these to designated persons in other areas. They were given the name, address, occupation, and a little more information about the "addressee" and were asked to send the booklet to anybody with whom they were personally acquainted who would be more likely to know the "addressee" than they were. In one case, a Kansas wheat farmer was given a booklet destined for the wife of a divinity student in Cambridge, Massachusetts. The wheat farmer passed the booklet to a minister in his home town, who sent it to another minister he happened to know in Cambridge. The Cambridge minister was personally acquainted with the wife of the divinity student and handed the booklet to her when he saw her on the street.

This was an unusually short chain, involving only two intermediaries. Most chains that were completed had from five to six links. And a number of chains broke down: Someone failed to forward the booklet.

To find out how well such chains operate when the sender is a member of one ethnic group and the addressee a member of another, 18 residents of New York City, half black and half white, were asked to serve as "target persons." The booklets were then given to 540 white residents of Los Angeles, who were instructed to mail them to any person they knew who was more likely to be acquainted with the target individual than they were. Many more of the booklets for the white New York residents actually reached the addressees (33 percent) than the black addressees (13 percent), but the white-black chains were only slightly longer than the white-white chains. The intermediaries, whose acquaintanceships crossed racial lines and made it possible to complete a white-black chain, were primarily professionals—doctors, lawyers, teachers, and so on. A smaller number of these intermediaries were managers, officials, and sales or clerical personnel; but practically none of them belonged to blue-collar groups. Most of the white-black chains that were not completed never crossed the racial barrier (Korte and Milgram, 1970; Travers and Milgram, 1969).

While it is true that person-to-person communication *can* span racial, occupational, and other groups, it is much more intense within groups that are relatively homogeneous. Business people talk with business people more than with others; lawyers more with lawyers;

and so on. The informal links among scientists who are working within the same area are most impressive. These groups of scientists are sometimes called "invisible colleges." The members of these "colleges" are in almost constant communication with each other regarding what is going on within their fields; and what they say or write to each other is likely to have a strong influence on the professional work that each one does. (Crane, 1972).

In contrast to the precise and authoritative messages that circulate within "invisible colleges," news that circulates mouth-to-mouth throughout the public in general is often referred to as rumor. Ordinarily, the source of a rumor and the information it contains are difficult to verify. Most rumors express hostility (as in the case of stories about racial incidents), reflect fear (there are ten thousand cans of poisoned sardines in supermarkets throughout the state), or are based on hopes (a sure cure for cancer has been found). They circulate most widely when the subject matter is important to a given population and when the people who are concerned cannot obtain all the information they would like to have on the subject, or suspect that information about it is being withheld. Rumors are especially likely in wartime, when people know that some matters are secret and doubt that the government is giving them full information. Thus, during World War II, when a coal transport sank off the coast of Cape Cod as a result of an accident, rumors circulated in New England to the effect that the ship had been torpedoed and that thousands of nurses on board had drowned (Allport and Postman, 1954).

As this example suggests, most of the reports that we refer to as rumors are untrue or are greatly exaggerated. Even if a message is fairly close to the facts at the outset, people who repeat it are likely to leave out some details, overemphasize others, and add new details as it passes from mouth to mouth. These phenomena of "leveling," "sharpening," and "assimilation" can be observed in laboratory experiments or in games where a report is introduced at one end of a human chain and then whispered from person to person down to the other end.

But not all reports passed from person to person are untrue. Some rumors represent pooling of information by many people, all of whom are concerned with learning as much as possible about something that is going on. Sociologists have referred to this kind of rumor-mongering as a collective problem-solving transaction. It gives rise to the spoken equivalent of a newspaper and helps people to cope with changes that are going on around them (Rosnow, 1974; Shibutani, 1966). Some scholars, however, would say that reports which are not untrue or exaggerated should not be classified as rumors. In an election, for instance, people who are wondering how to vote may share with each other what they know about the various candidates. Over a period of time, through these informal conversations, a substantial body of fairly accurate information develops.

Sociologists have pointed out also that any social organization in which people interact with each other frequently can provide channels for person-to-person communication. Verbal reports circulate easily throughout schools, churches, factories, clubs, and other social institutions. Most of the messages circulating through these channels are related in some way to the organization itself ("the word is that the office is going to close at four o'clock today") but some may be of a more general nature.

There is a border area between person-to-person communication and mass communication that one researcher has labeled "quasi-mass communication." When large numbers of salesmen, political party workers, or religious spokesmen deliver fairly standard messages throughout the country, millions of people may be reached. The messages may be spoken and they may be delivered face-to-face. In these respects they resemble person-to-person communications. But the size of the total audience and the fact that the content of the message is standard makes them more like mass communications. There is some opportunity for audience reaction (or "feedback)—more than in mass communication but not as much as in most person-to-person situations. Quasi-mass communication is particularly important in political and social movements: Those who are working to promote the movement are likely to try to speak to potential converts wherever they can be found—on streetcorners, outside supermarkets, at meetings of church groups or social clubs—yet the message is always substantially the same (Menzel, 1971). The governments of China and the Soviet Union make extensive use of quasi-mass communication.

CHANNEL INTERACTION

When something important happens, people learn about it through a variety of information channels. Some are informed first through television, some through radio, some through newspapers, and some through personal conversation. Which channel brings the news to most people first depends mainly on how important the event is and at what time of day it occurs. If an event is one that has tremendous significance for almost everyone, then those who hear about it first are likely to tell others immediately. Therefore, person-to-person communication plays a larger role. If the event takes place in the late afternoon or early evening, then most people are likely to get their first information from television; if news bulletins are sent out in the morning, then radio may reach a larger audience first.

When President Kennedy was shot on November 22, 1963, the bad news travelled with amazing speed. One study of this event, conducted in California, found that nearly 90 percent of those in a random sample were informed of the shooting (even before death was confirmed) within 45 minutes of the first announcement. Since the event took place in the morning, when many people were not at home, about 30 percent of these "early knowers" first heard the news from the radio and only about 20 percent from TV; the remainder first learned about it from someone else. Obviously, those who had happened to have their radios or TV sets on rushed to tell other people as soon as they heard the news (Greenberg, 1964; Greenberg and Parker, 1965).

The attempted assassination of Governor George Wallace during the afternoon of May 15, 1972, while he was campaigning for the presidency, produced a different pattern. Telephone interviews with a random sample in New York City that evening showed that nearly half of the respondents first heard the news from television, about a quarter from radio, and the rest from other people (Schwartz, 1973–74).

An example of a less cataclysmic, but still important, event was the release of a papal encyclical on family planning in March 1967. Immediately after the release, telephone interviews were conducted with random samples in 15 American cities to find out, among other things, how many people had heard of the encyclical and from what source they had learned about it first. In this case, newspapers were the most significant source of first information, being named by more than one-third of the respondents. Television and radio were each mentioned as a first source by somewhat less than a third of the sample, and interpersonal communication played a very small role as a first source. About 55 percent of the respondents said that they had heard about the encyclical by the time they were telephoned (Adams, Mullen, and Wilson, 1969).

All studies of news diffusion make it clear that no one channel informs the public; many are involved. It is interesting to know which channel reaches most people first, and under what conditions, but it is more important to document the extent to which channels interact and multiple channels are consulted.

When asked to describe their behavior after hearing about a major news event, most people make it clear that they engage in further communication activities. They inform someone else, or they ask about the reactions of others. They frequently check other channels. When Senator McGovern decided against keeping Senator Eagleton as his running mate in the presidential election of 1972, all respondents who had learned of the McGovern decision remembered having had at least one personal conversation about this shortly after they had first heard the news (Ostlund, 1973–74). Following the shooting of Governor Wallace, more than 80 percent of the respondents said they intended to learn more about this event from radio and television, and almost three-quarters planned to read about it in a newspaper the following day (Schwartz, 1973–74). About half intended to obtain additional information from both print and broadcast media.

The process by which information carried by the mass media is given wider dissemination through person-to-person channels has been called the "two-step flow" or the "multi-step flow." These flows take place according to certain patterns since, as we have seen above, people are more likely to talk with others who are like themselves than with those who are different. Thus, in a study carried out in the 1940s, it was found that young people were especially likely to read motion picture magazines (and also to see more motion pictures) and that it was these "experts" from whom others were likely to obtain information about Hollywood and its products. Another study found that those who read news magazines are likely to be sources of information about national and international affairs (Katz and Lazarsfeld, 1955; Merton, 1949). Certain people thus serve as links between the mass media and interpersonal channels of communication in so far as particular areas of information are concerned. But, as the diffusion studies remind us, those who obtain information from somebody else may then turn to the mass media to verify it or enlarge on it. The mass media and interpersonal channels constitute a network for the flow of information that interlocks at many points.

People who are approached for advice or information on a particular topic, or on a broad range of subjects, are sometimes called "opinion leaders." They tend to be similar to those whom they influence, and to belong to the same social group as their "followers" but they usually are slightly better educated, of somewhat higher status, more active in the community, and more exposed to the mass media. They are more likely than others to adopt new ideas and to have contacts outside their place of residence. Opinion leadership is a relative matter, since some leaders are followers of other opinion leaders. For instance, one study found that 68 percent of opinion leaders on foreign affairs sought information from others. In general, opinion leaders are likely to be more active both in person-to-person communication and in linking mass media and interpersonal channels (Rogers, 1973).

A person who is faced with a decision commonly consults several information channels. When 141 physicians were queried about the information sources they had used before deciding to prescribe a recently introduced drug for their patients, nearly all mentioned at least two sources, and about two-thirds mentioned three or more sources. Most of them first heard about the drug from a representative of the manufacturer—the "detail man." Then they read about it in a professional journal or in some other written source. Then they talked with one or more of their colleagues about it. Of course, not all followed the same order of decision. A few read about the drug first, then talked with the "detail man," and then heard the drug discussed at a meeting or lecture. But the significant fact is that most consulted several sources (Coleman, Katz, and Menzel, 1966).

Somewhat similar patterns have been disclosed in other studies. Members of professional associations (economists, engineers, dentists) were asked to mention the sources of information they had used in deciding whether or not to attend the annual conventions of their associations. Most of them reported multiple sources. The first source was usually a brochure or program sent out by the association or an announcement in a professional journal. Then came one or more discussions with friends and colleagues. It is significant that when they were asked to name the most influential source of information, nearly half of them replied that this was not a relevant question. It was apparently the totality of sources to which they were exposed, rather than any one source, that helped them make up their minds. There did, however, seem to be a division of function among the channels. Printed sources provided the initial information; while discussions with other individuals provided supplementary information that was necessary for the decision (Booth, 1969–70).

The "mix" of mass media and interpersonal channels that people use to inform themselves depends on many factors: the education of the individual, the availability of media or of human sources, the subject itself, and the importance of the subject to the individual. Studies of consumer behavior have found in general that person-to-person channels play a large role in helping people to decide among products; mass media sources seem to be more important in providing information about specialized matters (for example population growth) and also about topics that are currently in the news. One study found, somewhat surprisingly, that *less* educated people made-

more use of the mass media than of interpersonal channels when they wanted to inform themselves about local schools. With better educated people the pattern was just the other way around. Apparently, those who had not been to college felt self-conscious about going to parent-teacher meetings or talking with school personnel, while the college-educated made extensive use of these sources (Chaffee, 1972).

Another case in which well-educated people were found to make greater use of interpersonal communication was in Israel during the October 1973 war. Those with more education were likely to be suspicious of reports about the fighting carried by the Israeli mass media, and partly for this reason relied on information obtained from other people. The less educated were more likely to trust the domestic mass media. As this instance suggests, the degree of confidence that one has in different sources is another important factor in determining the mix of channels that will be used (Blumler and Katz, 1974).

There has been considerable discussion about which are more persuasive: mass media channels or person-to-person channels. You could easily design an experiment to explore this question. Choose a local election in which there is not very much interest. Then, select two random samples of about 100 each from the voter registration lists. Compose an appeal urging people to vote—tell them that it is their duty as citizens, that the quality of local government depends on it, and so forth. Have this appeal printed up in leaflet form and distributed to the members of one sample. At the same time, you and your friends should call on the members of the other sample and make the same appeal to them orally. You will find that the percentage of those you approached in person who actually turn out to vote is higher than the percentage of those to whom you sent the leaflets. At least, this is what previous experiments have found (Gosnell, 1927; Lazarsfeld, Berelson, and Gaudet, 1944).

Does this mean that interpersonal channels are more persuasive than mass media channels? Perhaps. But then again, the mass media appear to be more persuasive when it comes to certain topics. Other studies have found, for instance, that the mass media often have more effect on attitudes regarding current events than interpersonal channels (Chaffee, Ward, and Tipton, 1970).

Still, the bulk of the evidence so far is that personal communications are more persuasive than the mass media in many situations. Two researchers who studied how voters made up their minds regarding candidates concluded that "people appeared to be much more influenced in their political decisions by face-to-face contact with other people . . . than by the mass media directly" (Lazarsfeld and Menzel, 1963:96). And, as mentioned above, studies of how people choose among various consumer products have come to similar conclusions.

The opinion of most students of communication is, however, that it is not very rewarding to try to identify one channel as more influential or persuasive than another. All have a role to play, and different people prefer different channel mixes. Some researchers have found that the mass media are important in making people aware of a new idea or a new technique, and that interpersonal communication plays a larger role in later stages of the decision process. This tends to be true, for instance, for farmers who are thinking about adopting a new agricultural technique. But the situation is complex, and in some cases the order may be reversed. In our society, at least, it is more useful to think of interpersonal communication and mass media as interconnected and complementary channels than as unrelated and self-sufficient (Wright, 1975:100).

Thus, if you are trying to persuade or inform someone, it is wise to consider first which channels are likely to do the best job of conveying the ideas you have in mind, which channels this person is most likely to use, and how they might best reinforce each other. As one researcher remarks, a combination of media and interpersonal channels used in complementary roles could be an unbeatable force (Rogers, 1969).

Numerous attempts have been made to use combinations of channels systematically. One example is provided by "farm radio forums." These were first developed in Canada, where groups of farm people were assembled to listen to radio broadcasts, which they discussed afterwards. The technique has also been used in Japan and in such developing countries as India, Nigeria, and Brazil. In Italy, television programs have been used in a similar manner, and in other countries groups have been assembled to discuss the content of newspapers or other print materials (Rogers, 1973). All these "media forums" seem to have been successful in informing people and in influencing their attitudes and behavior, but the effects have been tested systematically only in India. Media forums usually have a discussion leader who has at least some training, but informal groups that view television or listen to the radio may also include people who lead discussions of what has just been seen or heard. In many cases, these self-appointed discussion leaders are those who have read an article or a book on the same subject. There are thus countless impromptu media forums going on all the time.

It is important to take account of the differing characteristics of information channels when it comes to keeping yourself informed. If you rely too much on a single channel, you may be informed only superficially, or you may not be aware how important a given event or idea is for others. A revealing discussion of the problem of keeping informed occurred recently in the columns of the *Columbia Journalism Review* (March/April, 1975). A history professor condemned television news as a "random mishmash" that, by emphasizing a personality or an event of the moment, "obscures causes and effects, and fragments information to the point of incomprehensibility." To this, the director of news information of the National Broadcasting Company replied in a letter to the editor (May/June, 1975) that this professor demanded something of television evening news programs that they could not provide; that his students should be encouraged to read newspapers and magazines and watch network news specials to learn the fuller meaning of news events. He concluded: "Only a combination of newspapers, magazines, and some TV news specials can fill these gaps."

We might add that books and personal conversation should also be part of the information diet of the person who wishes to be informed. The communication network is composed of many different channels. To make use of some channels and not others is to invite ignorance. And to study the effects of one channel without taking the others into account is to risk misunderstanding.

Most people do, in fact, make use of more than one of the mass media, and all of us engage in person-to-person communication. Television, newspapers, and radio reach nearly all American adults. Specialized segments of the population are exposed to magazines, motion pictures, and books. Information received from any one medium is likely to be augmented, modified, or contradicted by information from another. Person-to-person conversation gives further currency to some media content, and often helps us decide how important or reliable this content is. The effects of any communication on a person are determined, in part, by the total mix of channels to which that person is exposed.

But availability of communication channels and exposure to them do not by themselves account for the effects that they have on individuals and groups. People select certain kinds of information from each channel, and what is selected can vary widely from individual to individual. What happens as a result of exposure to a channel depends in large part on what information is selected and what use is made of it. So it is to this process of selection and utilization that we turn in the next chapter.

FURTHER READING

The *Handbook of Communication*, edited by Ithiel de Sola Pool, Wilbur Schramm, and others (Rand McNally, 1973) contains several chapters that are useful in gaining an overview of communication channels and their audiences. These include "Communication Systems," by Pool; "Channels and Audiences," by Schramm; "The Audience," by Raymond A. Bauer; "Mass Media and Interpersonal Communication," by Everett M. Rogers; and several others. For further information on nonverbal communication, see the chapter by Randall P. Harrison in the *Handbook* and also the classic *Silent Language* by Edward T. Hall (Doubleday, 1959). An excellent treatment of the television audience is found in *Television and the Public*, by Robert T. Bower (Holt, Rinehart and Winston, 1973). Research on newspaper audiences is summarized in seven small volumes entitled *News Research for Better Newspapers*, published by the American Newspaper Publishers Association Foundation, Washington D.C. The latest volume was published in 1975, and all seven can be purchased for $15.00. They are fine for browsing.

A fascinating research study that describes interpersonal communication among physicians and the way interpersonal channels interact with mass media channels is *Medical Innovation*, by James S. Coleman, Elihu Katz, and Herbert Menzel (Bobbs-Merrill, 1966). *Current Perspectives in Mass Communication Research*, edited by F. Gerald Kline and Phillip J. Tichenor (Sage, 1972), includes two chapters that summarize a large amount of research on interpersonal communication and information diffusion: "Mass Communication and Information Diffusion," by John P. Robinson; and "The Interpersonal Context of Mass Communication," by Steven H. Chaffee.

CHAPTER FIVE
Selectivity

OR HOW WE COPE WITH INFORMATION

Almost a century ago, the psychologist William James wrote: "although we are besieged at every moment by impressions from our whole sensory surface, we notice so very small a part of them (James, 1961:84)." He referred to this "narrowness of consciousness" as one of the most extraordinary facts of our lives. Latter-day social scientists refer to this ability to confine our attention to a relatively few messages as "selective attention" or "selective perception."

Today, with the development of the mass media and the exploitation of these media by advertisers, politicians, educators, and others, we are bombarded with communications more than ever before. A person forced to attend to or remember *all* available communications would have time for little else and would run the danger of becoming completely disoriented. Fortunately, we are equipped to make a selection from the stream of messages to which we are exposed.

You can observe the principle of selectivity at work if you perform a little experiment on yourself. Try to write down one-line summaries (or headlines) of stories that you remember from the last time you read a newspaper or saw a TV news program. Your list will probably be a rather short one. Then, ask yourself: "Why did I remember these stories?" If you are trying to recall newspaper articles, go back to the paper and see how many items you couldn't remember at all. A second question then is: "Why didn't I pay attention to these stories, or why did I forget them right away?" You may find out some interesting things about yourself.

This chapter presents several explanations social scientists have advanced for why people absorb some information from the mass media while ignoring or forgetting even more. It also describes various kinds of information that people look for in the mass media, and the uses that they make of this information. Not all of these observations will apply to you—each person has different ways of handling the flood of communications—but some of them will.

Which media we expose ourselves to, what we think of these media, and what kinds of content we look for depends in large measure on our habits and attitudes. Some of these habits and attitudes are formed rather early in life; others take shape later. By the age of six or seven children are likely to be aware that television commercials are trying to sell something and at eight or nine they tend to be cautious about believing advertising claims (Ward, 1971). Middle-class children who feel frustrated because they have strict and not very affectionate parents become heavy television viewers, probably to get away from the parents (Maccoby, 1954). Children in working-class families tend to become heavy television viewers, whether or not they are frustrated, because it is the dominant family activity. Some studies have found that children whose parents are heavy newspaper or newsmagazine users are somewhat more likely than other children to develop the habit of news reading (McLeod and O'Keefe, 1972; Roberts, 1973).

However our habits and attitudes toward the media are formed, the result is that each individual is likely to read certain newspapers or magazines, to watch television or listen to the radio at given times, and to trust or not trust the information obtained from particular sources.

At the same time that our attitudes toward the media are taking shape, we develop attitudes about a great many other subjects: politics, music, sex roles, and sports. We also develop values, or deep-seated criteria, by which we judge what is desirable or not desirable, what is good and what is bad. Thus, some people value money more highly than others, some put more stress on honesty, for some it is very important to be liked. We build up in our minds a picture of the world that is consistent with our attitudes and values, and each person's picture is unique. One individual may see most other people as basically friendly and well-intentioned; anything that goes wrong is an accident or an exception to the general rule. Another individual may have a mental picture of life as a battleground, where each takes what he can and the devil takes the hindmost. Our stereotypes, or mental images, of politicians, nations, businessmen, or beagles, summarize what we know or think we know about a great many aspects of the world around us.

As Walter Lippmann wrote more than fifty years ago, "there is economy in this" (Lippmann, 1922:66). We couldn't make the decisions that we have to make every day of our lives if we faced each new situation with no existing attitudes and values and without a mental map of the world to guide us. It would be difficult for a person even to make a simple purchase without knowing in advance what kinds of things he or she liked, how much it was worth paying for them, and whether merchants by and large could be trusted. Of course, we sometimes have specific knowledge about individual people, things, and situations, and this knowledge serves to guide our actions. But very often we don't. How one decides to behave in an airplane, a doctor's waiting room, or a government office depends largely on attitudes, values, and stereotypes.

CONSISTENCY THEORIES

According to one group of theories, we subconsciously or consciously select from the flow of communications those ideas that fit in with our attitudes, values, and pictures of the world—that are congruent with our existing ideas. At the same time, we ignore, dismiss, misunderstand, or forget those communications that would be "dissonant"—that would not fit in. If our beliefs are shaken, but not changed, by a dissonant piece of information, we may seek out other people who share our beliefs to obtain reassurance. Or we may decide the information is incorrect, is unimportant, or is outweighed by other information. There are three principal theories in this group, known as the theories of balance, congruity, and dissonance. They are closely related to each other, so we will discuss them together (Zajonc, 1960).

There is substantial evidence to support consistency theories although, as we will see later, there is some evidence that does not support them. But let's look first at the data that indicate the theories are correct.

If you examine your own experience, or observe the behavior of friends, you will find that people ordinarily expose themselves to certain communications and ignore or avoid others. A common reason for watching a particular actor or actress is that he or she plays a role the way you think it should be played; the performance is in harmony with at least some of your existing ideas and attitudes. You may read a particular columnist because he is usually "right"—that is, you agree with him, or because you like his writing style—that is, he writes the way you feel columnists should. Conversely, there are actors and columnists whom you avoid. This often means that you don't like their ideas or their style.

Social scientists have verified that selective exposure to communications does take place. They have done this by observing what people do in the normal course of their lives and by setting up ingenious experiments. Here are a few examples of their findings. After a Republican senatorial candidate in California staged a marathon appeal for votes on television, lasting 20 hours, researchers found that Republicans were about twice as likely as Democrats to have seen some of it (Schramm and Carter, 1959). Another researcher sent questionnaires to members of a liberal organization (The Americans for Democratic Action) and a conservative organization (the John Birch Society) asking which magazines they read and whether there was a nationally broadcast news program that they regularly followed. The replies showed 36 percent of the ADA'ers regularly watched a TV news show, but only 12 percent of the Birchers. On the other hand, 36 percent of the Birch Society members named a conservative radio commentator—Fulton Lewis, Jr., and Paul Harvey being the favorites—while only 11 percent of the ADA members did so. Edward P. Morgan was mentioned most frequently by the liberals (Grupp, 1970). The members of the two organizations differed even more sharply with respect to their preferences for political magazines. Not surprisingly, the ADA'ers tended to read the *New Republic* or the *Nation,* while the Birchers named *American Opinion* and the *National Review* (Grupp, 1969).

During the presidential campaign of 1972, researchers at the University of California designed an experiment to test whether Republicans and Democrats would each be more likely to open and read mailed material supporting their respective political opinions than to expose themselves to the opinions of the other party. They sent 202 envelopes—half with the return address "Voters for Nixon" and half "Voters for McGovern"—to samples of registered Democrats and Republicans. Actually, the envelopes contained a letter explaining that this was a research project to find out how many people opened their political mail and asking those who did open the envelope to mail back a postcard (which was also enclosed). The results strongly supported the "congruity" hypothesis. Twice as many people who presumably expected to agree with what they found in the envelopes (Democrats receiving McGovern letters and Republicans receiving Nixon letters) returned their postcards as those who did not expect to agree (Barlett et al., 1974).

Selective exposure involves both active information-seeking and avoidance of information. In the example mentioned above of radio and television habits of liberals and conservatives, we don't know whether the liberals really liked television news shows, and actively sought them out, or whether they just didn't object to them enough to turn them off, and therefore watched regularly. The conservative John Birch Society members, on the other hand, obviously sought out conservative radio commentators, and they probably avoided television news shows on purpose.

Active avoidance of unwelcome communications can be observed in the case of children who clap their hands over their ears when there is something they don't want to hear. During the 1950s, many schools introduced air raid drills, which had the effect of terrifying some children. One Columbia University student, recalling this period, wrote in 1974:

> I can remember hiding on the floor of the back seat of the family car, with my hands over my ears, whenever the hourly news came on the radio. I didn't want to hear that atomic war had broken out, so I refused to listen— not hearing the news would somehow make it not happen.

A well-known journalist has mentioned similar experiences:

> I don't like fighting. Since I've been a child I've always covered my eyes with my hands and crouched low in my seat at the movies when the shooting and punching begins. (Brownmiller, 1973)

For most older people it is not necessary to put the hands over the ears or to close the eyes. We tend to develop the ability to "handle" at least some unwelcome communications even while seeming to see or listen. For instance, we may attend to dissonant information but downgrade its importance. It has been found that people who are under pressure from their families to vote for one candidate in an election but are being urged by their friends to vote for another, frequently show little interest in the election itself. In order to escape "cross pressures" they give less attention to both sets of communications (Lazarsfeld, Berelson, and Gaudet, 1944). A study of attitudes toward the Soviet Union among Roman Catholics who were members of a leftist-dominated labor organization, conducted during the 1940s, led to a similar observation. Respondents who were exposed to communications from both the church and the union regarded America's policy toward Russia as less important than those who were exposed primarily to either pro-Soviet or anti-Soviet communications. Apparently, by withdrawing interest they could escape the unpleasant mental conflict that otherwise might have been caused by exposure to the conflicting points of view (Kriesberg, 1949).

The ability to avoid perceiving dissonant information while absorbing ideas that we agree with is known as selective perception. The extent to which most of us actually have such an ability is open to question, but there is some evidence indicating that we do. Two people who have different ideas may read the same news story or watch the same TV program and end up with quite different impressions. Thus when John F. Kennedy and Richard Nixon engaged in a series of television debates prior to the 1960 election, the supporters of each tended to believe that their favored candidate had "won" the

debates (Kraus, 1962). Similarly, researchers studying the 1970 gubernatorial races in Wisconsin and Colorado found that most voters saw
the televised "spots" of both candidates but they gave closer attention to the publicity of the candidate they favored and as a result
learned more about this candidate than about the other one (Atkin,
et al., 1973).

Experimental studies suggest that people may actually perceive dissonant information but then consciously or subconsciously reject it
or reinterpret it. In a classic experiment, a series of persons who had
previously been identified as prejudiced against ethnic minorities
were shown cartoons ridiculing prejudice. The central figure in the
cartoons was a disagreeable old man labeled "Mr. Biggott," who was
shown doing silly things, such as refusing to give an American Indian
a job because he was not "100 percent American." Many of the prejudiced respondents seemed to understand the cartoons when they
first saw them, but when they realized that their own attitudes were
being ridiculed they managed to misunderstand the message and
ended up missing the point completely (Cooper and Jahoda, 1947).

A recent study of people who watched the popular television program "All in the Family" also showed the ability of different people
to derive different meanings from the same material. In this program,
the central character (Archie Bunker) is roughly comparable to "Mr.
Biggott," in that he frequently makes ridiculous ethnic slurs and gives
other evidence of prejudice. When two samples of viewers (American students and Canadian adults) were divided into groups of those
who showed high prejudice and low prejudice, it was found people
with high prejudice were more likely than others to misunderstand
the purpose of the program. They perceived Archie Bunker as a like-
able character who usually won his constant arguments with other
members of his family. People with less prejudice, on the other hand,
were more likely to realize that the intent of the program was to
make Archie's ideas look ridiculous (Vidmar and Rokeach, 1974).

Even if we perceive the meaning of a communication accurately,
we are likely to be selective about the extent to which we believe it,
or the weight we give to it. A former government official recently
wrote about a conversation he had with an industrialist in New York
City "who believed everything he read in the press about politicians
in Washington, but insisted to me that everything I read in the newspapers about businessmen in New York was inaccurate" (Hess, 1974).
The same former official also recalled that Washington politicians
often accepted at face value most political stories that did not involve them, but rejected the stories in which they were participants.
Here again, it would appear that existing stereotypes, attitudes, and

values were affecting the way communications were being interpreted—in this case influencing the extent to which they should be believed.

Memory, too, plays a role in preserving the integrity of our existing
view of the world. This applies not only to *what* is remembered, but
also to *the form* in which it is remembered. We learn and remember
information more easily if it fits in somehow with what we already
know. The psychologist Hermann Ebbinghaus demonstrated this by
showing that it took about one-tenth the time to memorize mean-
ingful material (he used Byron's "Don Juan") as it did to memorize
nonsense syllables (Ebbinghaus, 1885). Later experiments have indicated that people remember material that is in accord with their
attitudes and values more easily than material that conflicts with
them. For instance, if a prejudiced person is given a list of statements
half of which support his prejudices and half of which conflict with
them, he is likely to remember more of the supportive statements.

In a well-known series of experiments, a British researcher asked
students to read a brief story taken from American Indian lore, called
"The War of the Ghosts." Then, at intervals, he asked them to write
down what they could remember of the story. Naturally, they forgot
some of the details, and the story grew shorter with each rendition.
But what was more significant, some details were changed, or even
added, and the effect of these changes was to make the story more
reasonable and believable to people brought up in a European culture. Incidents involving the supernatural were dropped, or they
were changed in such a way as to make them more easily explained.
Details that were added served to make the story more "Western."
Thus, the selective process involved in memory brought the story
closer to the world the students were familiar with (Bartlett, 1932).

It is often impossible to determine whether a communication has
been misperceived or whether selective memory is at work. Both are
probably involved in many cases. One of the authors has frequently
conducted an experiment in which subjects are asked to read ten
newspaper headlines mounted on a poster or flashed on a screen.
They are not told why. Then, a few minutes later, they are requested
to write down as many of the headlines as they can remember. Invariably, some of the headlines are recalled incorrectly, and the changes
nearly always have the effect of making the message conform more
closely to the subject's attitudes and stereotypes. One headline, tak-
en from a newspaper at the time of the war in Vietnam, ran: NEGRO
OFFICER OPPOSES WAR PROTESTS. The original story below it (not
shown to the subjects) had told how the army officer, stationed in
Vietnam, had been critical of student demonstrators back home. But

since the story was not shown to the subjects, many of them changed the headline so that it would accord more closely with their own view of the world. Most commonly, the headline was recalled as NEGRO OFFICER FIGHTS WAR POLICY, or some variant of this. A few subjects, their minds more on domestic problems, wrote: BLACK COP JOINS WAR PROTESTERS, or in some other way changed "officer" to "policeman." Another headline, STOCK MARKET RISES ON BROAD FRONT, was frequently remembered as having reported a decline in the market, especially when the experiment was conducted in a time of economic recession.

Both misperception and memory may play a role in the process by which people "change" the stand of their preferred political party on an issue in order to bring it more into line with their own attitude regarding that issue. For example, if a person favors stronger government action to reduce unemployment, and thinks the Democrats are more likely to take this action, but prefers the Republican Party, then this person's mental map of the political world is in a state of "dissonance." It contains conflicting components. Over a period of time, many such poeple will change one of these components so as to eliminate the conflict, and in most cases will convince themselves that the party they prefer would do the most to reduce unemployment (rather than changing their party preferences or changing their ideas about the importance of unemployment as an issue (Kirkpatrick, 1970). Similarly, it has been found that voters are likely to see the position of a candidate they favor as being fairly close to their own position, regardless of how the stand of that candidate is seen by the total population. That is, a person who feels that the government has an obligation to guarantee a decent standard of living for members of minority groups will probably attribute these views to his preferred candidate, even though most people may see the candidate as having other views (Sherrod, 1971–72).

There are thus many situations in which the principle of consistency has been found to govern people's behavior. They choose to expose themselves to information which is in accord with their existing ideas; they selectively give their attention to communications with which they expect to agree; and if they learn something that conflicts with their attitudes or values, they forget it, dismiss it as unimportant, or reinterpret it so as to minimize the dissonance.

But there are also situations in which the principle of congruity does *not* hold. Especially in laboratory experiments, it has been found that subjects will often choose to read or view material that is *opposed* to their attitudes, values, and view of the world in general. One experimenter used as subjects a group of cigarette smokers, some of whom believed that there was convincing evidence linking cancer with smoking and some of whom thought the evidence was not very convincing. When these people were given the opportunity to read either of two articles—one of which supported their beliefs and one of which did not—most of them chose the nonsupportive article; they chose to expose themselves to dissonant information. In another experiment, subjects were asked to evaluate a candidate for an overseas assignment (based on what they had heard about him) and were then offered a choice between two other evaluations of the candidate by people who supposedly knew him well. One of these evaluations was very favorable to the candidate; the other very unfavorable. In nearly every case, the subjects chose to expose themselves to the opinions that *conflicted* with their own. Not all experiments have come to the same conclusions. Some experimenters have found that the principle of balance or congruity holds true, but a great many have found that it does not (Sears and Freedman, 1967).

You will probably find that your own behavior sometimes supports consistency theory and sometimes does not. Even though you have a favorite columnist who expresses opinions similar to your own, you may also read a columnist with whom you expect to disagree—perhaps just to see what he or she has to say. And you might even be persuaded to change your opinions a little. Furthermore, you are unlikely to turn off, or forget, the weather forecast that predicts rain on the day you are planning a picnic.

UTILITY THEORY—"USES AND GRATIFICATIONS"

Uitlity theory offers another way of explaining why we expose ourselves to some communications and not others, why we perceive a fraction of these to which we are exposed, and why we remember—correctly or incorrectly—only some of these. According to this theory, often known as the "uses and gratifications approach," we will attend, perceive, and remember information that is pleasurable, or that will in some way help to satisfy our needs. This information may or may not be in accord with our existing ideas, but we will attend to it if we expect it to be useful or think that it will give us satisfaction.

Conversely, according to utility theory, if we expect a communication to be irrelevant or unpleasant we will probably not expose ourselves to it. Or, if we are exposed anyway, we will disregard or forget it. For example, most people who live in downtown urban areas learn to screen out the noises of the city. These noises do not tell them anything useful. But if they visit the country they may be awakened early by bird songs or the sound of wind in the trees—noises that country people often learn to disregard. Many newspaper reporters can concentrate on writing a story in the middle of a city room where there are conversations going on within a few feet, telephones constantly ringing, and typewriters clacking. Those who have not learned to screen out these sounds would find concentration difficult. Reporters have learned to disregard such noises not because they are unpleasant or dissonant but because they are irrelevant. Similarly, when you read a newspaper or watch TV you don't give equal attention to all the information that is made available. Some items have no significance for you, so you disregard them or forget them; other items are useful to you in some way, and these are the ones you remember.

Balance theory and utility theory are not necessarily opposed to each other; it is possible to reconcile them. One way to do this is by reference to the fact that most people seem to need reassurance that their ideas and attitudes are correct. Since they need reassurance, they seek out communications that are likely to support their existing views of the world. Thus, these supporting communications are useful. Dissonant information tends to be unsettling and unpleasant. Therefore, information of this kind may be avoided *unless* it has some other utility. According to this view, reassurance is only *one* of the needs that we commonly feel. We will pay attention to dissonant information if it helps us in some other way. For instance, it might warn us of impending danger. Or it might help us to impress others with the breadth of our knowledge.

A problem with utility theory is that it requires researchers to specify the needs that are served by the media. If we explain selectivity by saying that some content is useful and some is not, then we have to answer the question: useful for what? An answer is not easy to give, since people use different words to describe the needs they feel, and sometimes they are unable to describe them at all.

Researchers have used several different strategies to identify needs that mass communications can help to satisfy. One of these is to ask people why they make use of one or more of the mass media. The needs of the respondents can then be inferred from their replies. For example, in a recent study, English schoolchildren were asked to write essays on "Why I like to watch television." They were assured of anonymity and that the teacher would not read their essays. The needs that these children felt were satisfied by television fell into six groups:

To Learn—about myself and others; how I'm supposed to act.

To Be Aroused—it excites me; it cheers me up.

To Have Companionship—it helps me forget I'm alone.

To Relax—it calms me down.

To Forget—about school and homework; to get away from the family.

To Pass the Time—because there's nothing else to do. *Pass,*

Some of the children also indicated that they used television mainly out of habit, making such statements as: "I just like to watch" (Greenberg, 1974). *Pass,*

Two other researchers asked a sample of adult Americans why they watched, or didn't watch, television programs dealing with political matters. The principal reasons given by the American respondents can be summarized as follows:

Surveillance—to keep up with the main issues of the day, or to judge what the candidates are like.

Vote Guidance—to help make up my mind how to vote.

Anticipated Communication—to use as ammunition in arguments with others.

Excitement—to judge who will win, or to enjoy the election race.

Reinforcement—to remind me of my candidate's strong points.

The members of this sample also gave three principal reasons why they did *not* watch political television:

Partisanship—because my mind is already made up.

Relaxation—because I prefer to relax when watching television.

Alienation—because the candidates hardly say anything; they talk over your head; you can't trust them.

In addition, a number of respondents said that they did not watch political television because they were not interested in politics (McLeod and Becker, 1974).

As you can see, several of the needs that the British children tried to satisfy by watching television are quite similar to the needs referred to by American adults, even though members of the latter group were asked only about political television. "To learn," as the children put it, is fairly close to keeping up with the issues of the day, a reason for watching given by some of the adults. A number of those in both groups were looking for "excitement" or "arousal." The children mentioned a need to relax as one reason for watching, while the adults mentioned this need as a reason for *not* watching political television. Presumably, these adults preferred entertainment programs.

Another way of finding out about the uses and gratifications offered by the mass media is to compile in advance a list of widely shared human needs and then to ask people whether and how much each of these needs is satisfied by newspapers, radio, television, personal conversation, and so on. This approach was followed by three Israeli researchers, who compiled a list of 35 different personal needs—using the psychological literature as well as their own insights—and then asked respondents how well each was served by various media. Some of these needs, for instance, the need to "overcome loneliness," were very similar to those mentioned spontaneously in other studies. But some needs were quite specialized and had to do with the fact that the study was conducted in Israel. One, for instance, was the need "to feel pride that we have a state." This need was rated as "very important" by 90 percent of the respondents, and they also reported that radio, television, and newspapers were helpful in satisfying it (Katz, Gurevitch, and Haas, 1973).

Needs that the mass media help to satisfy can be inferred also from observing how people behave under varying conditions. For instance, the usefulness of the media in providing material for personal conversation was neatly brought out by a study conducted by researchers from the University of Wisconsin. During a hotly fought election campaign, they offered a sample of adults in Madison, Wisconsin, the opportunity to receive one or more political pamphlets about the contending candidates. It was found that the more a person reported discussing the campaign, the more likely he or she was to request a pamphlet favoring one or the other of the candidates. Similarly, if a person said that he expected to talk with someone about the election prior to election day, he was more likely than others to want to read about the candidates (Chaffee and McLeod, 1973).

The fact that people rely heavily on the media to supply them with material for personal conversation was brought out by a study using a different observational technique. Students at Wayne State University listened to over 800 conversations, but did not take part in them. They found that some public issue was the main topic in about a quarter of the conversations, and some mention of the mass media was made in 76 percent of these "political" discussions. There were, in addition, references to the media in 40 percent of the "nonpolitical" conversations. The media were cited most often by persons who were trying to convince others of something, or who were resisting attempts by others to persuade them (Greenberg, 1975).

The extent to which mass communications provide material for personal conversation can be well documented, but a psychologist has suggested that people also can use the media in just the opposite way—that is, as a substitute for conversation. In making this suggestion, he illustrates still another method of studying uses and gratifications—drawing inferences from psychological theory. According to his reasoning, interacting with others is hard work. It involves listening, reacting, accommodating, compromising. Therefore, we may use mass communications to escape from these demands, since the media provide the illusion of interaction without the costs. Those who use the media in this way may feel that they are in close touch with the world, though they rarely talk with others (Wiebe, 1969–70).

This thesis is difficult to prove, but seems reasonable. We know from a number of studies that those who are lonely because they have nobody to talk to frequently turn to the media. "It's a voice in the house," as one respondent remarked to an interviewer in an early study of radio listening. And since mass communications *can* be used in this way as a substitute for interaction with others, it follows that people who *don't* want human company might put the media to just this use. Most of us have experienced occasions when we are tired or discouraged and much prefer to read a novel or magazine article, or watch a mystery on TV, than to talk with someone.

Thus, there are quite a few different methods for finding out about the ways people use mass communications to satisfy their needs. The uses, needs, and gratifications that are identified depend in part on the research method that is employed. Fortunately, the results obtained by various methods usually do not contradict each other, but tend to be complementary and reinforcing. Widespread use of the mass media to obtain material for personal conversations, for instance, can be documented by several methods.

Whichever research method we prefer, it is obvious that the needs that can be satisfied by mass communications will vary from person to person. Because people have different attitudes, values, and interests, they will make different uses of the media and obtain different gratifications. It is less obvious, but well documented, that the needs people experience will depend in part on what is going on around them and on the social situations in which they find themselves.

The fact that special needs arise as a result of major events was illustrated by the uses that people made of the mass media following the assassination of President Kennedy. At that time, researchers noted that many people turned to television and the press for help in shaking off the shock they felt and expressing their grief (Schramm, 1965). Similarly, a study conducted in Israel during and after the October, 1973, war found that Israelis looked to broadcast news as a means of releasing the tension they felt and to obtain reassurance that things were going all right. Some (mainly the better educated) were suspicious that news bulletins put out by the government were unduly optimistic and therefore tuned to foreign news broadcasts in order to get a second opinion (Peled and Katz, 1974). That these needs were caused by the war is strongly suggested by the fact that they dropped off sharply after the war was over. During the height of the fighting, nearly half the Israeli population said they wanted television programs that would contribute to their feeling of pride in the state and the army and to their sense of solidarity with the leadership. A few months later, only about 12 percent called for programs of this type. Also, shortly after the war, many fewer people expressed a need for information that would help relieve tension and provide interpretation of current news, but when it became clear that a major political struggle between Israel and the Arab states was still going on these needs again became important.

Our social situation, too, helps to determine many of the needs we feel and the kinds of information we seek in order to satisfy them. If your friends like to talk about sports, you probably will pay attention to sports news, whether or not you are very interested yourself. The same is true of politics, music, and many other subjects. Your job, neighborhood, organizational memberships, and ethnic group will likewise shape your patterns of attention to the media. It has been found, for example, that people who belong to more organizations seek more information, possibly because they have greater opportunities than others to use this information in conversation (Chaffee and McLeod, 1973). Another inquiry, conducted several years ago, noted that liking for rock-and-roll music among high school students was related both to the student's family background and to his or her social adjustment in the school. Only 8 percent of the girls who were active in the school's social life and whose fathers had a college education expressed a preference for rock-and-roll, while 40 percent of the girls who were outside the social mainstream and whose fathers had a grade school education liked this type of music. The proportions for boys were 16 percent and 37 percent (Johnstone, 1974).

An even earlier study found that grade school children's use of the media was related to whether they were well integrated into play groups of children their age. Those who did belong to a play group were considerably less likely to read comic books about Bugs Bunny and other little animals than were those for whom the family was the only major social group. Apparently, this was because the children who were *not* members of peer groups used the comic books as a way of escaping from the demands imposed by adults. "He's a rascal," they would say of Bugs Bunny, "happy-go-lucky, but he gets away with it." The peer group members, on the other hand, could escape from parental demands when they were playing with their friends, and had less need of the relief offered by comic books (Riley and Riley, 1951).

This same study suggested that what children learned from the communications to which they exposed themselves also depended in part on whether or not they were members of peer groups. The peer group members were likely to select information from broadcast programs, such as Lone Ranger or Dragnet, that would be useful in playing games with their friends; nonmembers were more likely to use adventure programs for escape—"it gives me something good to dream about," as one said.

Adult uses of the media likewise depend in part on the social situation in which adults find themselves. Those who frequently call in to radio talk shows, for example, appear to do so because they are alone and feel a need for some kind of interpersonal contact. They tend to be people who are older, single, or in poor health—all of whom are less likely to be well integrated in social groups (Turow, 1974). In other words, group membership—or lack of group membership—plays a role in determining what kinds of communications are useful for particular people.

Social pressure may induce a person to buy a television set, subscribe to a certain newspaper or magazine, or otherwise give attention to a medium that previously had been ignored. During the 1950s, when television was spreading rapidly, many parents felt obliged to buy receivers because their children complained about being "out of it" at school when television programs were being discussed. One little girl said sorrowfully: "I was the only one who didn't know who Howdy Doody was." And a woman who had resisted television well into the 1970s reported that her friends believed she didn't have a receiver because she couldn't afford one. In five years she had been offered at least seven free TV sets. She concluded: "Nobody can understand how one can possibly survive today without having at least one television." Similarly, a man who was embarking on a career with a New York bank was advised by older colleagues that it would be a good idea if he subscribed to the *Wall Street Journal*; and a book publisher remarked: "The main reason people buy an expensive hardcover novel is because their friends tell them that they *have* to read the book."

In cases such as these, the initial utility of exposing oneself to a particular medium or communication is that this relieves the social pressure. Later, of course, it may turn out that the information obtained may satisfy other needs as well.

Because there are so many different kinds of people, and because these people find themselves in so many different kinds of situations, the number of needs that the mass media can sometimes help to satisfy is enormous. Nobody has attempted to draw up a complete list; it probably would be impossible. Nevertheless, there are several lists of *categories* of needs for the satisfaction of which the mass media have been found useful. One list (McQuail, Blumler, and Brown, 1972) is substantially as follows:

Diversion, including emotional release, escape from problems, a welcome change from the routine.

Needs having to do with personal relationships. Here the media may provide substitute companionship, or may furnish material for conversation.

Needs having to do with individual psychology: the desire to obtain reassurance, to understand oneself, to feel important, to gain a sense of personal identity.

Surveillance of the environment, including the need to know about events that might affect one and to obtain information that will help one do something or accomplish something.

Another list (Katz, Gurevitch, and Hass, 1973) contains substantially the same categories, but they are stated differently:

Cognitive needs, having to do with acquiring information, knowledge, and understanding.

Affective needs, having to do with emotional or aesthetic experience, including the need for love and friendship, the desire to see beautiful things.

Personal integrative needs, for confidence, stability, status, reassurance.

Social integrative needs, for strengthening contacts with family, friends, and other people in general.

Tension-release needs, for escape and diversion.

You will probably find that most of your own wants or needs will fall into one or another of the categories in the above lists, although a few may not. It is also likely that you will choose different mass media to satisfy different categories of needs. For information about the environment you may prefer newspapers or magazines; for tension-release you may choose television or motion pictures; and to satisfy the need for learning about yourself you may rely on books. Or you may find that each of the mass media contributes, in varying degrees, to the satisfaction of several needs.

It is important to remember, however, that some people may not select *any* of the mass media to help them satisfy a particular need, even though others might do so. For instance, one person might rely primarily on newspapers for reassurance that his or her views about the political situation were correct, while someone else might rely on conversations with friends to satisfy the same need. Or one person might like to listen to music on the radio in order to release tension and relax, while another might prefer to seek relief from tension by participating in a sport.

Indeed, at least two studies have indicated that personal conversation is the most important communication channel when it comes to satisfying needs. A Japanese researcher, for example, found that tenth-grade children chose conversation more frequently than any of the mass media when asked which would be the most useful for such purposes as providing enjoyment, releasing frustration, offering consolation, and solving problems in general (Furu, 1971). Research recently conducted in Israel came to much the same conclusion. In regard to only a few needs did most people find the mass media more helpful than some form of personal communication. Even when it came to the need "to be entertained" more people would rely on "friends" than on all the media together. On the other hand, the media were endorsed as "most helpful" for gaining knowledge, information, and understanding, and for strengthening feelings of confidence and stability (Katz, Gurevitch, and Haas, 1973).

To the best of our knowledge, no similar study has been conducted in the United States. It is possible that Americans might rely more on the mass media than Israelis and Japanese do. But it is certainly true that personal conversation is a popular communication channel in all countries. Nowhere do the media have a monopoly when it comes to satisfying major needs; there is always the alternative of talking with someone else. And this is an alternative that many people seem to prefer.

THE PASSIVE AUDIENCE

Consistency theory and utility theory both assume that people actively select certain materials from the stream of communications available to them—in the former case because these materials are congruent with their existing ideas; in the latter case because the selected communications might help satisfy some need. These theories thus postulate an *active* audience.

Some scholars, however, do not see the audience as primarily active. They may accept the concept of selectivity, but will maintain that people are likely to select for attention the communications that are most easily available to them. According to this view, those who control the media can manipulate popular tastes and attitudes, decide what information the public will receive, and thus maintain the status quo to their advantage (Schiller, 1973).

It is difficult to subscribe to the idea that mass media audiences are mainly passive, or to the frequently attached corollary that the media are all-powerful and devoted to maintaining the status quo. There is just too much evidence to the contrary. The data on audience activity marshalled by researchers exploring both balance and utility theories cannot be dismissed out of hand. Media sociology, too, argues against the concept of a passive audience, since many of the most basic decisions made by media managers are based in part on beliefs (whether correct or not) as to what the public wants. The mass media often appear to be engaged in a frantic race to keep up with public attitudes and tastes; the rise of new publications and broadcast programs and the death of old ones can be ascribed in part to changes in economics and technology, but may also reflect changes in popular attitudes and tastes (Mendelsohn, 1974).

If the mass media are devoted to maintaining the status quo, they clearly are doing a poor job of it. To all appearances, social change has never been so rapid as in the past generation. And as for the power of the media, this differs markedly from situation to situation, as we shall see in the next chapter. Advertising is remarkably successful in selling something for which many people feel a need, but some of the most massive propaganda campaigns have failed to accomplish their objectives. Even in countries where the entire press has been tightly controlled for many years it has proved impossible to root out all the ideas that are unacceptable to the governments in power.

Nevertheless, one should not reject the concept of the passive audiences completely. Passiveness is a matter of degree. Some media consumers are more passive than others; some people are active at some times and passive at other times. All of us occasionally find ourselves automatically reading a newspaper article or sitting in front of a TV screen passively accepting what is offered. We are not actively seeking any particular type of information or looking for reassurance. But if the material presented proves to be offensive or unduly boring, then we are likely to reject it—to put down the article or switch television channels.

Support for the idea that there is a large passive audience comes from the television ratings, which show that the total television audience is fairly constant at given times of the day and night. People who like to watch at a certain hour will find something to watch regardless of what is being shown.

Yet, there are exceptions. For instance, when in 1973 Senate hearings on the Watergate scandal were broadcast live during the day, the total audience size in Los Angeles jumped 31 percent in the mornings and 17 percent in the afternoons. Presumably, audience size increased similarly in the rest of the country as well (Besen and Mitchell, 1975). A rise in total audience size could also be observed for other television spectaculars, such as the first landing of a manned space craft on the moon. Thus, there are some people who actively seek out certain types of programming, in addition to those who will watch whatever is being offered.

Just how passive are those who automatically turn on the TV set at certain hours? They may still be active to the extent that they give close attention to only some of the material they are exposed to and remember only a portion of this. Researchers have been repeatedly surprised by the extent to which people can be exposed to information without absorbing it.

The outdoor advertising industry is fond of demonstrating its ability to penetrate this screen of indifference, and periodically conducts experiments to prove the power of billboards. Recently, for instance, the Institute of Outdoor Advertising sponsored a survey of over 15,000 adults in 44 metropolitan centers to find out how many could name Miss America for 1975. Only 1.6 percent could do so, in spite of the fact that the lady in question, Shirley Cothran, had already received extensive television and press coverage. Then 10,000 posters with Miss Cothran's picture and name went up in the 44 metropolitan centers and stayed up for two months. At the end of this period, a second survey found that 16.3 percent of the adults polled knew the current Miss America's name (*New York Times*, June 19, 1975). Of course, one could also point out that an even larger percentage of those who had presumably been exposed to the billboards *still* had not absorbed the message.

Psychologists have suggested that much advertising material is successful in gaining our attention because we do not feel strongly about it. It concerns essentially trivial matters and takes little effort to understand. While we do not seek out such advertising, we have no reason to reject it when it is easily available. One psychologist has labeled this phenomenon "learning without involvement" (Krugman, 1965). But it has also been noted that material learned under conditions of low involvement will soon be forgotten unless people are continually reminded of it (Zielske, 1959).

Not all advertising is of this "low involvement" character. One study found that publicity for products such as cigarettes tended to be accepted rather passively. Other advertising—for example, for foreign cars—aroused a much stronger response. Active selectivity would therefore probably play a larger role in regard to exposure to information about the latter category of products (Bowen and Chaffee, 1974). This observation is borne out by other research, which shows that people who have just bought an automobile are especially likely to read advertisements for the make of car they have chosen *after* completing the purchase—apparently to assure themselves that they have made a wise choice.

Political communications, likewise, may be of a high involvement or low involvement character, depending on the attitudes and interests of audience members. People who are interested in an election, and have a preference for one of the candidates, will actively seek out information. Both consistency theory and utility theory may apply to their behavior. But people who are *not* interested, if they pay attention to campaign publicity at all, are likely to give their attention to the information that is most easily available. A recent study of voter behavior in a city council election, for example, found that those who were undecided how to vote were twice as likely as those with a preference to ignore all news about the candidates. But it was also found that voters with less interest who nevertheless did read about the election in a newspaper were likely to read the stories that were given the most prominent page position, the largest headlines, and the biggest space. Their selection of material was based on availability (Atkin, 1971).

When political campaign managers flood television with spot advertising before an election, nearly all viewers are likely to remember being exposed to at least some of these appeals, but those with little interest in the election rarely give them close attention. The less interested people who *do* pay attention to the political advertising, however, are likely to give about equal attention to all messages of equal prominence. These uninterested and usually undecided voters are the ones campaign managers are most eager to reach. But the cost of reaching each one may be very high. As one research team concludes: "Saturation advertising strategies oriented toward high frequency of exposure may not be the most effective means of securing an attentive and responsive audience" (Atkin et al., 1973).

When you are attending to communications that don't have much to do with your needs or preferences, then a number of "cues" will probably determine how much attention you give them. If you are reading a newspaper, the size of the headline, placement of the story, and the amount of space given it will help you decide whether it is important or not. "Cues" on television include placement and amount of time, but also the tone of voice used by the announcer and the number of action shots. Given equal interest, the story that is designated as more important will receive more attention (Knapper and Warr, 1965).

On the other hand, if you are interested in a subject the cues that otherwise might help you determine how much attention to give it are less important. You will select what you want regardless of how important the editor thinks it is. Indeed, sometimes a small item will "jump out at you" as you read the newspaper, usually because it has some direct relevance to your interests.

We learn the cues that can be used to guide our attention as we grow up, and people living in different societies learn slightly different cues. A particular placement of a story in a newspaper, or a special tone of voice used by an announcer, may indicate importance in one society and not in another. A visitor to the United States, who understood very little English, told of hearing emotional language coming from the radio of the taxi that drove him from the airport. He couldn't understand the content, but realized from the tones of voice that something portentious had happened—perhaps war had broken out. He later learned that he had heard a report about the baseball world series. Another visitor expressed surprise when he learned that some American newspapers regard the space adjoining the comic strips as one of the most prominent locations in which to place a story. If you pick up a newspaper from another country, even if you know the language, you will find that it takes much longer to skim than the paper you usually read. Before you can read it rapidly, you have to learn the cues that the editors are using to guide your attention. These cues determine in part what information you will expose yourself to.

ORGANIZATIONS AS MASS MEDIA CONSUMERS

Many organizations, as well as individuals, select some of the content of the mass media for attention. If you get acquainted with almost any business organization you will find that it subscribes to a number of newspapers and magazines. It may also make use of a clipping service that keeps it informed of items relevant to its operations. Some governments maintain facilities for monitoring radio and television, and distribute to their officials summaries or even complete texts of broadcasts that concern current policies. Many other types of organizations—religious, labor, educational, welfare, and social—make extensive use of mass media content.

These communications actually go to individuals within the organizations concerned, so one could say that organizational use of the mass media is really one aspect of individual use. But the individuals give their attention to certain communications because of their position in the organization, and the purposes of the organization as a whole are served. If you change from one job to a very different type of job, you are likely to find that some of your reading habits and even your listening and viewing habits will soon change. In effect, you are behaving as part of an organization, in addition to behaving as an individual.

Little systematic research has been conducted on why certain organizations select certain communications for attention. We do not know, for instance, whether consistency theory is useful in explaining why an organization subscribes to one magazine rather than another. Common sense would suggest that sometimes it is. For instance, the New York *Herald Tribune* was banned from the White House at one point not many years ago because President Kennedy found some of its content offensive. And one can easily imagine that a very conservative organization would not subscribe to a liberal journal unless it needed this journal for "intelligence" purposes.

As this hypothetical example suggests, utility theory may be a better way of explaining organizational choices than consistency theory. Organizations often require enormous amounts of information if they are to function. It has been suggested that societies (which can be thought of as large and diffuse organizations) require communications for three principal purposes: to keep informed of any developments that may affect them; to enable different parts of the society to keep in touch with each other; and to pass on their culture from one generation to the next (Lasswell, 1948). More formal organizations, say, political parties or labor unions, require information for much the same purposes, which might be called "intelligence," "coordination," and "education." Organizations may use mass media content also to foster group morale and a sense of belonging.

Some of the informational needs of large organizations are taken care of by house organs. This is especially likely to be true with respect to coordination, education, and raising group morale. If you look at a house organ put out by almost any business organization, especially, you are likely to find some articles devoted to providing information on what various organizational units are doing, some containing instructions or advice on how to perform certain jobs better, and some devoted to self-congratulation and the promotion of teamwork.

But "intelligence"—the information that organizational leaders need in order to make decisions—usually has to come mainly from sources outside, and much of it is provided by the mass media. What are allied or competing groups doing? What political and economic developments might affect the organization's work? Large organizations usually monitor the mass media in order to get information on questions such as these.

Some information that is useful for coordination, education, and morale-building also may come from the mass media. Many U. S. Government officials read the *New York Times* or the *Washington Post* to keep up with what various agencies of the government are doing, as well as for other reasons. Educational functions in many large organizations are performed by technical and professional journals that keep specialized personnel in touch with the latest developments in their fields. And whenever a newspaper says something favorable about an organization, this is likely to be clipped, duplicated, and circulated to all personnel; it's good for morale.

It is difficult to estimate the total mass media usage that is made by organizations, but it is certainly very large. Indeed, the circulation of some technical periodicals is accounted for mainly by organizational subscriptions. On occasion, this may be true even of publications that are intended for a wider audience. During World War II, for instance, government agencies that were worried about domestic subversion subscribed to a number of extremist right-wing newspapers. When one such paper finally gave up publication it was found that it had been kept alive to that point mainly by large numbers of subscriptions from suspicious Washington watchdogs.

Whether organizations ever belong to the passive audience for the mass media is a matter for speculation. There is no research on the subject. Perhaps some organizations do in fact occasionally pay attention to information merely because it is available and not because they already have uses for it. If this is the case, it might help to explain why organizations—like individuals—are subject to fads. Certain systems of accounting, titles for organizational officials, computer techniques, and so on, may be adopted mainly because they are publicized by the mass media and not because they help the organization in its functioning.

In any event, it would be helpful at least to explore the possibility that all the various factors that are involved in the selection of communications by individuals also play a role for organizations. The fact that organizations constitute a major portion of the audience for the mass media is all too frequently ignored.

THE IMPORTANCE OF SELECTIVITY

Today one often hears references to "information overload." For many people, there is more information available than they can possibly absorb. Most of us deal with this overload by selecting some communications for attention and ignoring or skipping over the rest. But, as we have seen, selectivity cannot be explained by any single principle. There seem to be a number of factors involved. The most important ones include:

Habit. On the basis of experience we become accustomed to exposing ourselves to some communications and not others.

Consistency. We have a tendency to favor communications that are congruent with our existing ideas over information that conflicts with our mental map of the world.

Utility. We select communications that we think will be helpful in satisfying some need, or that will give us pleasure.

Availability. If we have no preference for one communication rather than another, we will expose ourselves to the one that is more easily available.

There is no agreement among scholars as to the relative importance of these factors. Common sense would suggest that all of them should be taken into account by anyone who is seeking to gain the attention of a particular audience. And this is essentially what practitioners of mass communications do.

If you write a book and take the manuscript to a publisher, the first thing he is likely to ask is: "What is the audience for this book?" Essentially what he is asking, but in a polite way, is: "Who needs it?" Unless you can answer this question to his satisfaction, and show that the book will be helpful in satisfying some need of a sufficiently large group of readers, the book is unlikely to be published. Utility theory thus plays a role in the decision about publication.

He is also likely to want to satisfy himself that the book will be in harmony with the ideas of the audience you are trying to reach. It is improbable that he will use such words as "congruence" and "dissonance," but he may tell you that people are tired of hearing about Vietnam or that readers are not likely to think that corruption in government is very funny. If your book deals with the large number of scientific discoveries made in Klopstockia, he is likely to anticipate a good sale among Americans of Klopstockian descent. All these considerations are relevant to consistency theory.

Once the book is published, the publisher and his salespeople will make every effort to ensure that it is widely available. The book trade is not very skillful at doing this, but frequent complaints by unread authors to the effect that publishers take delight in burying books are simply not true. They try to make them sufficiently available so that they will come to the attention of at least some members of the passive audience.

Finally, your publisher will probably belong to a trade association that encourages the habit of reading books. The more people who become addicted the better. The habit of book reading is not easy to inculcate. It may be a losing battle. But any energy shortage might help; a good reading light draws much less electricity than a color television set.

Practitioners in the different media place differing degrees of emphasis on the various factors involved in gaining attention. Motion picture producers and magazine publishers are making greater and greater efforts to tailor their products to the needs and interests of specific audiences. They emphasize utility. Commercial television has been widely criticized for attempting not to offend anyone—in effect, for giving too much weight to consistency theory. Entertainment programs, especially, have tended to become bland and noncontroversial. The American Newspaper Publishers Association, through its large-scale "newspaper in the classroom" project, is making valiant efforts to encourage the habit of newspaper reading. Radio is more and more appealing to specialized audiences, but also stresses availability: You can listen to the radio in the car, carry it with you to the beach, and it may even provide a welcome diversion when you should be concentrating on your work.

Nobody seems to be promoting personal conversation, except perhaps the people interested in sensitivity training, but for most of us it remains more available, useful, and habitual than any other channel. And one usually can choose a conversation partner with whose opinions one agrees.

But all channels, including personal conversation, are subject to selectivity. Attention does not automatically come with exposure. ("Excuse me, I wasn't listening to what you were saying.") And without attention there can be no effect.

How people select communications for attention is of vital importance to all mass media enterprises. It is of even greater importance to those who are engaged in persuasion—advertisers, propagandists, and public relations specialists. Indeed, as soon as a study that sheds new light on any aspect of selectivity is published, professional persuaders will attempt to see if the findings have practical applications for them. A great deal of research on selectivity is sponsored by these organizations, especially advertisers, testifying to the importance that they attach to it.

But the principles governing selectivity are also of great significance for individuals. In view of the impressive flood of communications to which we are all exposed, we somehow have to find ways of making the best use of our time and attention. Each person should ask: Given my purposes, and what I want to get out of life, have I formed the best possible habits to govern my use of communications? Am I avoiding information because it conflicts with my existing ideas, even though it might be important? How can I make the maximum use of mass media in helping to satisfy my needs? Do I pay attention to some information simply because it is most easily available?

No two people will find exactly the same answers to questions such as these, but all of us can benefit from thinking about them. In a world where knowledge is rapidly becoming the largest industry, the care with which we select communications for attention will have a profound effect on our lives.

Exposure to communications is likely to influence the behavior of individuals and groups. Whether we select information with which we agree or choose materials we think will be useful; whether we are eager to learn or absorb some ideas passively; whether we are concerned with our personal needs or with the needs of some organization or group to which we belong—in all these situations certain things may happen. For convenience, we refer to these resulting occurrences as "effects," although it would be more accurate to think of them as the result of processes that are frequently complicated and in which many factors in addition to communication may be involved. The following chapter will discuss some of the effects of communications that have been observed most frequently.

FURTHER READING

Much of the information on selective exposure and selective perception occurs within the context of literature on communication effects. A good summary, if somewhat dated, appears in Joseph T. Klapper, *The Effects of Mass Communication* (Free Press, 1960), pages 19–26. Frederic C. Bartlett's *Remembering* (Cambridge: The University Press, 1954), a charming, readable book, describes a number of experiments and observations on memory, several of which illustrate consistency theories. A critique of some of the literature on selective exposure and perception, by David O. Sears and Jonathan L. Freedman, is entitled "Selective Exposure to Information: A Critical Review." This can be found in the anthology *Communications and Public Opinion* edited by Robert O. Carlson (Praeger, 1975).

The "uses and gratifications" approach to the study of communication effects is beautifully presented by Elihu Katz, Jay G. Blumler, and Michael Gurevitch in *Mass Communication Research* (edited by W. Phillips Davison and Frederick T.C. Yu, Praeger, 1974). The uses of mass communications by organizations are discussed by Davison in the same volume. Recent research in the area of utility theory, some of it rather technical and complex, can be found in the volume *Uses of Mass Communication*, edited by Jay G. Blumler and Elihu Katz (Sage, 1974).

CHAPTER SIX
Effects of Mass Communications

Interest in communication effects is as old as human civilization. People in ancient times used some devices to transmit ideas that we might consider primitive—such as clay tablets, monuments, and runic inscriptions—but then as now the principal method of communication was by word of mouth. And they were preoccupied with fundamentally the same questions we face today: What are the powers of words to persuade? What happens as a result of communication?

One of the oldest documents in the world is an Egyptian poem, written in a time of revolution when the Old Kingdom of Egypt was in turmoil. Entitled "The Struggle with His Soul of One Who Is Tired of Life," it starts each verse with a question about communication (Bauer, 1929):

> To whom shall I speak today?
> People are greedy.
> Everyone seizes the possessions of his neighbor.

> To whom shall I speak today?
> Gentleness of spirit has perished.
> All the people are impudent.

> To whom shall I speak today?
> One laughs at crimes that before
> Would have enraged the righteous.

> To whom shall I speak today?
> There are no just men.
> The earth has been given over to evil doers.

We do not know to whom this poet of ancient Egypt had spoken previously, or what he expected words to accomplish, but it seems clear that he felt speech had lost its power; there was no one to whom he could appeal.

If you look at a slightly more recent document—the Book of Proverbs in the Bible—you will find much more explicit statements about communication. Indeed, the proverbs present a number of rules for communication in everyday life. Here are a few:

A soft answer turneth away wrath; but grievous words stir up anger. (15/1)

A talebearer revealeth secrets; but he that is of a faithful spirit concealeth the matter. (11/13)

Reprove not a scorner, lest he hate thee: rebuke a wise man, and he will love thee. (9/8)

We could take these and other proverbs and compare them with the findings of communication research in our own time. In a large number of cases the findings of communication researchers and the injunctions of the proverbs are similar. Indeed, the proverbs sometimes anticipate rather sophisticated research. To quote just one more: "A wise son heareth his father's instruction: but a scorner heareth not rebuke" (13/1). This anticipates the phenomenon known as "selective perception," which we have discussed in the previous chapter.

When we come to the writings of Aristotle, there is almost no need to translate into modern terms. Aristotle's *Rhetoric*, in which he laid down systematic rules for persuasion, is still studied by those who are interested in propaganda. Rhetoric, in Aristotle's words, is "the faculty of discovering in the particular case what are the means of persuasion" (Cooper, 1932:7).

Of these he tells us, "there are three kinds. The first kind reside in the character of the speaker; the second consist in producing a certain attitude in the hearer; the third appertain to the argument proper, in so far as it actually or seemingly demonstrates" (Cooper, 1932:8). He advises us that we should be able to argue on either side of a question. Of course, he says, we should not actually advocate the wrong side, but we should be *able* to do so in case our opponent makes unfair use of the art of persuasion; then we can refute him.

In medieval and early modern times, we find that princes were employing people we would now call public relations men. Pietro Aretino, a noted humanist who died in 1556, was in the service of both Charles V of Spain and Francis I of France. One of his contemporaries said that he knew how to defame, to threaten, and to flatter better than all others. Even earlier, Bishop William of Ely was attacked by his political opponents in England for hiring troubadours to extol his merits in public places, so that "people spoke of him as though his equal did not exist on earth." In other words, those who had developed persuasive skills could find a market for their services, much as is the case today (Bauer, 1929).

The purpose of this brief excursion through history is merely to show that the study of communication, and especially the study of persuasion, has been a persistent interest of mankind for many centuries. Those of us who study communication today are not breaking new ground, but follow in a tradition from which we can learn a great deal.

Modern research on communication effects differs from the older tradition primarily in three respects: it is concerned largely with the mass media, rather than with face-to-face relations; it places heavy emphasis on study of audiences—those who are exposed to particular communications; and it makes use of quantitative techniques that have been developed only in comparatively recent times.

In spite of the availability of new research techniques, our knowledge about the effects of mass communications remains spotty and incomplete. This is partly because the subject is a complex one, involving many aspects of individual psychology and social organization, and partly because certain types of communications have been studied more than others. Much of what we know comes from studies of election campaigns, of advertising messages, and of children's television viewing. Indeed, one social scientist located 2300 reports about research on television and human behavior, 60 percent of which had to do with television and young people (Comstock, 1975). There is also an extensive body of research on the effects of army training and indoctrination films, and of wartime propaganda in general, conducted during World War II (Hovland, Lumsdaine, and Sheffield, 1949).

In addition, a large number of laboratory experiments on communication effects have been conducted. These have led to impressive advances in knowledge, but their results must be used with caution. Most of the experiments have been performed under carefully controlled conditions, using students as subjects. For both these reasons one often cannot be sure that the results obtained in the experiment would be duplicated under other conditions and with other populations. In a laboratory, people can be induced to give their attention to communications that they would be likely to ignore in day-to-day living. And students tend to be quite different from other groups in the population; for instance, they are more oriented toward learning and more open to different points of view. Results obtained in the laboratory do not always occur under natural conditions (Hovland, 1959).

Relatively little attention has been given to the effects of television entertainment and news programs on the millions of adults who are exposed to them, and knowledge about the effects of reading newspapers, magazines, and books is limited. Indeed, the most comprehensive study on the effects of printed matter was published back in 1940 (Waples, Berelson, and Bradshaw, 1940). Researchers have found it difficult to investigate the effects of mass media over long time periods; most studies have focussed on shorter periods, such as the six months before an election, or have been confined to the effects of a single broadcast or advertisement. It is difficult and expensive to make systematic observations about the effects of communications over a period of years or decades, yet long-term effects are obviously of great significance. Perhaps the most striking lack is in regard to the effects of the mass media on groups, organizations, and society as a whole; the overwhelming proportion of studies have concerned themselves with effects on individuals. Consequently, although the air is full of charges and countercharges about the social effects of mass communication, there is little firm information on which to base these allegations.

In spite of gaps in our knowledge, some useful generalizations about the effects of the media can be drawn from existing research. As in all areas of social science, these generalizations are likely to be altered as a result of future investigation. Pending further study, they can serve as approximations of reality and they *do* enable us to make somewhat better predictions about what will happen as the result of exposure to the mass media.

SOCIALIZATION

Socialization is a process during which people (and young children in particular) learn what to expect from the world and what the world expects from them (Roberts, 1973). It has also been defined as the process of learning how to live in human society, or as the process by which human behavior is learned and maintained (McLeod and O'Keefe, 1972). Thus, a person who is socialized has acquired a basic minimum of knowledge about the society he or she lives in and also a number of basic attitudes and values: respect for the feelings of others; the importance of controlling destructive impulses; an appreciation for the worth of things people use or need, such as clothing, furniture, and tools.

Scholars agree that the most important part of the socialization process takes place in the home early in life and that the most important socializers are parents, brothers and sisters, and other children. Schools and churches also play a significant part. There is likewise agreement that the mass media have a role in socialization, but disagreement about how great this is. Does the small child, sitting in front of the television set, acquire some of the basic knowledge about how to behave from the flickering images on the tube? One researcher, working with not-so-young children (fifth graders), found that heavy viewers of crime shows did absorb the belief that criminals usually get caught and some knowledge about the rights of a person who is arrested. When asked to indicate the one person on TV they would most like to be, they were likely to mention one of the actors associated with law enforcement. But their attitudes toward the police were determined more by the attitudes of their friends and families than by what they saw on television (Dominick, 1974).

Television viewing has been found to affect the way children think about various occupations, and their beliefs about how one should behave in order to succeed in life. Heavy viewers, for instance, are more likely to believe that self-confidence is of great importance. They are also more likely to pay attention to the outward signs of social status and to agree with statements such as "You can tell how important a man is from the way he is dressed." In general, heavy viewers are more stereotyped in their thinking, seeing people as either good or bad, weak or strong; while children with less exposure to the mass media refer more frequently to specific reasons why a person would behave in a particular way in a given situation (Maccoby, 1964).

Most research on the role of the mass media in socialization has been concerned with television, but it is clear that the print media play a part in some cases. Several Columbia University students, who were asked to write essays on their early recollections about mass media exposure, mentioned newspapers and magazines. One woman, who grew up in a small country town, wrote:

> Through newspaper and news magazine articles on people in public life, I concluded that there were other occupations than teaching, nursing, or becoming a secretary . . . and that one could indeed survive in this world if one did not marry at the socially acceptable age—somewhere between 16 and 20.

She also recalled not liking television, because it usually showed women in traditional roles and also because disagreements about which program to watch caused arguments in the family.

A great deal of attention has been devoted to the question of whether exposure to violent content in the mass media causes aggressive behavior in children. A generation ago, the principal concerns were with the content of motion pictures and comic books. More recently, researchers have focused their attention on television.

Two massive attempts to determine whether violent television content does indeed foster aggressive tendencies in children were conducted in the first half of the 1970s. One was sponsored by the Surgeon General of the United States, acting under a mandate from Congress (U. S. Government, Surgeon General, 1972). The other was conducted by the National Broadcasting Company, and was still in progress when this book was written. Numerous smaller studies have been conducted on the same topic.

The Surgeon General's report concluded cautiously that violent content in television programs caused aggressive behavior among some children (who are disposed to be aggressive) and only under some conditions:

> There is a convergence of the fairly substantial experimental evidence for short-run causation of aggression among some children by viewing violence on the screen and the much less certain evidence from field studies that extensive violence viewing precedes some long-run manifestations of aggressive behavior. This convergence of the two types of evidence constitutes some preliminary evidence of a causal relationship. But a good deal of research remains to be done before we can have confidence in these conclusions. (U. S. Government, Surgeon General, 1972:17–18)

The results of the National Broadcasting Company study, which was based on close observations of two large samples of boys in a midwestern and a southern city over a period of several years, had not yet been reported as of the end of 1975. Preliminary analyses indicated that most of the boys seemed to be unaffected by exposure to violent programming.

Critics of the Surgeon General's report have objected that the broadcasting industry exercised undue influence in interpreting the data on which the report's conclusions were based. One critic wrote:

> The entire history of mass communications research has shown the tremendous difficulty of teasing out specific effects from the tissue of surrounding social influences. The absence of conclusive results, when rigorous criteria of statistical significance are applied, may reflect the limitations of our available research methodology more than any weakness in the influences being assessed. . . . No one knows how to *measure* the forces that shape character, although our society, in its finest expressions, *understands* what forces make for good character. Symbolic fantasies of violence are not among them. (Bogart, 1972–73:518–19)

A different kind of criticism was advanced by a social scientist who objected that researchers should be alert for other possible consequences of exposure to violence in mass media content, in addition to aggressive behavior. How, for example, does a child learn sentiments of sympathy and pity? One possible way is through identification with victims of fictional violence. Indeed, there is some reason to believe that children do help and protect others as a result of learning about violence through the media as well as by direct observation (Hyman, 1974). On the other hand, there is also evidence from experiments to indicate that children who are exposed to televised violence are slower to seek adult help when they see "real" violence among other children (Drabman and Thomas, 1975).

Politics is another area in which there is disagreement among researchers as to how much the child absorbs attitudes and beliefs from family, friends, and schools, and how much from the mass media. Until recently, most writing on political socialization emphasized personal influences. Indeed, a recent review of this literature criticizes it sharply for having largely ignored the mass media and especially television as potentially a major influence in the child's introduction to political life (Kraus, 1973). That the media help to form at least some political attitudes is indicated by a study of the attitudes of high school students toward war in general and the Vietnam war in particular. When asked to describe how they had learned about such subjects as the causes of the war in Vietnam and the results of this and other wars, the students mentioned the mass media twice as often as any other source. "Schools" came next, followed by "family," "friends," and "church." Television was cited as the major media source by half the students. About a quarter mentioned newspapers, with the remainder of the replies divided among magazines, movies, radio, and books (Hollander, 1971). A study conducted in Australia came to similar conclusions: that television was the most important source of political information for Australian children (Connell, 1971).

In spite of differences of opinion among social scientists as to how important mass media are in the socialization process—as opposed to family, friends, school, and church—it seems safe to conclude that they do help to shape a child's values, beliefs, and habits. The effects of mass communications are somewhat different for each child, depending on his or her temperament, needs, existing beliefs and values, and social surroundings, but nearly all children, while being entertained, absorb at least some information and attitudes that prepare them for roles that they will play in the future (Maccoby, 1964). This conclusion was based on a review of the literature more than ten years ago, but a researcher who examined approximately 1500 studies dealing with television and young people as of about 1974 confirmed that it does indeed affect both their beliefs and their behavior (Comstock, 1975).

There are many aspects of socialization through the mass media about which little is known, and which would be fascinating to explore. For instance, just how do the media exercise their influence? A German scholar suggests that they offer channels through which "socializers" present models of ways of behaving or thinking to those who are socialized. These "socializers" are of four types:

A media organization that you respect and trust.
A real person—perhaps a president or prime minister—speaking through the media, especially through television or radio.
A symbolic figure, such as a cartoon animal.
A hero, especially in an adventure story.

Which models are accepted depends, of course, on the individual reader, listener, or viewer (Ronneberger, 1971).

Another subject about which we know rather little is socialization later in life. Most research to date has focused on children. But people do enter different "worlds" as they grow older, and somehow they have to learn how to live in these worlds. For instance, when we become parents we have to learn to talk with our children and how to relate to them. These skills are quite different from the ones we learned in our early years so we could relate to adults. We also may enter positions of responsibility in business or the professions. How should we behave then? As we reach the age of retirement, we have to learn how to protect ourselves from fatigue and exhaustion. Our former behavior patterns are no longer adequate; we must learn new ones.

It seems reasonable that the mass media play an even larger part in socialization later in life than in our early socialization. Parents turn to baby books to learn how they should behave, as well as how the baby is likely to behave. The mass media provide numerous models of successful people who can instruct us on ways to get ahead in our chosen line of work. The general media offer role models for older people, too; and increasing numbers of specialized publications advise the aged on how to adjust to their new situation.

There are a great many rather subtle effects of the mass media in shaping our view of the world that we know rather little about. What, for instance, do maps do to us? Nearly all maps show the north on top and the south on the bottom. Does this somehow give us the feeling that north is superior to south? One commentator, reflecting about the potential role of maps in the socialization process, wonders why Australians and South Americans have not complained about this map-makers' custom (Hyman, 1974). Or, to take another example, is the way we think about some subjects influenced by the fact that reference books and other listings usually use alphabetical order as a device for making their contents accessible? Does "A" become more important than "Z"? Has Anne a better chance in life than Wendy, simply because her name begins with "A"?

One reason socialization is such an important subject for study by mass communication researchers is that the effects the media have on us depend in large part on the way we have learned to use them. People become "socialized" to the mass media just as they become socialized to family living, politics, academic life, and so on. As we saw in the discussion of selectivity in the preceding chapter, people gradually form habits and attitudes that help to govern their attention. They turn on the radio or television at certain times of the day, they may read a newspaper at breakfast, or they may customarily read the back pages of a news magazine before they read the front part. (Actually, this is very common.) Socialization to the media also helps to determine how much we trust information from various sources. Most people, for example, say that they trust television news more than news from printed sources. We do not know exactly why this is—perhaps it's because they can see the reporter, who nearly always looks and sounds honest.

The socialization process helps to determine how we select information from among the enormous number of communications available to us. If we select information that is consistent with our existing view of the world, as suggested by consistency theory, or if we give attention to communications that are likely to help satisfy needs or give pleasure, as held by utility theory, our behavior is still being governed in part by the socialization process. This is true for two reasons. First, our view of the world, our needs, and our preferences all result to a large extent from the way we have been socialized to live with other people. Second, the various ways in which we select communications to accord with our existing ideas or to serve our needs and preferences are learned. Some people learn to select more efficiently than others—or they use different criteria for selecting one source rather than another.

Understanding the socialization process is vital to understanding the effects of communications. The more we can learn about the former, the better we will comprehend the latter. If you can think back to your early childhood, or to a point at which you adjusted to a new phase in your life, you may be able to add to existing knowledge about the role of mass communication in socialization as well as about the role of socialization in determining communication effects.

LEVEL OF INFORMATION

The mass media make information about almost all subjects widely available. One would think that, for this reason, people who are exposed to the media would absorb this information; that their store of knowledge would grow as a result. Sometimes this is true; people do learn from the mass media. But sometimes it is not; an intensive information campaign on a given subject may not succeed in raising the level of knowledge about that subject among the people at whom the campaign is directed.

The difficulty of raising the information level through the use of mass communications was illustrated by a well-known study conducted after the end of World War II. At this time, many groups wanted to increase public support for the newly formed United Nations. A number of organizations in Cincinnati sponsored an information campaign that had the aim of making every adult in the metropolitan area conscious of and informed about the United Nations. The campaign, well-financed and well-organized, lasted six months. During this period Cincinnati's citizens were deluged with information about the world organization. Mass media, advertisers, schools, religious groups, and civic groups cooperated to din facts about the United Nations into the ears and minds of area residents, and to make them conscious of the slogan of the campaign: "Peace begins with the United Nations—the United Nations begins with you." Display cards carried the message in buses; newspapers stepped up U.N. coverage; thousands of matchbooks and blotters bearing the campaign slogan were distributed; and radio stations plugged the theme, one of them scheduling as many as 150 spot announcements each week.

In spite of this vigorous effort, the campaign had very little effect on the level of information about the U.N. in Cincinnati. A survey conducted by the National Opinion Research Center of the University of Chicago before the publicity started found 30 percent of the area's population almost totally ignorant about the purposes of the United Nations. After the campaign, a second survey found that the percentage of those informed had not changed significantly. Other techniques, too, were used to evaluate the impact of the campaign, but they all reinforced the same conclusion: The level of information about the U.N. had not been affected very much (Star and Hughes, 1950).

A similar experiment was conducted a few years later in West Germany. Officials of the South German radio decided to see whether they could raise the level of information among their listeners about the upper house of the Federal Legislature in Bonn, the "Bundesrat." Polls showed that at that time only ten percent of the station's listeners could give a satisfactory definition of what the Bundesrat was. For two years, Radio Stuttgart seized every opportunity to insert mentions of the Bundesrat in its news and public affairs broadcasts, together with a one-sentence description of this branch of the legislature and what it did. Listeners' knowledge about the Bundesrat was tested at the end of the first year and again at the end of the second, but on neither occasion could a significant change in the level of information be detected (Noelle-Neumann, 1959).

Even earlier, in a well-known article entitled "Some Reasons Why Information Campaigns Fail," two social scientists had pointed out that there is a hard core of chronic "know-nothings" with respect to almost any event or issue. The size of this group varies from one subject area to another. In the area of foreign affairs, which these researchers studied, about a third of the American adult population proved to be totally unaware of almost all major foreign policy stories that were receiving front-page headlines—which at that time included control of the atomic bomb, a very large loan to England, and the future of Palestine (Hyman and Sheatsley, 1947). If they had studied different subjects, they probably would have found different proportions of the population uninformed; the "know-nothings" might have been even more numerous as far as major scientific issues were concerned and less numerous with regard to domestic politics.

Nevertheless, people *do* learn a great deal of factual information from the mass media, and in many areas, publicity can substantially increase the level of knowledge. During World War II, for instance, army training films proved to be successful in acquainting American military personnel with the issues involved in the war (Hovland, Lumsdaine, and Sheffield, 1949). As a result of the televised hearings of the Senate Watergate Committee in 1973 there was a sharp increase in the number of people who could identify such major figures in the hearings as Senator Sam Erwin and John Dean (M. J. Robinson, 1974).

A particularly interesting information campaign dealing with the safe use of pesticides was conducted in Quincy, Illinois, in 1972. The campaign resembled in some ways the Cincinnati campaign about the United Nations, although it was on a smaller scale. The Quincy campaign, like the earlier one, had a slogan and it used a combination of channels. During a single month, four one-minute spots were aired 80 times by Quincy's two television stations. Four radio spots were carried 142 times, approximately five a day, by the city's radio stations. Two news articles and five public service advertisements were published in the daily newspaper. Four variations of a direct-mail appeal were sent to all heads of households in the city at one-week intervals.

After the campaign, about a quarter of those in a random sample of the adult population said that they remembered hearing or seeing the slogan: "Take a Look and Live." Of these, slightly more than half were able to recall some of the major points of the information that the campaign had intended to communicate—for example, "read the label on the pesticide container." Radio, television, and direct mail seem to have been about equally effective in raising the information level. The newspaper was somewhat less effective, although this probably was because it carried mentions of the campaign on relatively few days (Salcedo, et al., 1974).

One may feel that the proportion of the population that learned something from the campaign was relatively small. This is true, but this proportion still represented large absolute numbers. And there is a striking difference between the ability of the Quincy campaign to raise the information level, even if modestly, and the apparent inability of the Cincinnati campaign to do the same.

Why the difference? We cannot answer the question conclusively, but it is probable that the explanation is rooted in the human capacity to be selective about absorbing information, which was discussed in the previous chapter, and in the *previous* availability of information in the two cities. One must assume that in Cincinnati the mass media had already been giving extensive publicity to the United Nations on a day-to-day basis. As a result, all those who wanted information about the world organization already had been able to obtain it. After all, about 70 percent of the population knew about the United Nations prior to the start of the campaign. The remaining 30 percent, the hard-core know-nothings, probably consisted mainly of people for whom information about the United Nations had no utility. A few probably had not formed habits of paying attention to the mass media, and for some the information may have been dissonant—perhaps they resisted perceiving it because they felt that foreign policy was none of their business. These speculations are supported by the researchers who conducted the study of public response to the campaign, who reported: "the surveys indicate that people who have preexisting favorable attitudes are the ones who will pay attention to publicity, that is, that people seek information which is congenial to their attitudes" (Star and Hughes, 1950:398). They also found that those who felt that international relations affected them personally—for example, that they would benefit if foreign trade increased—were more interested in foreign affairs, and hence in publicity about the United Nations. Thus, both the principle of consistency and the principle of utility seem to have played a role in the behavior of those who paid attention to the campaign.

In Quincy, on the other hand, it seems improbable that the mass media had given extensive attention to pesticide safety prior to the start of the campaign. There were therefore presumably a number of people who found this information useful and who had not already received it. Furthermore, it may have been congruent with their attitudes about safety in general.

The success of a Denver film on alcohol and traffic safety in raising the information level among a substantial portion (37 percent) of its audience is also interesting, since it suggests that the effectiveness of a communication can be increased if it is designed with the various theories regarding selectivity in mind (Mendelsohn, 1973). Efforts were made to avoid clashing head-on with existing attitudes either about drinking or about driving, and to make the film as different as possible from hortatory traffic safety messages, which previous research had shown to receive little attention. It was assumed that people were interested in safe driving—that there was a need for the information—but that a successful film would have to avoid arousing defense mechanisms by which people protect themselves from being bored or scolded.

One possibly encouraging aspect of learning through the media was illustrated by a study conducted among college students in California. The students felt that they needed certain types of political information, and this need led them to expose themselves to the mass media. As their exposure to the media increased, their interest in politics increased also. A result of this greater interest was that they began to want additional kinds of political information and to give more attention to news magazines and newspaper editorials. That is, satisfying the need for information gave rise to a felt need for more information (McCombs, 1972a).

Perhaps the most important conclusion to be drawn from research on the effects of mass media on information level is that there is no direct relationship between *exposure* to information and *learning* of information. People can be exposed repeatedly to an idea but may not remember it. On the other hand, the mass media can raise the information level about a topic significantly if people can find a use for the information or if it is in line with their existing attitudes.

ATTITUDE FORMATION AND CHANGE

Just as people have the ability to disregard informative communications in which they are not interested, they also have an amazing capacity to resist persuasive communications. This was first documented systematically by researchers who made an intensive study of political propaganda in Erie County, Ohio, during the 1940 presidential campaign. They found that, in spite of the flood of persuasive material issued by and for the candidates in this election, only about six percent of the population changed their voting intention as a result of political propaganda (Lazarsfeld, Berelson, and Gaudet, 1944). The Erie County voting study was replicated in 1948 in Elmira, New York, and led to very similar conclusions (Berelson, Lazarsfeld, and McPhee, 1954). Few attitudinal changes were found as a result of the extended campaign on behalf of the United Nations in Cincinnati, which was described above. And a number of observers have noted that British taste in television fare did not seem to be changed by the fact that for ten years the British Broadcasting Corporation enjoyed a broadcasting monopoly, which it used in part to try to raise the level of public taste (Gans, 1974).

These findings and observations came as somewhat of a surprise to many social scientists. It had been widely assumed that mass communications could be highly persuasive. If not, why had political parties and candidates devoted so much money and effort to campaign publicity? Why had governments engaged in extensive international propaganda? Why had almost every interest group—whatever its field of interest—tried to mold public attitudes through the use of the mass media?

Furthermore, other studies showed rather impressive attitudinal effects. Well before researchers in Erie County, Ohio, found political propaganda to be relatively ineffective as a persuasive tool, other researchers at the University of Iowa demonstrated that political communications could be an important force in shaping attitudes. In this experimental study, subjects were divided into two groups, one of which was exposed to published material that praised Prime Minister Hughes of Australia. The other group read anti-Hughes material. The subjects did not know they were involved in an experiment. When their attitudes were subsequently tested, it was found that those who had read pro-Hughes material were much more favorable to him than those who had been exposed to the anti-Hughes articles (Annis and Meier, 1934). This was followed by numerous other experiments, and observations made under natural conditions, which likewise indicated that the mass media could have a powerful effect on attitudes. For example, political propaganda seemed able to influence large numbers of voters in some local elections. Children who were regular viewers of the Sesame Street public television program were found to have more positive attitudes toward children of other races as compared with children of the same age who did not view the program (Lesser, 1974). Careful statistical analysis of voting patterns in presidential elections from 1956 to 1972 showed that in some cases readers of a newspaper that gave its editorial endorsement to one candidate were considerably more likely to vote for that candidate as a result of the endorsement (J. P. Robinson, 1974).

Conflicting data as to the power of the mass media to affect attitudes were in part responsible for two developments in thinking among many social scientists. First, there was an inclination to reevaluate the data that showed little or no effect: Perhaps the time periods studied were not long enough; an election campaign may be too short to enable persuasive communications to achieve major effects on attitudes. It was also pointed out that in a close election a shift in attitude among a relatively few voters might be of great importance (Noelle-Neumann, 1973).

A second tendency among social scientists was to place more emphasis on the complexity of the problem. It was recognized that the question was not whether mass communications could or could not affect attitudes, but rather under what conditions there would be an effect and under what conditions no effect or very little effect. The large number of factors to be explored is suggested by the fact that, according to one estimate, about 1000 studies on persuasion are now reported each year in the psychological literature alone (McGuire, 1973).

Even to refer to all the factors that have been studied would be impossible, but most of them can be grouped under four headings: characteristics of the source of the message (for example, is it trustworthy or not trustworthy?); characteristics of the message content (is it clear or unclear? does it appeal to the emotions or the reason?); characteristics of the channel (is television more persuasive than the newspaper?); and characteristics of the audience. This classification scheme follows the description of communication by Harold D. Lasswell as: "Who says what, through what channel, to whom, with what effect?" (Lasswell, 1948). Other scholars have suggested that additional categories be included—for instance, the timing of the communication and the competing communications to which the same audience is exposed.

Research on the role of the source, the channel, and the message content in persuasion has confirmed many common-sense notions, but it has also turned up unexpected relationships. For instance, a source is likely to be more persuasive if perceived as expert (an obvious finding), but children are more influenced if praised by a stranger than if the praise comes from a person they know (not quite so obvious). Or, with regard to channel, people are more likely to be persuaded by a message delivered by a speaker who appears before them live than they are by the same message in recorded form (fairly obvious). But reading a magazine and viewing television cause different types of brain waves, which appear to be associated with different degrees of attention (not obvious at all). Finally, with regard to content, one is more likely to gain agreement with a succession of points if the most attractive ones are placed first (reasonable, if not completely obvious); but a moderate threat is more likely to achieve compliance than a very strong one or a weak one (less obvious).

Professional persuaders are often concerned with research on source, channel, and message variables (some of which have been discussed in Chapter 4), but audience variables have been given the most attention by students of mass communication. Why does the same message, delivered through the same channel, from the same source, succeed in affecting the attitudes of one person and not of another?

Four characteristics of audiences seem to be particularly important in accounting for different attitudinal effects. First, there are personality and educational differences; some people are more easily persuaded than others, some can understand more complicated arguments, and so on. Second, people are situated in a variety of social settings; one person's friends and family may be liberal, while another is in a more conservative milieu. Third, the attitudes that any one person has may vary in strength; he or she may be deeply committed to a given church or political party, may be more loosely attached, or may have no attitudes at all on some political and religious subjects. Fourth, external events may affect audience attitudes; a communication that is not very persuasive in peacetime may be quite compelling in time of war—or vice versa.

Research on the role of personality in persuasibility has indicated that some people are more easily persuaded than others, regardless of the nature of the topic. A person whose personality is high on this characteristic is more likely to be influenced by communications than one who is of low persuasibility, whether the communications are about medicine, culture, or politics. An experiment conducted at Yale University, for instance, had subjects first read a little booklet arguing in favor of a number of conclusions and then another booklet arguing the exact opposite. The subjects' opinions were tested three times: before any communication was presented, after reading booklet I, and again after reading booklet II. Some examples of the conclusions for which pro and con arguments were presented were: (a) "An effective cure for cancer can be achieved within one or two years if an all-out research effort is made; (b) Jack O'Keefe, a corny comedian who is trying to break into TV, is not worth watching and his TV show will be a complete flop." The results showed consistent differences in persuasibility among individuals: Some shifted their opinions as a result of the successive communications more than others, regardless of the topic (Hovland and Janis, 1959).

But when one asks what causes persuasibility, or what other characteristics are associated with it, the research results are confusing. At one point it was suspected that anxiety, low self-confidence, low intelligence, and a low education level were related to persuasibility, but further experimentation failed to bear these conclusions out. It may be, as one psychologist has suggested, that these factors can work both for and against being persuaded easily. A person with high intelligence and education, for instance, is likely to have more basis for his or her existing opinions, but at the same time is able to give more careful consideration to arguments on the other side. Similarly, a person with low self-confidence may not wish to risk paying attention to opposing arguments, while a person with high self-confidence will not be afraid to do so (McGuire, 1973). It may be that people who show moderate degrees of anxiety, intelligence, and self-confidence are the most persuasible, while those at either extreme are less so.

Research has been done on relationships between persuasibility and such characteristics as religion, race, and social class, but no very impressive correlations have been found. Children are, however, more persuasible than adults, and some studies have found women to be slightly more persuasible than men.

At present, therefore, it is difficult to predict what kinds of people will have their attitudes most affected by mass communications unless one is able to test them individually. This is not very helpful to professional persuaders, but the fact that persuasibility does exist as a personality characteristic may explain in part why the same communication can have different effects on the attitudes of different audiences.

If one wishes to predict the success of a communication in changing an attitude, it is more useful to know something about the social setting of the individuals who are exposed. This is because people who are well integrated in a group are unlikely to change their attitudes in any way that would disturb their relations with others in the group. Studies conducted during World War II, for instance, found that Allied propaganda had little effect on the attitudes of soldiers on the other side when they were members of well-integrated and well-led military units. But if the units started to break down—if leadership was poor, supplies didn't arrive, and there was no mail from home—then the propaganda might have the effect of depressing morale and building favorable attitudes toward surrender (Shils and Janowitz, 1948). An Allied propagandist, summarizing his experience during the war, advised aiming propaganda at "the marginal man"— the one who was dissatisfied and not fully accepted by the group. These were the people who were subject to attitude change. To direct persuasive propaganda to soldiers who were firmly identified with their unit was a waste of time (Herz, 1949).

The importance of the social setting was also emphasized by the election study conducted in Elmira, New York. It was found that individuals who were most likely to change their vote intention were those who initially had a candidate or party preference different from their family and friends. During the course of the campaign, many of these people changed their attitudes so as to agree with those whom they saw every day. They were prime candidates for persuasion (Berelson, Lazarsfeld, and McPhee, 1954).

A similar observation was made by social scientists who studied the attitudes and behavior of American soldiers during World War II. They noted that men who were transferred into an *existing* army unit tended to adopt the attitudes which were already current in that unit (Smith, 1949). As far as is known, the mass media were not involved in these attitude changes, but the research suggests that people can most easily be influenced to adopt those ideas that are already held by members of a group with which they become identified.

Laboratory studies also underline the importance of the group. When subjects are exposed to persuasive communications that are opposed to the beliefs endorsed by organizations to which they belong, they are less likely to be influenced if they are first reminded (indirectly) about their organizational membership. For instance, Catholics who were asked to state their religious preference before listening to a statement that conflicted with Catholic beliefs were less likely to be influenced than those who were not reminded of their religious affiliation (Kelley, 1955).

A third major factor affecting the likelihood of attitude change in response to communications is the strength of the attitude in question. If you feel strongly about something, even the most skillful propaganda is unlikely to change your opinion. This is why relatively fewer changes in voting intention are brought about by political communications during presidential campaigns, when most people have fairly well-formed attitudes, than during local elections, when public interest is likely to be low. Even in presidential campaigns, those people who have fairly weak opinions and relatively little political information are more likely to change their opinions than those with more information and better-formed attitudes.

Between major elections political interest tends to be lower and people hold their attitudes less strongly. It would seem logical, therefore, that the mass media would be more likely to affect political attitudes in these between-election periods than during major political campaigns. This is suggested by the work of two British researchers, who estimated that 36 percent of a sample interviewed in connection with elections in 1959 and 1964 changed their party preference during the interelection period. But they also found that campaign-induced change was "not negligible" (Blumler and McQuail, 1968).

Newspaper editorials are apparently more effective in changing attitudes with regard to rather obscure, technical issues than about matters that have been more widely discussed. For instance, a researcher who studied six types of voting decisions noted that newspaper editorials had the greatest impact on attitudes toward a measure involving taxation of insurance companies (McCombs, 1967).

In some cases, the influence of communications may be traced to the fact that very little information of any sort on a given topic is available. Those who want to make up their minds about this topic therefore may have to rely on a single article, editorial, or television item. That is, the influence of the media may not be due mainly to the weakness of the attitude being influenced but to the fact that there are no other sources of information (McCombs, 1972a).

Much the same is often true when new attitudes are formed. A person who has little or no information about a given candidate or issue may be influenced decisively by a newspaper or broadcast editorial. Many voters have had the experience of going through the newspaper on election eve looking for any tidbits of information on the contest for an obscure office—say, a judgeship—that might help them to decide how to choose among two or more candidates of whom they have never heard before. If someone's attention to a persuasive communication can be won, and if that person has no existing attitude on the subject, then the communication may be very important in shaping a new attitude. This is apparently what happened in the experiment involving Prime Minister Hughes of Australia. But there is an important qualification: Ordinarily, people have no attitude on subjects in which they are not interested, and therefore pay little attention to communications about them.

You can demonstrate the importance of communications in forming new attitudes and influencing weak ones by a simple experiment, which one of the authors has conducted often. Find a group of students, half of whom have studied politics in, say, Western Europe, and half of whom have not. Then give them a simple attitude test on a number of subjects, including attitudes toward a few prominent Western European politicians. Several days later, have a speaker talk to them about the situation in Western Europe. In the course of his remarks, the speaker should single out one political figure—for example, Foreign Minister James Callaghan of Great Britain—for particular praise, asserting that Callaghan is actually one of the greatest statesmen of the time. Then, after a few more days, test the attitudes of your subjects again.

The second test is likely to show that those students who have studied Western European politics will not change appreciably in their attitudes toward Callaghan, while those who are less well informed about European affairs will show more positive attitudes than before. The obvious inference is that the latter group had weak attitudes or no attitudes at all about Callaghan, and therefore were influenced by the speaker. The former group is likely to have had well-formed attitudes and a considerable amount of information on which to base them; therefore the speaker had little influence on their attitudes. Of course, you could perform this experiment using other subject areas as well. For instance, half of the students might be science majors and the other half humanities majors, and the speaker might try to influence their attitudes on some scientific question, such as the prospects for finding a low-cost substitute for gasoline.

A fourth major factor determining the degree to which communications can affect attitudes is what is happening, either in the individual's private world or in the world outside. Studies of propaganda during World War II found that leaflets advocating surrender might be quite effective on troops that were retreating but had little effect when those who were exposed to the propaganda thought the battle was going in their favor. Similarly, U.S. Supreme Court decisions ordering school integration seem to have caused many people to adopt more favorable attitudes toward the consolidation of black and white schools in the South (Hyman and Sheatsley, 1964). Much the same phenomenon could be observed with regard to changes in attitudes toward the rights of young people. Researchers found that respondents who, through the media, knew about changes in voting regulations that allowed 18-year-olds to vote, were more likely than others to favor participation of youth in political activities (Wade, 1973).

In such cases as these, one can ask whether it is really the power of the media that has caused attitude changes, or whether the changes should be ascribed to the events themselves. It seems probable that both are responsible: Events would have no impact if people did not learn about them, and the media would have little effect if they had nothing significant to report. One can bypass the question, however, by saying that mass communications are likely to affect even strongly held attitudes if they are able to report major events that have a bearing on these attitudes.

Up to this point, the discussion has focused on the power of the media to change attitudes, or to form new ones, but there is another category of effects that mass communications can have on attitudes: They may be reinforced and activated.

The ability of the mass media to reinforce and activate attitudes was first explored systematically in the Erie County election study mentioned previously. Some of the respondents in this study were interviewed seven times during and after the campaign period. It was found that political propaganda had the effect of strengthening the attitudes of those who were already leaning toward one party or the other. People who considered themselves Democrats but didn't have very strong political attitudes at the start of the campaign were much more enthusiastic Democrats as election day drew near. The same was true of those who were leaning toward the Republican party.

Furthermore, there were some people who had voted for one party or the other in past elections, but who really didn't feel very strongly about either candidate at the start of the 1940 campaign. In many cases, the political propaganda seemed to have the effect of activating the latent attitudes of such people. They rediscovered their political preferences.

Subsequent investigations have confirmed the existence of these important categories of effect. For instance, a study of two gubernatorial races in 1970 found that 31 percent of those who had already formed a preference before the start of the campaign felt that the political advertising of their preferred candidate strengthened their intention to vote for him. Their existing attitudes were reinforced. (On the other hand, it should be noted that 65 percent said that their candidate's political advertising had had no effect at all on their voting intention.) The activation effect could be noted, too. About half of those respondents who decided for whom to vote late in the campaign said that political advertising had had some effect on their decision (Atkin, et al., 1973).

We can conclude that if a person's attitudes are strongly held, and especially if family and friends share these attitudes, the mass media are unlikely to change them; instead, the media are more likely to activate and reinforce them. The principal way in which mass communication can modify such strongly held attitudes is by reporting some event, or some change in the environment, that makes these attitudes less appropriate.

On the other hand, the media may be quite influential in forming new attitudes and in altering those that are weakly held. These effects depend, however, on the ability of the media to secure attention—something that cannot be taken for granted.

It is important to keep one further reservation in mind when trying to evaluate the influence of the media on attitudes. This is that person-to-person communication may be even more powerful. Indeed, most studies of political attitudes that have compared the persuasive effects of the mass media with those of interpersonal communication have concluded that the latter are more influential. The Erie County study, for instance, found that more switches in voting intention could be attributed to conversation than to the campaign publicity.

An experiment conducted in West Germany not long ago documented the relative inability of mass media to shape attitudes in the face of contrary pressures from the social environment. The researchers were primarily concerned with observing the effects of prolonged exposure to a newspaper with a particular point of view. They therefore wrote to samples of students who were about to enter two German universities and asked them if they would be willing to participate in a study of newspaper reading. Those who agreed to participate also promised to read a particular daily newspaper during the entire year and were given a free subscription to it. Half of the students read a paper with liberal-left tendencies; the other half a conservative daily. The attitudes of the students toward political subjects were tested before the start of the experiment and again at its conclusion without, of course, revealing that these tests were part of the newspaper reading study.

It turned out that the attitudes of *both* groups of students became more leftist during the year. Indeed, those who read the conservative newspaper tended to veer even more to the left than the others. The explanation seemed to be that the atmosphere among students at both universities during this period was a radical one. Even though half of the sample was subjected to prolonged exposure to a conservative point of view, via the conservative daily, the effects of the total atmosphere were much more powerful. This involved person-to-person communication and, one must assume, exposure to other mass media. The fact that the students who read the conservative paper became even more leftist than the others may be because they grew more conscious of the differences between the ideas they found in the paper and those that were favored by their peers at the university (Franke et al., 1971).

ATTENTION

While people have an impressive ability to disregard communications in which they are not interested, the mass media exercise a powerful influence in determining the *degree* of attention they give to subjects in which they *are* interested. For instance, if you are interested in sports in general, but stories about a particular tennis tournament dominate the headlines for several days, you are likely to devote more time to thinking about tennis than, say, golf or boxing.

This ability of the media to channel attention has frequently been noted by social scientists studying letters sent to newspapers or to public officials. It is often said that "the mail follows the headlines." When one story dominates the news for several days, then a large proportion of the letters will be about this story, whether it concerns taxes, corruption in high places, or foreign policy (Davison, 1949).

The attention of organizations, too, is directed by the mass media to certain subjects. A political scientist, studying the role of the press in foreign policy, noted that one of the most influential documents circulated in the State Department at that time was a daily summary of international news stories that appeared in principal American newspapers. The document was influential not because it had an impact on the content of U.S. foreign policy, but because it had the effect of directing the attention of high officials to one problem rather than another. Indeed, subjects that were dealt with in these news summaries often were moved higher on the agenda of the Secretary of State's daily staff meeting. This researcher concluded from these and other observations that: "The press may not be successful much of the time in telling people what to think, but it is stunningly successful in telling its readers what to think about" (Cohen, 1963:120).

Propagandists have long recognized the importance of capturing headlines, of getting as many people as possible to talk about a given subject. In time of war, for instance, the propagandists on each side are likely to focus attention on areas where their own forces are doing well. This technique is supposed to raise morale among one's supporters and depress the opponent's morale.

"Agenda setting" is the label often given to the ability of the mass media to direct attention to one subject rather than another. Several researchers have attempted to determine whether people do in fact judge the importance of issues by the emphasis they are given in the mass media. In one study, conducted in Chapel Hill, North Carolina, people who had not yet decided for whom to vote were asked to outline the key issues, as they saw them, in the 1968 presidential campaign. At the same time, a content analysis was made of the mass media serving these voters, in order to determine which issues were given greatest prominence. The two lists of issues were very similar. Indeed, there was almost perfect agreement between voter emphasis on certain issues and the degree of coverage given these issues in *The New York Times*. Correlations between voter emphasis and coverage in other newspapers were only somewhat lower. The researchers noted that these correlations did not *prove* the agenda-setting capability of the press—other explanations are possible—but that it seemed very likely that the voters' priorities had been influenced by the extent of media coverage (McCombs and Shaw, 1972).

Researchers at the University of Kentucky undertook a similar study, centered on the 1971 elections of the Kentucky governor and the Lexington mayor. They found a much less clear relationship between voter interest in issues and media coverage of those issues. Furthermore, there was as much evidence to indicate that the media were reflecting public concern as that they were influencing it. Some of the differences between the results of this study and the one conducted in North Carolina may have been that the Kentucky study was of a local rather than a national election. Nor did the principal newspapers and broadcasting stations in Lexington and Louisville themselves agree on what the principal issues were. The study thus did not offer much confirmation for the agenda-setting hypothesis, but did not disprove it either (Tipton, Haney, and Baseheart, 1975).

While it is difficult to prove conclusively that the mass media are successful in telling people what to think about, there is considerable indirect evidence that this is true. The Erie County study found that issues to which voters had previously given little attention took on greater importance when they were stressed by campaign propaganda. The study in Elmira came to somewhat similar conclusions. It seems probable that agenda-setting is especially likely among people who do not already have strong convictions about what is important. To this extent, the power of the mass media to focus attention is similar to their power to influence weakly held attitudes and to help form new attitudes.

Several social scientists have suggested that the media can have the effect of building up the importance of personalities, as well as issues, in the public mind. As two sociologists put it back in 1948, if you are important you will be a subject of mass attention and if you are the subject of mass attention you must be important (Lazarsfeld and Merton, 1948). An earlier study of a war bond sales campaign conducted by a popular radio personality (Kate Smith) found that her success was due in substantial degree to the way in which the mass media had previously built her up as a person of sincerity and competence (Merton et al., 1946). And a post-war study indicated that the mass media had portrayed General MacArthur as an almost unanimously acclaimed hero to such a degree that it took a brave politician to side with President Truman when the president decided to fire the general (Lang and Lang, 1959). It seems to be true that public relations specialists, through their use of publicity, can turn almost any client into a public figure. Whether this figure will meet with public approval or not is another question, as is the duration of the celebrity.

Many implications of the agenda-setting and attention-focusing capacities of the mass media remain to be explored. In particular we do not know nearly enough about the conditions under which people's attention can be focused on certain issues and personalities. That there are grounds for caution when it comes to generalizing about the power of the media is indicated by a number of studies that have concluded that personal concerns nearly always take precedence over public issues. One of the best-known of these was conducted by a Harvard sociologist at a time when the United States seemed to be in the grip of anticommunist hysteria. Yet, when he asked two national cross-sections what they were most concerned about, less than one percent of the respondents in each survey mentioned the internal communist threat or the threat to civil liberties. By contrast, 97 percent mentioned some personal or family problem (Stouffer, 1955). The media may be powerful in shaping our attention as far as public issues are concerned, but most of us are still more preoccupied with questions involving our own lives.

BEHAVIORAL IMPLICATIONS

The effects of the mass media on level of information, attitudes, and attention may influence us in what we do. And then again, they may not. If we want to do something anyway—say, buy a given product— then an advertisement may immediately affect our behavior by telling us where we can find the product and at what price. But a great deal of information gained from advertising does not lead to sales (Bogart, 1973). Similarly, campaign publicity may be successful in changing a person's attitude toward a candidate, but this person may not take the trouble to vote on election day. And our attention may be focused on a problem that we can do nothing about. On the other hand, it has been demonstrated many times that some advertising does result in sales, election publicity can help bring some people to the polls, and some of those whose attention is focused on an issue will write a letter to a newspaper or their representative in Congress.

The complexity of the relationship between the effects of publicity, on the one hand, and behavior on the other is illustrated by statistics on cigarette smoking in the United States. From 1870 to 1949, the growth in cigarette consumption was very regular, interrupted only by three periods of economic downturn, while the amounts expended for cigarette advertising varied sharply. Yet there seems to have been little relationship between volume of advertising and number of cigarettes sold. Indeed, when advertising expenditures reached a high in the 1920s, the rate of growth of cigarette production started to fall (Marcus-Steiff, 1969).

Consumption of cigarettes continued to rise until 1963, when it reached a high of 217 packs annually for each member of the adult population (nonsmokers as well as smokers). Then the Surgeon General's report appeared, linking cigarette smoking with cancer. Consumption fell off to 210 packs per capita in 1964 and continued down to 199 packs in 1970. But then it started to rise again, and by 1974 was at a level of 214 packs. One must assume that both advertising and the continuing antismoking publicity have affected information level, attitudes, and attention, but the resulting behavioral trends are difficult to interpret.

SOCIETAL EFFECTS

Just as the mass media may have behavioral effects on individuals, they also have effects on social organizations and on society in general. These effects may occur because of the cumulative impact on individuals, or because social organizations themselves make use of mass communications.

The full range of societal effects of mass communication has never been studied or indeed ever identified. This is partly because effects of this type are very difficult to study. One cannot put a whole society in a laboratory (although there have been attempts to build small replicas of various types of societies), and in the real world there are so many variables that one scarcely knows which to measure, if indeed they can be measured at all. Furthermore, almost every imaginable type of effect is possible, and researchers are constantly stumbling on implications they did not anticipate. For example, research conducted by students from Columbia University's Graduate School of Journalism during a New York newspaper strike in the 1960s disclosed that the machinery of municipal government tended to slow down. This was partly because city officials and workers were no longer under the watchful eyes of reporters, and partly because the municipal government itself depended to a degree on newspapers for its own communication (Knowles and Hunt, 1963).

Because of the multiplicity of societal effects possible, only examples of the kinds of effects observed—or suspected—in various sectors of society can be given. Let us look briefly at the political, economic, cultural, and social spheres.

In democratic politics, the mass media play a significant part both in enabling the government to govern and the opposition to form. The dependence of government in the United States on the mass media is illustrated by the increasing frequency with which the president appeals to a national audience on television (Minow, Martin, and Mitchell, 1973), and also by the extent to which governmental officials rely on the mass media for information necessary to perform their jobs. As a State Department official told a researcher: "The first thing we do is read the newspaper—*the* newspaper—*The New York Times*. You can't work in the State Department without *The New York Times*" (Cohen, 1963:135).

The media affect the functioning of local government as well. A study of newspaper coverage of city council meetings in Durham, North Carolina, concluded that this coverage tended to support the authority of the city council and to insulate it from public scrutiny. This was because reports of the council's meetings made them appear more efficient and rational than they really were, and because the selection of material that was provided tended to reassure people that the council was responsive to the community's needs, when this was not always the case (Paletz, Reichert, and McIntyre, 1971).

Political party life is heavily dependent on the mass media network, enabling leaders both in and out of office to rally their supporters and marshal votes. Indeed, some students of politics have maintained that the formal political party machinery in some parts of the United States is weak precisely because it is not necessary. The mass media can be used to lead the party faithful and recruit new supporters; there is no need to maintain a small army of paid workers and a network of political clubs and offices (Truman, 1951).

The close relationship between mass communication and the political process is illustrated by the fact that changes in the media frequently bring about changes in political practices. For instance, before television saturated the United States, political candidates sought to speak in as many population centers and shake as many hands as possible. Now, while they still travel from city to city shaking hands, their public appearances are timed so as to be carried on the evening television news. Appearances in person have become less important. Political candidates are interested in the latest findings of mass communication researchers, too. They frequently employ communication specialists to advise them on techniques of mass persuasion, on how to reach the largest possible audience, and on how to gauge the effectiveness of their publicity. In recent years, many political campaigns have been directed by specialists in political advertising.

At one time, social scientists feared that the mass media would give political leaders undue power over the populations of their countries, and possibly would even undermine democracy. According to this theory, the media would give rise to a "mass society," in which communications would tie each individual to the central government, while the influence of local affiliations would decline. This fear, however, appears to have been exaggerated. It is true that the ability of central governments to use mass communications seems to have strengthened central executive authority. In the United States, the president can appeal to the voters over the heads of Congress by using radio and television; and in Western Europe election contests are now dominated by party leaders who are candidates for the office of prime minister rather than by individual races for parliamentary seats, as was formerly the case. But at the same time, the media appear to have strengthened other political forces as well. For instance, mass communication has been used to increase the self-awareness of ethnic groups, to bring out Catholic, Protestant, or Jewish voters, to rally labor union members, and so on. In politics, at least, a unitary "mass society" does not seem to have been created.

The ability of the media to link together those with common interests, to focus attention on certain issues, and to enable minority groups to state their case to the public at large has important political implications, even though it has effects in nonpolitical spheres as well. The role of the "elite" press in the United States and many other countries is of particular interest. "Elite" newspapers are those that are read by people who are better educated, more affluent, and in positions of leadership. In the United States, about two-thirds of industrial executives, labor leaders, high civil servants, and members of Congress are regular readers of the New York Times. Heads of voluntary associations and mass media executives are even more likely to read the Times. The next most important papers, in terms of their readership by influential people, are the Wall Street Journal and the Washington Post (Weiss, 1974). In England, a survey of people listed in Who's Who, conducted in 1963, found that 70 percent of them regularly read the Times, while 43 percent read the Daily Telegraph. In France, Le Monde is the favorite newspaper of influential people. These elite newspapers make it possible for leaders in all sectors of society to keep in touch with each other, to exchange ideas, and to form opinions about major issues. They serve as a coordinating mechanism for people who, together, exercise an enormous influence on what happens in their societies. The editorial policy that these newspapers adopt is not necessarily important, although in some cases it may be. What is significant about them is that their news coverage helps influential people to focus their attention on major issues—political and otherwise—and to know what other influential people think about these issues. They make a kind of national town meeting possible (Merrill, 1968).

Just as the elite press enables public opinion to form among influential members of a society, other mass communication channels facilitate the formation of public opinion in a society as a whole, in certain geographical regions, or among certain population groups. This also has important political implications. Media reporting of the Watergate scandal is usually credited with influencing public opinion with regard to the Nixon administration and ultimately forcing the president to resign. On a local level, newspapers, radio, and television reporting often helps to shape public opinion about city and state officials, school bond issues, highway construction, and many other subjects.

The media also enable minority groups and special interest groups to gain the attention of a wider public and to state their cases. Advocates of women's rights, opponents of racial discrimination, consumer groups, and many others have found it possible to reach large audiences through the mass media. Sometimes they have been able to influence legislation.

It has not always been easy for such groups to gain access to the news columns. For many years, as noted above in connection with media sociology, the press in the United States simply ignored the black population, except when reporting a race riot or a crime committed by a black person against a white. But the media do ordinarily report mass demonstrations, dramatic acts of protest, and major scandals. Consumerism in the United States was given impetus as a result of reporting about the efforts of General Motors to silence consumer advocate Ralph Nader. Nader hit the headlines at that time and has been in the news ever since. The prominence given him by the media seems to have played an important part in his ability to influence legislation affecting consumers and the quality of the environment. Similarly, television reporting of racial protests in the 1960s, and of the brutal tactics that were sometimes used in controlling these demonstrations, is generally credited with having hastened the passage of civil rights legislation. In instances such as these it is difficult to prove conclusively that media coverage actually did have specific political effects. Perhaps consumer and civil rights legislation would have been passed in any case. The most one can say is that these and other media effects seem very probable.

What is the impact of the mass media on economic activity? One can speculate about this by asking what would happen to economic activity if there were no mass media, or if mass communication were structured very differently—for instance, if no advertising was allowed on television, or if newspapers did not carry classified ads.

Some indication of the effects of newspapers on economic activity can be gained from examining the reasons for the introduction of newspapers, and of advertising, in the first place. The publisher of the first newspaper to appear in France, in 1631, argued that newspapers were beneficial because "they serve the practical business man in that they enable a merchant to avoid trying to do business with a city that is under siege, or has been destroyed, they enable the soldier to avoid looking for employment in areas where peace prevails," and so on (Bauer, 1929). Over 100 years later, in 1761, when the Prince of Nassau-Saarbrücken introduced the first weekly newspaper in his diminutive state, he gave a more detailed description of the economic benefits it was expected to bring:

> Whoever wishes to borrow or to loan money, or other things; whoever wishes to buy or sell, to exchange or to barter . . . he needs only to have a notice inserted in the weekly paper, and thereby can save himself a great deal of tiresome inquiry from house to house and even from town to town . . . . Persons who wish to hire themselves out, including those who would like to earn something honorably by working privately, can offer their services through this medium in the most convenient manner without being publicly named, and thereby do a service both to themselves and to others.
>
> Those who live here, and foreigners who have goods to sell at the fair in the Saar or somewhere else, can in this manner make the availability of these goods known throughout the whole land . . . and there are many other conveniences of such a nature that we shall not mention here. (Bauer, 1929)

It is significant that some of the large banking houses in early modern Europe maintained private news services. The most famous of these services, the Fugger Newsletters, instituted by the Augsburg bank of the same name, included detailed news about court intrigues, battles, and diplomacy, as well as gossip about prominent people. All this information could have had an effect on business, in that it would have been useful for decisions about who was a good credit risk, which states were more stable than others, and so on (Matthews, 1959). Bankers still make use of private newsletters, but much of the information they need comes from the general mass media (Bauer, Pool, and Dexter, 1963).

As these fragments of historical testimony indicate, the mass media are associated with quickening economic activity. The media enable buyer and seller, employer and employee, to find each other more rapidly than would otherwise be the case. They also help a large enterprise to do business throughout a wide territory and to deal with numerous people. Advertising is an essential element in making mass production and mass distribution possible. Unless a firm can reach thousands or even millions of buyers it may not be able to afford the investment required to produce items at a low cost per unit. But then the expenses of advertising must be added to the cost of the product, thereby canceling out some of the economies achieved by mass production. More than two percent of the United States' gross national product is spent for advertising.

The huge expenditures required to reach millions of consumers tend to restrict competition in some product lines by making it impossible for all but the largest firms to enter the market. On the other hand, advertising also makes it possible for smaller firms dealing in more specialized products to come into existence and to prosper. The fact that some socialist countries, after having excluded advertising from the mass media, have more recently allowed it on an increasing scale, suggests that its benefits to the economy are regarded as important. The question remains, however, whether the benefits justify the huge amounts spent for advertising in the United States. Other industrialized nations spend much less. Canada and the United Kingdom, for example, devote only about 1.6 percent of their gross national product to advertising expenditures.

It is probable too that the entertainment content of the mass media, along with news and advertising, affects the economy. Critics of television, in particular, have noted that portrayals of wealthy people living in opulent houses, using modern appliances, driving expensive cars, and frequenting elegant restaurants may cause those who are less affluent to covet goods and services they cannot afford. But this effect has not been proved, any more than it has been demonstrated that people who prefer to watch Westerns on television long for a simple life in the open and want to ride horses. Nevertheless, common sense would suggest that some mass media entertainment content does indeed stimulate a demand for consumer goods.

It would be especially interesting to study the effects of specialized magazines and journals on various sectors of the economy. As has already been noted, there are thousands of magazines, large and small, in the United States that serve almost every imaginable special- ty: turkey breeding, steam fitting, chemical engineering, industrial psychology—you name it. But what effect do these magazines have? Do they promote innovation, or do they encourage conformity among those who specialize in a given area? Again, common sense would suggest that they would have the effect of stimulating a higher level of competence and a stronger sense of group pride among those who read them. But this remains to be demonstrated.

Knowledge about the effects of the mass media in the cultural sphere is equally deficient. Critics accuse television and radio, espe- cially, of having debased popular taste and of offering fare that caters to the least common denominator. Their defenders point out that they carry a large number of high-quality programs—well-done do- cumentaries, serious music, scientific features, and interviews with some of the best minds in the country. True, these programs occupy only a small proportion of the total broadcast hours, but at the same time they make quality cultural materials more easily available to more people than ever before. At present, there is no firm evidence to indicate how the mass media have changed the level of taste in the United States.

Regardless of the media's effect on the level of taste, it does seem probable that they have homogenized popular culture in the United States. One social scientist suggests that they have speeded up the demise of folk cultures, since young people of varying backgrounds usually find mass-produced entertainment more attractive than the stories, songs, and dances that their parents or grandparents brought with them to the New World. Entertainment materials provided by the mass media have usually emphasized middle-class settings and values, virtually ignoring working-class culture (Gans, 1974). A rather old analysis of mass periodical fiction (from 1921 to 1940) showed that the heroes in the stories published were overwhelmingly busi- ness or professional people. Indeed, in *True Story Magazine*, 78 per- cent of the protagonists represented these groups. Even in the *Atlan- tic* more than a third of the heroes came from business or the professions, while the occupations of another third were not identi- fied. No magazine studied showed more than a sprinkling of work- ing-class heroes (Johns-Heine and Gerth, 1949). While the proportion of business people portrayed in more recent popular fiction—wheth- er in magazines or on television—probably has declined, the heroes are still predominantly middle-class.

Yet there is also a countertrend to homogenization. FM radio, mo- tion picture films, and specialized magazines have increasingly appealed to particular subaudiences. A devotee of the "counterculture," for instance, can find broadcasting stations, magazines, films, and "underground" newspapers that have little good to say about middle-class culture. An adherent of high culture can listen to classical music, read avant-garde novels, and patronize art films. Even though commercial television and the daily press encourage a common life style, many contemporary media support other life styles. It seems probable that the two trends will coexist for many years to come.

As in other spheres, one must be cautious about ascribing cultural effects to the mass media. Do they mainly cause changes in taste, or do they reflect changes that have already occurred? Probably they do both.

It also seems probable that the media affect the way people and groups relate to each other. Perhaps they make individuals more or less honest and law-abiding, more or less tolerant; perhaps they bring different groups in a society together, or promote divisiveness. This diverse category of influences may be labeled "social effects."

But here again it is difficult to determine whether the media stimulate trends or merely follow them. For example, does newspaper reporting about crimes stimulate more crimes and thus affect the crime rate? This question has long interested law enforcement officials and social scientists, some of whom speculate that a detailed description of a robbery or murder will provide "how-to-do-it" information or will suggest such courses of action to people who have criminal tendencies already.

Researchers have made several attempts to establish whether there is a relationship between crime reporting and the incidence of crime. In one recent attempt, a researcher at the University of Iowa examined crime rates in three cities—Cleveland, Minneapolis, and Vancouver—during periods of two months or more when newspapers in these cities had been closed down by strikes. He concluded that there was not a significant relationship between crime rates and newspaper blackouts. Some types of crime (auto theft, rape, murder, and larceny under 50 dollars) were slightly lower in Cleveland during the period when there were no newspapers, as compared with the average for the same months in other years, but the relationship did not apply to other types of crime and was so small that it probably was due to chance. And there was no consistent relationship in the other cities (Payne, 1974).

As we have seen above, there is evidence that viewing of violent content on television increases aggressive tendencies among some children, but we do not know whether this affects the crime rate. It may be that heightened aggressiveness is expressed in other ways than through engaging in crime. Or the media may exercise a countervailing influence that has not yet been identified.

Certainly the mass media have played some part in bringing about changes in the way women and minority groups are treated in American society, but we do not know how great a part. It seems reasonable to assume that the civil rights movement and women's rights movement would have developed more slowly if they had not received so much attention from mass communications, but they might have developed anyway. Perhaps the media activated and reinforced existing attitudes to a point where they led to behavior that advanced these movements: for example, demonstrations, the passage of legislation, and changes in employment policies. ✳

Some social effects of the media are important, but rather subtle. Thus, researchers have established that those who are better educated take more advantage of new sources of information than those who are less educated. As a result, a "knowledge gap" develops, giving better educated (and usually more affluent) people even more of an advantage than they enjoyed before. For example, if newspapers emphasize information on health and medicine, and carry more articles on these topics, the better-educated will learn more, even though it is the less-educated who are in greater need of the information (Tichenor, Donohue, and Olien, 1970). Recent research has indicated, however, that when publicity is very intense, and especially if a controversy is involved, then the less-educated tend to catch up and narrow the gap in the information level (Tichenor et al., 1973).

Some social scientists have maintained that the mass media tend to preserve the status quo by reinforcing existing values, increasing the power of those who already have power, and focusing attention on subjects of interest to the elite. Others have seen media as promoting social change through their capacity to help new interest groups and political movements to form, to acquaint people with ideas and life styles other than their own, and to focus attention on grievances and injustices. One can make a case for either position. At some times and places, and with regard to some social arrangements, one position appears to be more reasonable; under other circumstances the other would seem to have greater merit. Research in developing countries, especially, has shown that the mass media can have the effect either of encouraging rapid modernization or of reinforcing old customs and practices. In some Middle Eastern countries, for instance, radio popularizes new life styles; in others it has emphasized traditional music and verses from the Koran (Lerner, 1958).

Part of the reason it is so difficult to isolate specific effects of the media in almost any area of society is that they ordinarily are only one of several factors involved. What, for instance, is the role of the media in either advancing or retarding the birth rate? The publicity given to family planning must have some effect—as well as publicity given to fertility drugs. But economic factors also enter in: The birthrate tends to decline in times of recession. There are also laws and regulations affecting the sale of contraceptives, the positions adopted by churches, the degree of urbanization of a society, and many other factors. And here, as in regard to nearly all effects of the mass media, person-to-person communication also is important. What relatives and friends think and say about family planning may be more significant than any information obtained from the channels of mass communication.

The multiplicity of factors that are involved in gauging the social effects of mass communication can be seen even more clearly when one asks whether the media promote cohesion in a society or, contrariwise, encourage disunity and separatism. Obviously, they can do both, depending on how they are used. And how they are used depends on the political structure of a society, the degree of control a central government exercises over communication, the ethnic and language patterns within the population, the principal trade routes and markets, and a host of other considerations.

Analysis of communication flows within and between societies has indicated that one condition for national cohesion is that people communicate more with others in the same country than they do with those who are citizens of another state. When the principal channels of communication cut across borders of a country, or when they fail to link all areas of a country with each other, then the probability of instability is enhanced (Deutsch, 1953). Thus, bilingual nations such as Canada and Belgium have been subjected to severe strains in part because of the tendency of communication patterns to follow language patterns. Some of the French-speaking, English-speaking, or Flemish-speaking citizens of these nations have tended to live, so to speak, in different worlds. Yet at the same time that some mass media, whether intentionally or unintentionally, were encouraging separatism in these nations, other media were helping to bind the Canadian and Belgian societies together. But can either social cohesion or a tendency toward divisiveness be listed as an "effect" of communication? Certainly, both are possible effects that can occur, but only as a result of the interaction of communications with other forces.

THE DIVERSE POTENTIALITIES OF THE MASS MEDIA

This chapter has summarized some of the available data about the ways in which mass media can affect the socialization of the individual, as well as his or her level of information, attitudes, and attention. We have tried to indicate more generally the types of effects that the media may have on a society as a whole.

Enough is known about the effects of some communications on individuals to provide rough guidelines for predictions as to what will happen when certain kinds of individuals are exposed to these communications under certain conditions. Many professional persuaders—advertisers, propagandists, political party workers—attempt to apply these general guidelines in specific situations. In a fairly recent handbook for political party workers, for instance, we read: "You should make absolutely clear to canvassers that their principal job is not to argue issues with voters, but to evaluate voters in terms of candidate preferences. The emphasis must be on mobilization, not conversion" (Movement for a New Congress, 1970:28). The handbook does not say so, but one can assume that this statement is based on research showing that communications are more likely to activate and reinforce political attitudes than to convert people to new attitudes. Somewhat similar statements, based on the research literature, can be found in handbooks dealing with advertising, public relations, or propaganda.

Nevertheless, the guidelines based on the research literature are, in most cases, merely approximate ones. They do not hold in all cases; exceptions can usually be found. The use of communications to socialize, to inform, to persuade, or to focus attention remains as much an art as a science. Professional users of communications are frequently surprised by the unintended effects they achieve—assuming that they are able to find out what effects *do* result from their activities. Product advertising, in some cases, has been found to *reduce* sales (Bogart, 1973). Political advertising on behalf of a candidate may lead as many people to vote *against* that candidate as to vote for him (Atkin, et al., 1973). The political candidate who has the most money to spend for campaign publicity will not necessarily win the election. Indeed, in the 1970 senatorial campaigns the winner spent less than the loser in 14 out of 32 contests (Seiden, 1974). A more detailed study of candidates' expenditures for television and radio publicity in the 1970 congressional elections concluded that the amount spent did indeed seem to influence the number of votes a senatorial candidate received, but that in races for seats in the House of Representatives expenditures for broadcast time did not influence election results (Dawson and Zinser, 1971).

News bulletins can sometimes confuse people, rather than enlightening them. Before seeing a news bulletin dealing with defense questions, 90 percent of a sample of television viewers in England were able to describe NATO correctly as a defense organization. But after the broadcast only 57 percent linked it to defense and 34 percent thought it had something to do with trade (Anon., 1974).

When it comes to social effects of communication, knowledge is even more approximate. While research on communication effects makes possible somewhat better predictions than would otherwise be the case, it is far from a sure guide as to what will happen.

But one effect of the mass media about which one can speak with considerable confidence is that they open up new possibilities, both for individuals and for societies. A person can learn French via television; keep in touch with a particular religious cult via radio, newspapers, or magazines; or bathe in the strains of an exotic musical tradition via recordings. The individual is far less dependent than before on the resources of a single community. Societies, too, have many choices open to them. They can put the mass media at the service of the government or ruling party; they can use the media to help their citizens achieve their private goals; or they can fashion communications so as to encourage a rich diversity of subcultures. The enormous number of linkages between individuals and groups made possible by the mass media multiplies the choices with which people and societies are faced. How should the potentialities of both the old and the new means of communication be used?

Scholars have been fond of pointing out that new communication technologies, merely by the fact of their existence, alter conditions of human life—just as other technologies have done. After the explosion of the first atomic bomb, the world was not the same as before. This point of view has been popularized, in the case of communications, with the slogan, "the medium is the message" (McLuhan, 1964). But the fact of a technology's existence does not necessarily tell us what results this technology will have; these results depend on choices—some conscious, some unconscious, made by people.

Much of the time we cannot predict the effects of the mass media with any confidence, but modern research techniques enable us to learn more about the kinds of results that flow from them. Communication research thus can help us make some of the choices with which we are faced.

What are these choices? They are too numerous to enumerate, even if one could identify them all. They concern individuals, groups, and whole societies. Our final chapter will discuss a few of them.

FURTHER READING

A readable summary of quantitative research on the effects of mass communication is Joseph T. Klapper's *Effects of Mass Communica-*

tion (Free Press, 1960). More technical and somewhat more recent summaries are Otto N. Larsen's "Social Effects of Mass Communication," in *Handbook of Modern Sociology*, edited by Robert Faris (Rand McNally, 1964); and Walter Weiss's "Effects of Mass Media of Communication," in *Handbook of Social Psychology*, edited by Gardner Lindzey and Elliot Aronson (second edition, Addison-Wesley, 1968).

Two classic monographs that provide rich insights into the effects of political communication and the communication process in general are *The People's Choice* by Paul F. Lazarsfeld, Bernard Berelson, and Hazel Gaudet (third edition, Columbia University Press, 1968); and *Voting* by Bernard Berelson, Paul F. Lazarsfeld, and William Mc-Phee (University of Chicago Press, 1954).

The role of the mass media in socialization is discussed by Herbert H. Hyman in his chapter entitled "Mass Communication and Socialization," in *Mass Communication Research*, edited by W. Phillips Davison and Frederick T. C. Yu (Praeger, 1974). A summary of the research literature on socialization is presented by Jack M. McLeod and Garrett J. O'Keefe, Jr., in "The Socialization Perspective and Communication," in *Current Perspectives in Mass Communication Research*, edited by F. Gerald Kline and Phillip J. Tichenor (Sage, 1972). A chapter by Donald F. Roberts, "Communication and Children: A Developmental Approach," in the *Handbook of Communication*, edited by Ithiel de Sola Pool, Wilbur Schramm, and others (Rand McNally, 1973), also includes some useful material on socialization.

EPILOGUE

YOU AND THE MASS MEDIA

How do the mass-media issues discussed in this book affect you? They can do so in many ways, but these can be divided into two broad categories—private and public. As a private individual, you have to make decisions as to the part the mass media will play in your life, whether the role you choose is that of a professional in communication or that of a media consumer. As a citizen, you should be aware of the role of the media in society and you should be able to take well-informed positions on policy issues regarding the mass media—their relationship with government, their structure and financing, their technological progress.

If you are considering a career in communication—as, say, a journalist or a researcher—then the development, process, and effects of mass communication will be of great personal relevance. As a journalist, for example, you would most likely be serving a specific function in the media structure; your understanding of your job would be enhanced by knowledge of the media and the ways that people select communications. As a communication research specialist—if, for example, you wanted to become a public opinion analyst—you would require an even more intensive knowledge of what has been found out about communication processes. If you expect to become a specialist, you ought to start reading such publications as *Public Opinion Quarterly, Journalism Quarterly, Journal of Communication, Columbia Journalism Review,* and books and articles written by journalists and scholars. You ought to pay attention as well to coverage of media issues in newspapers and news magazines.

THE MEDIA AND DAILY LIFE

Even as a member of the general public, you can use knowledge about the mass media. For example, few people plan their mass media diet systematically. Their attention is governed by habit, by the suggestions of their friends, by professional necessity, or by chance. Few are aware, either, of the range of media fare available to them. They are selective in their attention to those communications that come their way—mainly VHF television, the daily newspaper, radio, and some mass magazines—but they rarely stop to ask themselves what other media content might be more useful to them or might give them greater pleasure.

There are many accounts of people who have stumbled upon a book, a magazine, or a television program that gave them particular satisfaction. In some cases, this chance encounter has led them to become devoted to an author, a journal, or an actor. Dramatic accounts come from developing countries, where exposure to a new medium has caused striking changes in a person's life. A Turkish scholar has written:

> You may wonder where I get this passion for newspapers. When I left the primary school . . . I had no notion that anything was published other than schoolbooks. . . . Then . . . I suddenly got a taste for papers and periodicals. . . . It was as though whole worlds of fairy tales were disclosed to me in the pages of every newspaper, magazine, and book, and that terribly narrow world of mine became wider and wider. (Makal, 1954, quoted in Hyman, 1974:55–56)

Researchers studying the role of mass media in the Middle East shortly after World War II found numerous individuals whose outlook on life had been affected by even fleeting contacts with one or another of the mass media. A young Arab shepherd, who lived in a Bedouin camp in Jordan, had seen an American movie once—and thereafter had become restless. He missed the opportunity to watch "good things," such as beautiful girls and horses; camp life seemed narrow and confining (Lerner, 1958:326).

The discovery of new media content by people in industrialized society is less likely to lead to startling consequences, but it still may make a difference. An American businessman reported that his chance finding of the "news capsule" in the *Wall Street Journal* had resulted in a saving of about 20 minutes a day; the capsule gave him all the general news he wanted or, so he believed, needed. A teacher who first encountered *Consumer Reports* magazine rather late in life said that from that time he never made a major purchase without consulting the magazine first. The number of those who "discover" public television programs to which they become firmly attached has grown rapidly in recent years.

All of us can benefit from making periodic surveys of the mass media available to us, by deliberately going off our habitual media paths. We can occasionally tune in television programs or radio stations to which we have never been exposed; we can spend a few minutes in the library examining magazines that we ordinarily do not see elsewhere; we can sample different newspapers at the newsstand. Book reviews, television magazines, and newspaper columns that comment on other media are also helpful. There is no single best method of making an inventory of available media content. The most important thing is to remain alert for new sources of information and entertainment that might help us attain our goals or satisfy our needs. Perhaps some day there will be a computerized system that will enable us to punch in our interests, tastes, and values, and then to receive a listing of the sources of information that would be most useful to us, but that would never be as stimulating as exploring on our own.

As consumers of the mass media we should develop skill not only in locating the best sources of information but also in utilizing those sources to the fullest extent. You may have noticed that some people seem to learn more from a given news item than others do; some can enjoy a work of art more fully; and so on. The skills involved in utilizing communications are complex. They include the ability to read or listen carefully and selectively, a store of background knowledge about the subject being dealt with, and an appreciation of the strengths and limitations of the channel in use. Reading and listening ability, as well as background knowledge, are developed through the whole process of formal education and self-education, but familiarity with the way the mass media operate can help us utilize their content a little better.

Perceptive reading of news is one such skill. Journalists, when reading a newspaper, usually notice things that most other people pay little attention to. They may recognize the byline—the name of the writer or agency given credit for a story. In many cases they will know a lot about the writer, even in the absence of personal acquaintance—whether the writer has a reputation for accuracy and careful investigation, and whether he or she has specialized in the subject with which the story deals. They may also check to see which sources of information are cited, and whether one source confirms another. If the identity of a source was withheld, why was this and how might it affect the story? They usually can tell about how much time was available to write the story before the deadline for filing it, and whether the writer was under great time pressure or not. Since they are familiar with professional news criteria, they can make a good guess as to why the item was included and why it was placed where it was. They may look at another newspaper or listen to a news broadcast to see whether the story is handled in the same way or differently. If the story is credited to a news service or an anonymous "special correspondent," they can still make an estimate about its quality and completeness: perhaps the item comes from a wire service that has a reputation for checking out facts more carefully than another.

Without hoping to duplicate the expertise of an experienced journalist, if we have some knowledge of media sociology we can still make many of the same inferences. Indeed, the media sociologist can sometimes gain insights that elude the journalist, since the former may be aware of social pressures that the latter takes for granted. For example, the journalist may not be aware of the extent to which his or her professional news judgment is influenced by the opinions of other journalists as to what is to be defined as news at the moment. A story that is regarded as of little interest at one point may be headline news at another. Thus, a former reporter for the *National Observer* recalled having discovered a case in which a local welfare agency was denying assistance to unwed mothers who refused to practice birth control. He wrote a story about this, but it was killed by his editor, who felt it had little news value. Yet, a few months later, similar stories were receiving front-page treatment throughout the country, the subject having by then been accepted as newsworthy by the journalistic community.

At one time or another, nearly all of us will want to make use of the mass media to reach a wider public than we can address through person-to-person and other channels of communication normally open to us. We may have an idea that we feel is important—for ending unemployment, for solving an international dispute, or for creating more local recreational facilities. We may be trying to raise money for a worthy cause, or we may feel that we have been dealt with unjustly by some government agency. It is important to know how to gain access to the mass media.

The most obvious methods of gaining access are to write a letter to the editor, or to offer material to radio programs that invite contributions from the audience, such as talk shows. Some radio stations regularly feature "bulletin boards," where they present announcements that have been sent to them. Many small magazines welcome contributions that they think will be of interest to their specialized audiences. Often, a friend who happens to be in media work can give you worthwhile advice on approaching a particular outlet.

Such methods of gaining access depend heavily on communication skills. A person who can write or speak succinctly and forcefully will do better than one who rambles. Most publications will print only a limited number of words in letters from readers, and broadcasters will not permit anyone to go beyond allotted air time, unless he happens to be a president or a quarterback.

Communication skills are even more important when it comes to writing press releases. If you write a release that meets an editor's definition of news, and is brief and to the point as well, it is probable that local weeklies or local dailies will use part of it, or even all of it intact, however much journalism textbooks frown on the practice. There are many books that describe how to write a good news story or press release, and the subject is dealt with in many courses on journalism or public relations. Ideally, any literate person ought to be able to write a basic news story.

If you are an accomplished writer and have something significant to say, you probably will be able to place longer articles in newspapers and magazines. Most newspapers accept such articles only for such special sections as a magazine or travel, although some, like the *Christian Science Monitor*, welcome them on many subjects. But the number of magazines that print articles sent in "over the transom" (as editors sometimes refer to unsolicited material that is mailed to them) is substantial. If you look at one of the publications that lists potential outlets, such as the *Literary Marketplace* or *Writer's Digest*, you may be amazed at their number. Furthermore, they serve a wide range of interests and attitudes, so that if you are a radical or a conservative, a beekeeper or a yachtsman, you will probably be able to find a publication that is hospitable to your views. The limiting factor in each case, however, is that the editor must agree that what you have to say is important enough to take precedence over other possible uses of the space. It is often useful to ask an editor by telephone or letter whether he would like to see an article on a given subject before sending the whole manuscript.

Suppose you have something to say that you feel is very important, but you can't find any editor who shares your opinion of its importance. You can still gain access to the mass media if you are willing to invest enough effort or if you can find a substantial number of other people who share your views. You can climb to the top of the flagpole in front of city hall and stay there for two days, perhaps throwing down leaflets from time to time; or you can organize a mass demonstration in the park. The news media are likely to report either event, and probably—or so you hope—will include at least a few sentences as to why you climbed the flagpole or why the demonstration took place. If you are arrested for violating local ordinances, then the publicity is likely to be even greater. People who feel disadvantaged and discriminated against have increasingly used such techniques to tell their story.

A less dramatic, but probably more effective, way of gaining access to the mass media is not to approach them directly, but to work through a sympathetic organization. If you can persuade a political group or a religious, labor, business, or other organization to adopt a resolution expressing your point of view, it is likely to be reported. You might join Common Cause, Americans for Democratic Action, the John Birch Society, or a local conservation club because you agreed with the purposes of these associations. Elected officials may be of some help, too. Congressmen frequently have letters from their constituents printed in the *Congressional Record,* where they are sometimes picked up by the media.

But perhaps you feel that a newspaper, magazine, or broadcasting station has failed to fulfill one of its obligations, that it is not serving society adequately. What then? Of course, the fact that we read a certain newspaper or watch a particular television program is in itself an expression of opinion. But it is not always a clear expression. The newspaper may be the only daily in town, and the program may be the "least bad" one being aired at a given hour.

A letter is a more forceful way of exerting influence. In some cases, you can influence media decisions by a personal letter—or one signed by a number of individuals. Even though they are not likely to influence an editor's definition of news, or even his decisions on a given story, letters have more of an impact than commonly supposed. A few newspapers have appointed ombudsmen to respond to reader complaints. Large broadcasting networks pay careful attention to communications from private citizens that praise or condemn programs or programming. And even a modest number of letters to a large newspaper complaining about some aspect of the paper's policy—for example, a failure to cover a given type of story—are likely to exert some influence. "The public's responsibility," a student of mass communication has written, "is to be an active, discriminating audience, to make its needs known to the media . . . and if we do not exercise [this responsibility] we deserve only what we get" (Schramm, 1957:364–365).

INFLUENCING POLICY: THE CITIZEN'S ROLE

If your dissatisfactions with the media are more basic than one-at-a-time complaints—if you feel, for example, that they should be organized or structured differently, if you feel that they fail to perform services the public needs, if you feel that their relationships with government ought to be changed—then your strategy will have to be different.

Your first objective must be to prepare yourself. Few of us are equipped—by education or experience—to campaign intelligently for changes in the mass-media system. To start with, few of us even know what to advocate or how to advocate it. In fact, we will find that most people do not want any changes at all—that they are fairly well satisfied with the current output of the media. Even those who are dissatisfied have rarely thought through alternatives, beyond the most rudimentary. To advocate changes requires, first of all, a basis for advocacy—a thought-out conception of what might be the most fruitful relationships between the media and the society, as well as an understanding of some of the implications of technology, financing, and organization of the media.

Not that we should all aspire to be instant experts; rather, we should acquaint ourselves with media issues much as we acquaint ourselves with political issues in a campaign. As in politics, the media questions we avoid may be answered for us. The voter who stays away from the polls, pleading ignorance, nonetheless influences the outcome of the election. The individual who fails to try to grasp issues concerning the media that are supposed to serve the public not only will be unable to understand his or her own media environment but will be unable to affect its quality.

You must be warned, however, that exerting influence on media policy is, in most ways, far different from voting. The American media system operates with considerable independence, not only from government but from its clientele, as well as from pressure groups and other organized influences. Nonetheless, there is a slowly growing body of organizations and publications devoted to study and criticism of mass media performance. In addition, private citizens can make use of the provisions in government regulation—notably of broadcasting—for making their views heard. Large, private associations may concern themselves with aspects of the press: Churches, political parties, and labor organizations have all started their own newspapers in other countries; in America, they have tended to serve as critics of particular aspects of press performance. Still other groups have taken direct action by starting alternative newspapers, magazines, or even news services; to the extent that these widen the spectrum of media available they affect the total communication structure, and may influence the style and content of preexisting media.

Before discussing in detail some of the possible avenues to influence an individual may follow, let us first glance at some of the major policy issues that may be encountered along the way.

MEDIA IN THE AMERICAN SYSTEM

As already noted, the privately owned media in America operate with considerable autonomy. They are only indirectly accountable to the public—usually only to the extent that the public might decline to consume their output—and they are largely free of government direction as well.

Yet the relationships of the media to functions of government at several levels—be they judiciary, regulatory, or executive—are important, even critical to their existence. In theory, all media forms in what the scholar Thomas I. Emerson has called "the system of freedom of expression" fall under the protection of the First Amendment to the Constitution, which provides that "Congress shall make no law . . . abridging the freedom of speech, or of the press" (Emerson, 1970).

In practice, First Amendment guarantees have shielded some media more than others from government intervention: Newspapers and magazines have been curbed the least; historically, the federal government has moved to censor or suppress their content only rarely, usually in emergencies supposedly affecting national security—in federal closings of newspapers in the Civil War, or in the government's unsuccessful challenge in 1971 to publication by *The New York Times* of the Pentagon Papers, the secret documents dealing with the Vietnam War. They have also found themselves subject to federal and state laws regulating business—for example, statutes concerning labor organization—despite protests by publishers that such enforcement violated their constitutional guarantees. In addition, postal rates—although low in the past—have become increasingly burdensome; and the Post Office has occasionally played the role of censor as well.

By and large, the courts, and especially the Supreme Court, have been a force for increasing the strength of the First Amendment as it applies to print media; the justices have weakened libel and privacy laws that in the past have subjected the press to costly legal retaliation. Possibly the only major claim of the press to fail thus far is the right of protecting the confidentiality of news sources, a practice reporters consider an invaluable adjunct of investigative journalism.

By contrast, other types of media have encountered, more restriction. Books that have shocked or offended certain groups have provoked local prohibitions. Film has been subject to state and local licensing and censorship, and Hollywood itself long ago established a self-censoring system that was even more restrictive than official scrutiny; only in recent years has film escaped these fetters.

Broadcasting remains the most compromised major medium. It has been on a federal leash from the beginning—tied directly to the Federal Communications Commission, and indirectly to Congress, which oversees the FCC. All stations must be licensed, all transfers must be authorized, and, in the interest of diversity, all holdings by a given company must be limited. In addition, the FCC sets rules that affect broadcast content—notably the fairness doctrine, which requires balanced discussion of issues and opportunity for reply. In addition, stations applying for licensing or relicensing must commit themselves to specific program categories.

However loose these reins may appear to critics of commercial broadcasting, they are nonetheless restraints and—broadcasters say—an unfair, even unconstitutional discrimination between print and broadcast media. The original rationale for licensing—that broadcasters needed to be allocated specific frequencies to assure orderly broadcast practices, and that the public owned these frequencies—has become a kind of myth, an excuse for regulation far beyond the original necessity. The issue that will be fought out, possibly in the next decade, is whether broadcasting can win full constitutional guarantees.

One relatively small branch of broadcasting is under government control by definition, but still realizes considerable autonomy. Public radio and television—that is, noncommercial, nonprofit broadcasting with some form of governmental or other quasiofficial sponsorship—has struggled ahead in recent years on a combination of financing from foundations, private contributions, and government appropriations. Despite the contests for control among those allied with these various sources, public broadcasting has been able to offer in many instances a more varied, richer fare than has commercial broadcasting. Yet it remains vulnerable—most particularly to the retaliation of Congress, which must continue to vote money for PTV. To date, public broadcasting has remained an adjunct to commercial broadcasting, not its rival.

Journalists and others in the media often sound, to outsiders, hypersensitive about the First Amendment. This may be true because such persons may be more aware of—even participants in—the functioning of the media as critics of government, and more aware of government's power to retaliate. They see themselves as representing the public in an adversary relationship that challenges and oversees government actions. There are two sides to their task—the goal of disseminating discussion of government and its objectives, and equally important, gaining the right of access to information about government. This long struggle, dating from the campaign to publish the proceedings of colonial assemblies, has produced laws on the state and federal level that open a good many meetings and records to public (or press) scrutiny. But at the same time, government has grown bigger and more complex, and often able to conceal more in its labyrinth.

Much of the research described in this book has dealt with the media as they play a role—indirect or direct—in the American political system. Their ventilation of public issues, their dissemination of information or advertising supporting candidates or positions, their own statements of positions all enter into the workings of politics. Although this active political role for the media is as old as the press itself in the United States, it has become if anything more important with the passage of time, as the distribution of almost all political information beyond the interpersonal and strictly local level has come to depend on one instrument or another of mass communication. This very magnitude of political communication has led to constant dispute over whether the mass media operate as common carriers, transmitting material without distortion, or whether they are structured so as to favor a party, a power, or an ideology.

What is the individual citizen's stake in such controversies? It would seem to lie on the side of defending the First Amendment, but at the same time exercising vigilance that freedoms claimed on the public's behalf are actually exercised in the public interest. People who operate the mass media tend to think of themselves as always operating for the public good; it is up to the public to tell them when they have gone astray.

Government and political influence on the destiny of mass media extends well beyond questions of freedom and suppression. Through its policymaking processes, on both the domestic and the international scene, government helps to shape the structure, economics, and technology of media. Agencies such as the Federal Communications Commission, the Federal Trade Commission, and the White House Office of Telecommunications Policy all influence media operations directly. Acts of Congress—such as the law exempting newspapers from certain antitrust provisions and the bill forbidding some television blackouts of professional football games—also bear on media operations. Beyond these are myriad agencies and laws that affect the media indirectly.

THE IMPACT OF TECHNOLOGY

Historically, government action has accounted for comparatively little of the development of communication policy in America. To a much greater extent, economic, social, and technological forces lying outside government have spurred media growth and guided their direction.

Part of the impact of technology in the late nineteenth and early twentieth centuries was described in the first chapter. There it was concluded that no single new mass medium appeared to be emerging now. But this did not mean that technological development had slowed, nor that the multiplicity of communication tools spewed out by the electronic age had run dry.

It has become almost trite to say that an ever-accelerating communications revolution is taking place in the world today and that new communication technologies present complex problems and opportunities. It is difficult to understand this process, but the responsible citizen cannot dismiss the question of new technologies with a gee-whiz or who-knows-what-will-come-next attitude. Nor can one afford to simply "let things work out themselves." New communication technologies create options that we may not fully understand; they can come into use, nonetheless, before they have been adequately studied. Ill-prepared though we may be, we are then nonetheless forced to choose among options and to live with the consequences of our choices (Parker, 1974).

The field of communication policy research, which deals with the larger questions posed by communication technology, is still relatively new. There was a time, not very long ago, when students of communication left some problems to engineers, some to psychologists, and some to political scientists or politicians. Communication policy research is designed to bring them together, to produce some understanding of our media system as a whole. These specialists must all wrestle with such innovations as direct satellite broadcasting, packet switching, telemedicine, integrated circuits, fiber optics, wave guides, pay-cable, solid state switching, and many more.

For the ordinary citizen, it is not important to know a long list of terminology; rather, one should seek to grasp some of the breadth and complexity of the problems presented by communication technology. One of these underlying concepts, for example, is what communication policy researchers call "convergence among modes." There are three main modes of delivery to the consumer in the present American communication system: telephone, broadcast, and the mail. They are institutionally independent; each has a separate job.

Very possibly—indeed, quite probably—each mode in the coming years will tread on the turf of the others. For instance, either telephone lines or CATV cables might be available to deliver new services such as checkless banking or remote education; each may offer as well to carry electronic mail.

An even more crucial issue facing the American public is, perhaps, a happy one. Massachusetts Institute of Technology scientists call it "abundance of choices." Their observation:

> New technologies are being invented every day. Many of them are alternatives to each other; often we must choose. Some satellite systems, for example, economize on the satellite component by requiring large ground stations. Others permit cheaper ground stations at the expense of more sophisticated satellites capable of radiating a stronger signal. For which system, or for what combination of them, should we plan? Science deluges society with a plethora of technical possibilities but economics compels society to choose. As is often said about the new communications facilities: we can do whatever we want; the issue is price and social goals.

A related problem is the rapid obsolescence of existing facilities. As one of the M.I.T. researchers has commented:

> We are now at the point, on the exponential acceleration of change, where major innovations in our communications system are coming every decade, and there is no reason to expect that acceleration to stop. We are entering a period in which the whole communications system will be in a process of constant flux. (Pool, 1974:33)

Such breathtaking change means that billions of dollars worth of equipment are always in danger of discard. To take but one example: Cable systems, satellites, and digital equipment all exist in forms that can—technically speaking—replace enormous amounts of present investment. And yet replacement does not always occur; too many interests resist. To achieve changes in the face of such resistance requires almost that we make a separate field of study of the problems of easing change.

Although technology is constantly providing newer, faster, and often cheaper means of distribution—partly in response to the growing number of events and ideas to be processed in a world where population and complexity of social organization are still growing—the information in the end must be found, selected, and processed through but one human brain at a time. As the amount of information transmitted increases, the number of forms, channels, or processes through which it is reported expand: more media, more communications, more output. But the increase in sources and channels scarcely means that even the interested citizen will have a more balanced diet of information or receive more enlightenment than before. We have been hearing for years about "information glut" or "information overload." (A magazine cartoon shows a physician advising a run-down patient to "cut down on your media intake.") New technologies may improve our ability to communicate in some ways; in other ways, they contribute to the breakdown in our communication.

Coupled with the complaint about the surfeit of communication is the charge that modern communication is impersonal and unresponsive to individual needs. To a great degree, this is true; yet new technologies also hold the promise of unheard-of flexibility and adaptability. Already we have had adequate demonstration of techniques for on-demand access to increasingly large volumes of information, both through cable television channels and through computer retrieval systems. Moreover, the development of such inexpensive, easily used materials as half-inch videotape holds the promise of permitting hitherto silent groups in society to offer their presentations over what is becoming an increasing abundance of wired channels. The outlook is for increasingly individualized information capabilities that will break the mold of mass-media impersonality (Maisel, 1973).

Yet the techniques of mass communication will continue to develop, for they will continue to serve important social needs. The mass media have helped to create and to integrate national societies, and to convey urgent information to whole populations promptly, almost instantaneously. Moreover, while new technologies can create individualized systems, reliance solely on such systems could create a new kind of isolation, a weakening of the coherence and commonality essential to a society. Indeed, we can read a danger in many of the most recent communications appliances—that they are contributing to a kind of "privatizing" of communication, sealing one family or individual off from the next.

Nonetheless, what is called "on demand communication," which permits audience (or user) to control the timing and content of messages received, will assume increasing importance. Many of its uses, of course, will be in business or the professions, notably those—such as science, medicine, law, news, or social research—that depend on the retrieval of quantities of material. Yet the possible social impact of these forms remains unclear. A group of leading communication policy researchers has reported that "to estimate the 1980–1990 demand for on-demand communication is technological forecasting at its hardest." They add:

We are asking about a technology that is not yet deployed. We are asking not only whether it is technically feasible and at what cost but also how far ordinary people will accept innovations that will change their way of life. We do not believe that a categorical forecast is possible. People themselves seldom know how they will act and what they will desire in a totally new situation. . . . On the other hand, total defeatism would be just as wrong as exaggerated confidence. Social research is often able to predict what people will do even though they are quite unsure themselves. (Pool, 1973b:266)

One encouraging circumstance is that a new communication technology is emerging in which individuals can use communications devices by themselves without relying upon a class of professionals. Not long ago, one had to be at least literate to participate in certain aspects of communications. To a certain extent, the use of computers is still the almost exclusive right of programmers or other professionals. But this situation is not going to last long. Computer and audio-video media "literacy" will eventually become important and near-universal skills. The trend is already well under way in industrial nations; it is discernible in some developing countries.

The new technologies are also having an impact on such an older technology as that of printing and publishing. On an increasing number of publications, computerized typesetting is already in use, and its effects are gradually flowing back into the editorial departments: A newspaper copy editor may now use a light beam instead of a greasy black pencil when making changes. Moreover, newspapers and other publications are being pressed by economics to seek new means, such as facsimile transmission, to supplant the cumbersome, expensive method of distributing tons of printed copies from a central point.

A word now about communications at the global level. Satellite systems could, potentially, have the greatest impact not only on the world's communications system, but on its societies. Their capabilities for transmitting to the earth's populations has scarcely been explored. Moreover, they are data collectors as well on an entirely new scale. Students of world resources, for instance, are already working on such techniques as "remote sensing" to collect periodic data on the entire planet.

The very breadth of satellite communication has made it the source of international policy clashes. It is too easy to proclaim satellites, as did too many Americans in the 1960s, the automatic carriers of a new era of "open-skies" communications. The Soviet Union, for one, has proposed a convention making satellite broadcasting illegal without prior consent of the receiving country. While many small nations are interested in the prospects of satellite communication, others are equally worried about their ability to resist satellite penetration.

Even after a decade of experimental use of satellites, their full impact remains unclear. But it is probably a safe guess that, because of the economics and complexity of satellite technology, they will continue to be controlled and managed by investors in industrialized countries. The residents of the "global village" will be hard-put to find a significant role in satellite planning or policymaking.

Although this and other aspects of the flourishing technology of communications may sound a gloomy note, in fact there is reason for encouragement. In the long run, although technological development has presented and will present humanity with enormous and complicated problems, these are more subject to human choice and control than other, purely economic or social issues. This is all the more reason for intelligent understanding of communication policy by specialists and nonspecialists alike.

ECONOMICS, SOCIETY, AND THE MEDIA

The opening chapter discussed briefly the economic organization of the mass media in the United States, and chapter 2 compared the American system with those of other nations. In some countries, government policy has all but created the media system, but in the United States it has grown largely through a combination of economic and social opportunities, seized by private innovators, both corporate and individual. In the long run, mass media organization has taken forms, with a few peculiarities, similar to the rest of American private business, with increasing combination, diversification, and complexity.

Where will these economic trends lead in the long run? Ben H. Bagdikian, the press critic, has projected that if newspapers continue to be absorbed into groups (or "chains") at the present rate, there will be no singly owned, independent newspapers left by 1984. In broadcasting, there appears to be a stability—much like the combination that has dominated the automobile industry—permitting survival of three major companies. Similarly, book and magazine publishers have sought survival by alliance with or absorption into large entities, some of them these same broadcasting-based corporations. Yet it would be foolish to predict either stagnation or security for even the largest conglomerates. The debacle of the Curtis Publishing

Company in the 1950s and 1960s showed how rapidly shifts in audience and economic support can erode even the most successful media enterprise. Change and perishability have been the marks of the age of mass media, and there is little evidence that the future will be different.

Yet mass media will continue to exist as long as there is demand—and the persistence of demand by the American consumer is as much a constant as any other factor. As has been frequently noted in these pages, Americans, with such other countries as Great Britain and Japan, evince an enormous appetite for mass-produced media products, and in general have had sufficient affluence to purchase them.

Still, there have been signs, faint and scattered, of possible overload—of the American consumer's limitations in money and time beginning to overtake the appetite for print, sound, and pictures. It is possible that in this age of the maturity of the mass media that outer limits are being reached in the degree of consumption that can be expected, even given a continued expansion of the economy. As hinted in the discussion above of technology, consumers may want to turn to more individualized communication—as many have, say, in the use of records and taping equipment. Or they may turn away from media as recreation to other, more active forms; the striking increases in sports participation by adults may be symptomatic.

Although students would agree that the general shape of mass media social and economic development is molded by forces beyond the control of most individuals, American media have shown, nonetheless, their adaptability to changing sensitivities and requirements. They are operated by human beings who, for the most part, wish to please or influence other human beings. There are surprisingly numerous avenues open to influencing the conduct of the media. Some of the methods were described in the first section of this chapter.

But if you wish to influence policies affecting the ownership, structure, organization, or long-term operation of the media, you will probably have to work through larger entities.

Many of the governmental avenues have been mentioned already. The FCC, given supervisory power over broadcast licenses and economic organization, is directed by court order to give the public—and groups from the public—a voice in consideration of license renewals. One organization that has used this grant to campaign for minority employment and minority access to broadcasting is the Office of Communication of the United Church of Christ, which has gained several agreements from reluctant broadcasters. Opinions about broadcasting can also be directed to members of Congress, particularly those who serve on the communications committees that oversee the FCC.

The government has less jurisdiction over the printed press, but one aspect—advertising—is subject to regulation. The Federal Trade Commission, Food and Drug Administration (for medical and pharmaceutical advertising), and the various federal, state, and local consumer agencies can hear complaints about the truthfulness of advertising and, by implication, the efficacy of what is advertised.

The individual's voice is much magnified—although probably blurred—if one chooses to speak through a large association. The interests of such organizations in the press are as varied as the reasons they came into being in the first place. In other countries, labor organizations, churches, or political parties have undertaken their own media to compete with the existing ones. With a few exceptions—such as strike-period newspapers run by unions or broadcasting stations operated by religious sects—such steps are uncommon in the United States. Most associations, be they political, economic, philanthropic, cultural, or religious, have preferred to try to influence the existing media to serve their interests. Nor have the media been unresponsive. Television has altered or even canceled broadcast material that offended ethnic or other groups. The nature of news coverage of such topics as race, sexuality, and dissenting politics has changed, partly in response to organized pressure groups. One caution should be added: It is difficult to justify pressure group tactics that lead to simple censorship, for these result in an entire public's being deprived of material on which it may have a right to make its own judgment. Such tactics can be more justifiably (and effectively) directed to expanding and illuminating media content, in demanding access, rather than exclusion.

Recent years have seen the creation of groups that take a general interest in media operations, rather than concentrating on a special aspect. Such bodies are called press councils. In the United States, they are brought into existence privately, rather than by official action, as in Britain. Typically, they have been either inspired or supported by the media themselves, seeking contact with the public. The most ambitious of these is the National News Council, established in 1973 by the Twentieth Century Fund with aid from a consortium of foundations, to hear complaints concerning media and news suppliers with national scope; its membership, drawn from both the public and the media, has no powers beyond those of publicity. In addition, a state press council (Minnesota) and a few local councils have been in operation for a short time. Their results, obviously, are not tangible, but they have promise of exerting a steady influence on the news media in their areas.

In all likelihood, you do not live in a locality where a press council functions. Nonetheless, if you feel that such a body would be useful to your community, you might try to interest a local organization, or a group of local organizations, in organizing one. By all means, you should seek the cooperation of the local media outlets, although you should be prepared to go ahead even if they do not cooperate.

In all such forms of activity—and their type and number will undoubtedly increase as people realize their stake in the media—the first requirement for useful criticism is the base from which to make it. One should not campaign for changes simply on the basis of hunch or irritation. It helps to know what you really want and, moreover, the obstacles that stand in the way.

Although a career in any type of mass media requires special study, members of the general public can exert influence on the media as well. Many, however, lack the skill to seek out the most useful media sources and to exploit them; much can be learned in this respect by study and evaluation of media content. Nor do many know how to produce a communication that will have a chance of media dissemination, although these skills are readily developed, and the media are generally open to them. The media are likewise open to individual criticisms, if reasonably presented.

The individual with more basic criticisms of the media—of their structure, operation, or organization—must first be aware of the contending forces that shape the media today. Among these is government—through court decisions, legislation, administrative regulation, and even political confrontation. Technology is another force influencing the media to change. The complexity and diversity of communications forms is multiplying, but the changes are limited by the ability of humanity to pay for and absorb the output. Similarly, economic and social forces are constantly pressing the formats, and at the same time are undergoing change that makes those organizations obsolescent unless they change too.

Those who wish to work to change media policy can do so through varied avenues. One possibility is to communicate with the government agencies that regulate or otherwise affect media performance. Another, if one has a special interest, is to work with a private organization that has an effective means for voicing that interest. A third is to seek out or attempt to create an organization that specializes in criticizing media performance or policy, such as a press council. The results may not be immediate or striking, but in the long run the people who operate media have proved themselves willing to listen.

Appendix

**Some Statistics on Journalism and Journalists:
Numbers, Characteristics, Incomes,
Working Conditions**

Massive quantities of statistics concerning the mass media are collected each year. If you want current information on newspapers, a good place to look is the latest edition of *Editor & Publisher International Yearbook* (New York: Editor & Publisher Co., Inc.). It lists the newspapers published in the United States and Canada, their circulation, ownership, principal personnel, and a great deal of additional information. Briefer mention is made of newspapers published in other parts of the world. For data about radio and television, look in the *Broadcasting Yearbook* (Washington, D.C.: Broadcasting Publications, Inc.).

There are many other sources for statistics on the mass media: the *International Motion Picture Almanac,* the *Standard Dictionary of Periodicals,* and the *Ayer Directory of Publications,* to name only a few. Most libraries have these sources in their reference collections.

Further data are gathered from time to time by trade groups and professional associations, such as the American Newspaper Publishers Association, the National Association of Broadcasters, and the Association for Education in Journalism. These data are often reported in news releases from the Television Information Office, in the Newspaper Information Service Newsletter of the Newspaper Publishers Association, or in such magazines and journals as *Broadcasting, Editor & Publisher,* and *Journalism Quarterly.*

A third source of statistical information consists of surveys, often conducted by academic researchers. These surveys are reported in the journals devoted to communication research and sometimes in books. One of the most ambitious studies of the characteristics of journalists was conducted in 1971 by the National Opinion Research Center (NORC) of the University of Chicago, under the sponsorship of the John and Mary R. Markle foundation. NORC interviewed a probability sample of 1313 American journalists, representing editorial personnel in daily and weekly newspapers, news magazines, wire services, and the news departments of radio and television stations and networks. The results of this study will be reported in John W.C. Johnstone, Edward J. Slawski, and William W. Bowman, *The Newspeople: A Sociological Profile of American Journalists.* (Urbana: University of Illinois Press, forthcoming).

Numbers and Characteristics of Personnel in Mass Communication

Based on the NORC survey, Johnstone, Slawski, and Bowman estimated that there are approximately 70,000 editorial personnel employed by the media they studied. But, of course, they did not include book publishing, motion pictures, the entertainment side of television, the recording industry, magazines (other than news magazines), advertising, public relations, and a number of other enterprises and professions that are involved in mass communication. The total number of professional personnel involved is in the hundreds of thousands. Among the news media, daily newspapers are by far the largest employer, accounting for over 55 percent of all editorial personnel. Broadcast news employs about 20 percent, weekly newspapers about 17 percent, news services about 5 percent, and news magazines about 3 percent. But these media are not the only employers of journalists. When the Newspaper Fund surveyed 4458 journalism graduates from 106 colleges and universities in 1974, it was found that nearly 20 percent of them had gone into advertising or public relations (ANPA Newspaper Information Service Newsletter, Vol. 15, No. 6, June, 1975).

Journalism and related occupations are still mainly populated by white males, but are becoming somewhat less so. Based on a study of "mass media image makers," as of 1973 the Journalism Council reported that women accounted for 37 percent of owners, managers, and professionals in periodicals, 21 percent in advertising, 18 percent in newspapers and motion pictures, and 14 percent in broadcasting. As compared with 1969, the proportion of women in all these fields, except motion pictures, had increased. Periodicals showed an increase of nearly 5 percent, broadcasting 4 percent, newspapers 2 percent, and advertising less than 1 percent.

The proportion of "image makers" who were minority group members in 1973 was found to be 9 percent in broadcasting, 8 percent in motion pictures, 5 percent in advertising and periodicals, and 3 percent in newspapers. As in the case of women, the proportions had increased slightly since 1969 in all fields except motion pictures. Broadcasting led the increase with 5 percent; the other fields showed increases of less than 2 percent (ANPA Newspaper Information Service Newsletter, Vol. 15, No. 8, August, 1975). The NORC survey found very similar proportions of women and minority group members among the employees of the media they studied in 1971: women comprised 19 percent of the sample and minority group members 3 percent.

How well educated are professional personnel in mass communication? Data are available only for editorial employees of daily newspapers, and here it turns out that degree of formal education varies sharply with the size of the newspaper. In newspapers with a circulation of *more* than 150,000 that were surveyed by the NORC, nearly half of the editorial personnel had a college degree and another quarter had a graduate degree or some graduate training. The rest had a smaller amount of formal education. But in newspapers with a daily circulation under 150,000, nearly half had no college degree. It is clear that many of these journalists learned their skills on the job. This is likely to become less common, however. When the Southern Newspaper Publishers Association Foundation asked a sample of editors and publishers where they looked for new employees, the predominant response was that they preferred journalism or liberal arts college graduates (*Editor & Publisher,* November 14, 1970).

The Satisfactions of Journalism

It is clear from several studies that most people do not go into journalism primarily to make a lot of money—and that those who do are likely to be disappointed. The satisfactions of journalism are many, but they are not mainly financial. In 1974, the median starting salary of journalism graduates was just about $7500—up approximately $500 from the previous year (ANPA Newspaper Information Service Newsletter, Vol. 15, No. 6, June, 1975). The NORC survey, checking income of journalists as of 1970, found that the median salary for those under 25 years of age was about $6200 at that time. For editorial personnel of all ages, the 1970 median was just over $11,000, with the highest salaries going to those in the 35–44 age bracket.

Salary varied sharply with the size of the editorial staff, the population of the city where the medium was located, and the region of the United States. For media with editorial staffs of 10 or fewer, the median was $8545; for those with staffs of over 100 it was $13,515. For cities under 10,000 inhabitants the median was about $8000; for those over one million it was close to $15,000. Journalists in the Southern states were receiving a median salary of just under $10,000, while those in the Pacific states were making $13,390.

Differences according to medium were less impressive, except in the case of weekly newspapers and news magazines. For weekly newspapers, the median figure was low—$8698; for news magazines it was high—$15,571 (although the sample of news magazine personnel was rather small and the figure may not be as reliable as the others). Salaries in daily newspapers, radio, wire services, and television news all ranged between $11,000 and $12,000, with the dailies offering a median of $11,351 and the wire services $11,833.

To translate these salaries into those of 1976, a very rough correction would be to add one third to each median value, since the Consumer Price Index rose from 119 to 160 between 1970 and 1976.

In spite of these rather modest salary figures, editorial personnel expressed themselves as highly satisfied with their jobs, when queried by the NORC interviewers. Indeed, the most satisfied were the ones who were paid the least—the employees of weekly newspapers. Of these, 61 percent said they were "very satisfied," and 32 percent said "fairly satisfied." Only 6 percent were "somewhat dissatisfied" and 1 percent "very dissatisfied." Employees of the other media seemed quite happy with their jobs, too. The most dissatisfied were those in radio, but even here only 15 percent were "somewhat dissatisfied" and 2 percent "very dissatisfied." The rest were enthusiastic or at least content.

One reason journalists are, in general, so satisfied with their work is that the reporters among them feel that they have great freedom in selecting stories to work on and in deciding how to handle these stories. Here again, there are some variations among media. Of the reporters on weekly newspapers, 52 percent said that they had "almost complete" freedom in choosing what stories to write, and 93 percent felt that they had "almost complete" freedom in deciding where to place the emphasis in the story. Smaller proportions in other media reported "almost complete" freedom in choosing and handling stories, but it was still high: in television 68 percent and 84 percent, in radio 75 percent and 72 percent, and in daily newspapers 50 percent and 70 percent. Interestingly enough, the editors who were queried said that reporters had somewhat less freedom than the latter thought they did. Only about half of the editors on weekly newspapers replied that reporters had "almost complete" freedom in choosing and handling stories, and there were similar differences between editors and reporters in the other media.

When journalists were asked to specify the most important aspect of jobs in the mass media, two-thirds replied that the opportunity to help other people was most important. The next most important aspect was "freedom from supervision" and after that came "job security." Salaries were given the lowest rating.

That journalists seem to find their jobs satisfying is also indicated by the fact that two-thirds of those interviewed by the NORC said that they would stay in the same type of work if they could choose what they wanted to do. About a third said they would like to try something else, but most of them wanted to stay in the communication field. The editors and publishers who were surveyed by the Southern Newspaper Publishers Association also suggested that most journalists looked for psychological rewards in their jobs. Over half of them thought that most people who decided to work for newspapers were looking for self-fulfillment more than anything else.

It would appear that the rewards of journalism are considerable, even though largely intangible. Few of those who choose journalism as a career seem to regret their choice.

References

Adams, John B., James J. Mullen, and Harold M. Wilson. 1969. "Diffusion of a 'Minor' Foreign Affairs News Event." *Journalism Quarterly* 46:545–551.

Allen, Frederick Lewis. 1931. *Only Yesterday: An Informal History of the Nineteen-Twenties.* New York: Harper.

Allport, Gordon W., and Leo J. Postman. 1954. "The Basic Psychology of Rumor." In Daniel Katz et al. (eds.), *Public Opinion and Propaganda.* New York: Dryden.

Ames, William E., and Dwight L. Teeter. 1971. "Politics, Economics, and the Mass Media." In Ronald T. Farrar and John D. Stevens (eds.), *Mass Media and the National Experience.* New York: Harper & Row.

Annis, Albert D., and Norman Meier. 1934. "The Induction of Opinion through Suggestion by Means of Planted Content." *Journal of Social Psychology* 5:65–81.

Anon. 1974. "Who's Gromyko?" *Intermedia* 2, no. 2.

Aspen Handbook on the Media. 1975–76. Palo Alto, Ca.: Aspen Program on Communications and Society.

Atkin, Charles K. 1971. "How Imbalanced Campaign Coverage Affects Audience Exposure Patterns." *Journalism Quarterly* 48:235–244.

Atkin, Charles K., Lawrence Bowen, Oguz B. Nayman, and Kenneth G. Scheinkopf. 1973. "Quality versus Quantity in Televised Political Ads." *Public Opinion Quarterly* 37:209–224.

Bagdikian, Ben H. 1972. *The Effete Conspiracy and Other Crimes by the Press.* New York: Harper & Row.

Bagdikian, Ben H. 1974. "Professional Personnel and Organizational Structure in the Mass Media." In W. Phillips Davison and Frederick T.C. Yu (eds.), *Mass Communication Research.* New York: Praeger.

Bales, Robert F. 1950. *Interaction Process Analysis.* Cambridge: Addison-Wesley.

Barlett, Dorothy L., et al. 1974. "Selective Exposure to a Presidential Campaign Appeal." *Public Opinion Quarterly* 38:264–270.

Barnet, Richard, and Ronald Muller. 1974. "Global Reach." *New Yorker,* December, 2 and 9.

Barnett, A. Doak. 1965. *Communist China in Perspective.* New York: Praeger.

Barnouw, Erik. 1966. *A Tower in Babel. A History of Broadcasting in the United States,* vol. 1, to 1933. New York: Oxford.

Barnouw, Erik. 1968. *The Golden Web. A History of Broadcasting in the United States,* vol. 2, 1933–1953. New York: Oxford.

Barnouw, Erik. 1970. *The Image Empire. A History of Broadcasting in the United States,* vol. 3, from 1953. New York: Oxford.

Barnouw, Erik. 1974. *Documentary: A History of the Non-Fiction Film.* New York: Oxford.

Barnouw, Erik. 1975. *Tube of Plenty*. New York: Oxford University Press.

Bartlett, Frederic C. 1954. *Remembering*. Cambridge: The University Press.

Barton, Allen H. 1974–75. "Consensus and Conflict among American Leaders." *Public Opinion Quarterly* 38:507–530.

Batscha, Robert M. 1975. *Foreign Affairs News and the Broadcast Journalist*. New York: Praeger.

Bauer, Raymond A., Ithiel De Sola Pool, and Lewis A. Dexter. 1963. *American Business and Public Policy*. New York: Atherton.

Bauer, Wilhelm. 1929. *Die Oeffentliche Meinung in der Weltgeschichte*. Potsdam: Akademische Verlagsgesellschaft Athenaion.

Bent, Silas. 1927. *Ballyhoo: The Voice of the Press*. New York: Boni & Liveright.

Berelson, Bernard, Paul F. Lazarsfeld, and William N. McPhee. 1954. *Voting*. Chicago: University of Chicago Press.

Berger, Meyer. 1951. *The Story of the New York Times 1851–1951*. New York: Simon & Schuster.

Besen, Stanley M., and Bridger M. Mitchell. 1975. "Watergate and Television: An Economic Analysis." Santa Monica, Ca.: The Rand Corporation, May.

Bessie, Simon Michael. 1938. *Jazz Journalism: The Story of the Tabloid Newspapers*. New York: Dutton.

Blumler, Jay G., and Elihu Katz (eds.). 1974. *The Uses of Mass Communications*. Beverly Hills, Ca.: Sage Publications.

Blumler, Jay G., and Denis McQuail. 1968. *Television in Politics*. London: Faber.

Bogart, Leo. 1968. "The Overseas Newsman: A 1967 Profile Study." *Journalism Quarterly* 45:293–306.

Bogart, Leo. 1968–69. "Changing News Interests and the News Media." *Public Opinion Quarterly* 32:560–574.

Bogart, Leo. 1972–73. "Warning: The Surgeon General Has Determined That TV Violence Is Moderately Dangerous to Your Child's Mental Health." *Public Opinion Quarterly* 36:491–521.

Bogart, Leo. 1973. "Consumer and Advertising Research." In Ithiel De Sola Pool, Wilbur Schramm, et al. (eds.), *Handbook of Communication*. Chicago: Rand McNally.

Bogart, Leo. 1974. "The Management of Mass Media." In W. Phillips Davison and Frederick T.C. Yu (eds.), *Mass Communication Research*. New York: Praeger.

Boorstin, Daniel J. 1962. *The Image or What Happened to the American Dream*. New York: Atheneum.

Booth, Alan. 1969–70. "Personal Influence Networks and Participation in Professional Association Activities." *Public Opinion Quarterly* 33:611–614.

Bowen, Lawrence, and Steven H. Chaffee. 1974. "Product Involvement and Pertinent Advertising Appeals." *Journalism Quarterly* 51:613–621.

Bower, Robert T. 1973. *Television and the Public.* New York: Holt, Rinehart and Winston.

Breed, Warren. 1955. "Social Control in the News Room." *Social Forces* 33: 326–335.

Breed, Warren. 1958. "Mass Communication and Sociocultural Integration." *Social Forces* 37:109–116.

Brown, Robert U. 1975. "What the Public Doesn't Know," *Editor & Publisher,* September 27, 1975.

Brownmiller, Susan. 1973. "Street Fighting Woman." New York: Alicia Patterson Foundation, February 27, 1973 (mimeo).

Buckalew, James K. 1974. "The Local Radio News Editor as Gatekeeper." *Journal of Broadcasting* 18:211–222.

Carlson, Oliver. 1942. *The Man Who Made News: James Gordon Bennett.* New York: Duell, Sloan & Pearce.

Carlson, Robert O. 1975. *Communications and Public Opinion.* New York: Praeger.

Chaffee, Steven H. 1972. "The Interpersonal Context of Mass Communication." In F. Gerald Klein and Phillip J. Tichenor (eds.), *Current Perspectives in Mass Communication Research.* Beverly Hills, Ca.: Sage Publications.

Chaffee, Steven H., and Jack M. McLeod. 1973. "Individual vs. Social Predictors of Information Seeking." *Journalism Quarterly* 50:237–245.

Chaffee, Steven H., L. Scott Ward, and Leonard P. Tipton. 1970. "Mass Communication and Political Socialization." *Journalism Quarterly* 47:647–659.

Cohen, Bernard C. 1963. *The Press and Foreign Policy.* Princeton, N.J.: Princeton University Press.

Coleman, James S. 1957. *Community Conflict.* New York: Free Press.

Coleman, James S., Elihu Katz, and Herbert Menzel. 1966. *Medical Innovation.* Indianapolis: Bobbs-Merrill.

Comstock, George. 1975. "The Effects of Television on Children and Adolescents." *Journal of Communication* 25(1):25–34.

Connell, R.W. 1971. *The Child's Construction of Politics.* Melbourne: Melbourne University Press.

Converse, Philip E. 1962. "Information Flow and the Stability of Partisan Attitudes." *Public Opinion Quarterly* 26:578–599.

Cooper, Eunice, and Marie Jahoda. 1947. "The Evasion of Propaganda." *Journal of Psychology* 23:15–25.

Cooper, Lane. 1932. *The Rhetoric of Aristotle.* New York: Appleton.

Crane, Diana. 1972. *Invisible Colleges.* Chicago: University of Chicago Press.

Crouse, Timothy. 1973. *The Boys on the Bus.* New York: Random House.

Cutlip, Scott M. 1962. "Third of Newspapers' Content PR Inspired." *Editor & Publisher,* May 26.

Dajani, Nabil H. 1975. "Press for Rent." *Journal of Communication* 25(2):165–170.

Darnton, Robert. 1975. "Writing News and Telling Stories." *Daedalus,* 1975, 175–194.

Davison, W. Phillips. 1949. "More Than Diplomacy." In Lester Markel (ed.), *Public Opinion and Foreign Policy.* New York: Harper.

Davison, W. Phillips. 1965. *International Political Communication.* New York: Praeger.

Davison, W. Phillips. 1975. "Diplomatic Reporting: Rules of the Game." *Journal of Communication* 25(4):138–146.

Davison, W. Phillips. Forthcoming. "Communication Channels Since World War II." In Daniel Lerner, Harold D. Lasswell, and Hans Speier (eds.), *Communication and Propaganda in World History.* Honolulu: University Press of Hawaii.

Dawson, Paul A., and James E. Zinser. 1971. "Broadcast Expenditures and Electoral Outcomes in the 1970 Congressional Elections." *Public Opinion Quarterly* 35:398–402.

Deutsch, Karl W. 1953. *Nationalism and Social Communication.* Cambridge and New York: Technology Press of M.I.T. and Wiley.

Dizard, Wilson P. 1966. *Television: A World View.* Syracuse, N.Y.: Syracuse University Press.

Dominick, Joseph R. 1974. "Children's Viewing of Crime Shows and Attitudes on Law Enforcement." *Journalism Quarterly* 51:5–12.

Drabman, Ronald S., and Margaret Thomas. 1975. "Does TV Violence Breed Indifference?" *Journal of Communication* 25:86–89.

Drew, Dan G. 1973. "Attitude toward a News Source, Expected Reporter-Source Interaction and Journalistic Objectivity." Ph.D. dissertation, Indiana University.

Dube, S.C. 1967. "Communication, Innovation and Planned Change in India." In Daniel Lerner and Wilbur Schramm (eds.), *Communication and Change in Developing Countries.* Honolulu: East-West Center Press.

Dube, S.C. Forthcoming. "Communication and Change in Developing Countries: A Review of Last Ten Years." In Wilbur Schramm and Daniel Lerner (eds.), *Communication and Change: The Past Ten Years—and the Next.* Honolulu: University Press of Hawaii.

Ebbinghaus, Hermann. 1885. *Ueber das Gedächtnis.* Leipzig: Duncker und Humblot. (English translation entitled *Memory,* published by Teachers College, Columbia University, 1913.)

Efron, Edith. 1971. *The News Twisters.* Los Angeles: Nash.

Emerson, Thomas I. 1970. *The System of Freedom of Expression.* New York: Random House.

Emery, Edwin. 1972. *The Press and America,* 3d ed. Englewood Cliffs, N.J.: Prentice-Hall.

Emery, Walter B. 1969. *National and International Systems of Broadcasting.* East Lansing: Michigan State University Press.

Epstein, Edward J. 1973. *News from Nowhere.* New York: Random House.

Farrar, Ronald T., and John D. Stevens (eds.). 1971. *Mass Media and the National Experience.* New York: Harper & Row.

Fathi, Asghar. 1973. "Diffusion of a 'Happy' News Event." *Journalism Quarterly* 50:271–277.

Fedler, Fred. 1973. "The Media and Minority Groups." *Journalism Quarterly* 50:109–117.

Fielding, Raymond. 1972. *The American Newsreel, 1911–1967.* Norman: University of Oklahoma Press.

Filler, Louis. 1939. *Crusaders for American Liberalism.* New York: Harcourt.

Fowler, Joseph S., and Stuart W. Showalter. 1974. "Evening Network News Selection: A Confirmation of News Judgment." *Journalism Quarterly* 51: 712–715.

Franke, Joachim, et al. 1971. "Enkulturationsbewirkung des regelmässigen Lesens von Tageszeitungen." In Franz Ronneberger (ed.), *Sozialisation durch Massenkommunikation.* Stuttgart: Enke.

Funkhouser, G. Ray. 1973. "The Issues of the Sixties." *Public Opinion Quarterly* 37:62–75.

Furu, T. 1971. *The Function of Television for Children and Adolescents.* Tokyo: Sophia University.

Galtung, Johan, and Mari Holmboe Ruge. 1970. "The Structure of Foreign News." In Jeremy Tunstall (ed.), *Media Sociology.* Urbana: University of Illinois Press.

Gans, Herbert. 1974. *Popular Culture and High Culture.* New York: Basic Books.

Garrison, Martin B. 1973. "Pretesting Newspaper Article Headlines as a Means of Determining the Level of Wire Editors' Knowledge of Subscribers' Interests." M.A. Thesis, University of Tennessee.

Gartner, Jane E. 1972. "A Study of Verbal, Vocal and Visual Communication." Ph.D. dissertation, Columbia University.

Gieber, Walter. 1964. "News Is What Newspapermen Make It." In Lewis A. Dexter and David M. White (eds.), *People, Society, and Mass Communications.* New York: Free Press.

Gosnell, Harold F. 1927. *Getting Out the Vote.* Chicago: University of Chicago Press.

Greenberg, Bradley S. 1964. "Diffusion of News of the Kennedy Assassination." *Public Opinion Quarterly* 28:225–232.

Greenberg, Bradley S. 1974. "Gratifications of Television Viewing and Their Correlates for British Children." In Jay Blumler and Elihu Katz (eds.), *The Uses of Mass Communications: Current Perspectives on Gratifications Research.* Beverly Hills, Ca.: Sage Publications.

Greenberg, Bradley S., and Edwin B. Parker (eds.). 1965. *The Kennedy Assassination and the American Public.* Stanford, Ca.: Stanford University Press.

Greenberg, Saadia R. 1975. "Conversations as Units of Analysis in the Study of Personal Influence." *Journalism Quarterly* 52:125–131.

Grunig, James E. 1974. "Three Stopping Experiments on the Communication of Science." *Journalism Quarterly* 51:387–399.

Grupp, Fred W., Jr. 1969. "The Magazine Reading Habits of Political Activists." *Public Opinion Quarterly* 33:103–106.

Grupp, Fred W., Jr. 1970. "Newscast Avoidance among Political Activists." *Public Opinion Quarterly* 34:262–266.

Guillain, Robert. 1957. *600 Million Chinese.* New York: Criterion Books.

Gutman, Jonathan. 1973. "Self-Concepts and Television Viewing." *Public Opinion Quarterly* 37:388–397.

Hachten, William A. 1971. *Muffled Drums: The News Media in Africa.* Ames: Iowa State University Press.

Hall, Edward T. 1959. *The Silent Language.* New York: Doubleday.

Hall, Stuart. 1974. "Media Power: The Double Bind." *Journal of Communication* 24(4):19–26.

Halloran, James D., Philip Elliott, and Graham Murdock. 1970. *Demonstration and Communication.* Harmondsworth, England: Penguin.

Harrison, Randall P. 1973. "Nonverbal Communication." In Ithiel De Sola Pool and Wilbur Schramm (eds.), *Handbook of Communication.* Chicago: Rand McNally.

Herz, Martin F. 1949. "Some Psychological Lessons from Leaflet Propaganda in World War II." *Public Opinion Quarterly* 13:471–486.

Hess, Stephen. 1974. "Is the Press Fair?" *The Brookings Bulletin,* Summer/Fall.

Hollander, Neil. 1971. "Adolescents and the War: Sources of Socialization." *Journalism Quarterly* 48:472–479.

Hopkins, Mark W. 1970. *Mass Media in the Soviet Union.* New York: Pegasus.

Hoskins, Robert L. 1973. "A Readability Study of AP and UPI Wire Copy." *Journalism Quarterly* 50:360–363.

Hovland, Carl I. 1959. "Reconciling Conflicting Results Derived from Experimental and Survey Studies." *American Psychologist* 14:8–17.

Hovland, Carl I., and Irving L. Janis (eds.). 1959. *Personality and Persuasibility.* New Haven: Yale University Press.

Hovland, Carl I., Arthur A. Lumsdaine, and F.D. Sheffield. 1949. *Experiments on Mass Communication.* Princeton, N.J.: Princeton University Press.

Hyman, Herbert H. 1974. "Mass Communication and Socialization." In Davison and Yu (eds.), *Mass Communication Research.* New York: Praeger.

Hyman, Herbert H., and Paul B. Sheatsley. 1947. "Some Reasons Why Information Campaigns Fail." *Public Opinion Quarterly* 11:412–423.

Hyman, Herbert H., and Paul B. Sheatsley. 1964. "Attitudes toward Desegregation." *Scientific American,* July.

Inkeles, Alex. 1968. *Social Change in Soviet Russia.* New York: Clarion.

Innis, Harold A. 1950. *Empire and Communications.* London: Oxford University Press.

James, William. 1961. *Psychology: The Briefer Course.* New York: Harper & Row. (First published in 1892)

The Japanese Press, 1975. Published by Nihon Shinbun Kuokai (The Japanese Newspaper Publishers and Editors Association), Tokyo, Japan.

Johns-Heine, Patricke, and Hans H. Gerth. 1949. "Values in Mass Periodical Fiction, 1921–1940." *Public Opinion Quarterly* 13:105–113.

Johnson, Nicholas, and James M. Hoak, Jr. 1970. "Media Concentration: Some Observations on the United States' Experience." *Iowa Law Review* 56:267–291.

Johnstone, John W.C. 1974. "Social Integration and Mass Media Use among Adolescents." In Jay G. Blumler and Elihu Katz (eds.), *The Uses of Mass Communications.* Beverly Hills, Ca.: Sage Publications.

Johnstone, John W.C., Edward J. Slawski, and William W. Bowman. 1972–73. "The Professional Values of American Newsmen." *Public Opinion Quarterly* 36:522–540.

Johnstone, John W. C., Edward J. Slawski, and William W. Bowman. Forthcoming. *The Newspeople: A Sociological Profile of American Journalists.* Urbana: University of Illinois Press.

Kato, Hidetoshi. 1974. *Japanese Research on Mass Communication: Selected Abstracts.* Honolulu: University Press of Hawaii.

Katz, Elihu, Michael Gurevitch, and Hadassah Haas. 1973. "On the Uses of the Mass Media for Important Things." *American Sociological Review* 38:164–181.

Katz, Elihu, and Paul F. Lazarsfeld. 1955. *Personal Influence.* New York: Free Press.

Kelley, Harold H. 1955. "Salience of Membership and Resistance to Change of Group-Anchored Attitudes." *Human Relations* 8:275–289.

Key, V.O., Jr. 1961. *Public Opinion and American Democracy.* New York: Knopf.

Kirkpatrick, Samuel A. 1970. "Political Attitude Structure and Component Change." *Public Opinion Quarterly* 34:403–407.

Klapper, Joseph T. 1960. *The Effects of Mass Communication.* Glencoe, Ill.: Free Press.

Knapper, Chris, and Peter B. Warr. 1965. "The Effect of Position and Layout on the Readership of News Items." *Gazette* 11: 231–236.

Knight, Oliver H. (ed.). 1966. *I Protest: Selected Disquisitions of E.W. Scripps.* Madison: University of Wisconsin Press.

Knowles, Clayton, and Richard P. Hunt. 1963. "Public Policy in a Newspaper Strike." *Columbia Journalism Review,* Spring.

Korte, Charles, and Stanley Milgram. 1970. "Acquaintance Networks between Racial Groups." *Journal of Personality and Social Psychology* 15:101–108.

Kraus, Sidney. 1962. *The Great Debates.* Bloomington: University of Indiana Press.

Kraus, Sidney. 1973. "Mass Communication and Political Socialization." *Quarterly Journal of Speech* 59:390–400.

Kriesberg, Martin. 1949. "Cross-Pressures and Attitudes." *Public Opinion Quarterly* 13:5–16.

Krisher, Bernard. 1972. "What Public Television Can Be: Japan's NHK." *Columbia Journalism Review,* July/August, 21–25.

Krugman, Herbert E. 1965. "The Impact of Television Advertising." *Public Opinion Quarterly* 29:349–356.

Krugman, Herbert E., and Eugene L. Harley. 1970. "Passive Learning from Television." *Public Opinion Quarterly* 34:184–190.

Kuang Ming Jin Pao, Enlightenment Daily, Peking.

Lacy, Dan. 1965. *Freedom and Communications,* 2d ed. Urbana: University of Illinois Press.

Lang, Kurt, and Gladys Engel Lang. 1959. "The Mass Media and Voting." In Eugene Burdick and A.J. Brodbeck (eds.), *American Voting Behavior.* Glencoe, Ill.: Free Press.

Larsen, Otto N. 1964. "Social Effects of Mass Communication." In Robert Faris (ed.), *Handbook of Modern Sociology.* Chicago: Rand McNally.

Lasswell, Harold D. 1927. *Propaganda Technique in the World War.* London: Kegan Paul.

Lasswell, Harold D. 1946. "Describing the Contents of Communication." In Bruce Lannes Smith, Harold D. Lasswell, and Ralph D. Casey (eds.), *Propaganda, Communication, and Public Opinion.* Princeton, N.J.: Princeton University Press.

Lasswell, Harold D. 1948. "The Structure and Function of Communications in Society." In Lyman Bryson (ed.), *The Communication of Ideas.* New York: Harper.

Lazarsfeld, Paul F., Bernard Berelson, and Hazel Gaudet. 1944. *The People's Choice.* New York: Duell, Sloan & Pearce.

Lazarsfeld, Paul F., and Herbert Menzel. 1963. "Mass Media and Personal Influence." In Wilbur Schramm (ed.), *The Science of Human Communication.* New York: Basic Books.

Lazarsfeld, Paul F., and Robert K. Merton. 1948. "Mass Communications, Popular Taste, and Organized Social Action." In Lyman Bryson (ed.). *The Communication of Ideas.* New York: Harper.

Lee, Alfred McClung. 1937. *The Daily Newspaper in America: The Evolution of a Social Instrument.* New York: Macmillan.

Lemert, James B. 1974. "Content Duplication by the Networks in Competing Evening Newscasts." *Journalism Quarterly* 51:238–244.

Lerner, Daniel. 1958. *The Passing of Traditional Society.* New York: Free Press.

Lerner, Daniel, and Wilbur Schramm. 1967. *Communication and Change in Developing Countries.* Honolulu: East-West Center Press.

Lesser, Gerald S. 1974. *Children and Television.* New York: Random House.

Lippmann, Walter. 1922. *Public Opinion.* New York: Macmillan (page citations from Penguin edition, 1946).

Maccoby, Eleanor. 1954. "Why Do Children Watch Television?" *Public Opinion Quarterly* 18:239–244.

Maccoby, Eleanor. 1964. "Effects of the Mass Media." In Martin L. Hoffman and Lois W. Hoffman (eds.), *Review of Child Development Research.* New York: Russell Sage.

Maccoby, Nathan, and Eleanor E. Maccoby. 1961. "Homeostatic Theories in Attitude Change." *Public Opinion Quarterly* 25:538–545.

Machlup, Fritz. 1962. *The Production and Distribution of Knowledge in the United States.* Princeton, N.J.: Princeton University Press.

Maisel, Richard. 1973. "The Decline of Mass Media." *Public Opinion Quarterly* 37:159–170.

Mann, Leon. 1974. "Counting the Crowd: Effects of Editorial Policy on Estimates." *Journalism Quarterly* 51:278–285.

Mao Tse-tung. 1954. *Selected Works of Mao Tse-tung.* London: Lawrence and Wishart.

Mao Tse-tung. 1967. *Quotations from Chairman Mao Tse-tung.* New York: Bantam.

Marcus-Steiff, Joachim. 1969. "Les Effets de la Publicite sur les Ventes." *Revue Francaise de Sociologie* 10:279–311.

Matthews, George T. 1959. *News and Rumor in Renaissance Europe: The Fugger Newsletters.* New York: Capricorn Books.

McCombs, Maxwell E. 1967. "Editorial Endorsement: A Study of Influence." *Journalism Quarterly* 44:545–548.

McCombs, Maxwell E. 1972a. "Mass Communication in Political Campaigns: Information, Gratification, and Persuasion." In F. Gerald Kline and Phillip J. Tichenor (eds.), *Current Perspectives in Mass Communication Research.* Beverly Hills, Ca.: Sage Publications.

McCombs, Maxwell E. 1972b. *Mass Media in the Marketplace. Journalism Monographs,* 24 (August 1972).

McCombs, Maxwell E., and Donald L. Shaw. 1972. "The Agenda-Setting Function of Mass Media." *Public Opinion Quarterly* 36:176–187.

McCormack, Buren H., Stanley T. McBrayer, William D. Rinehard, Albert Spendlove, and Robert M. White, II. 1967. *A Study of the Printing and Publishing Business in the Soviet Union.* New York: American Newspaper Publishers Association.

McGuire, William J. 1973. "Persuasion, Resistance, and Attitude Change." In Ithiel de Sola Pool, Wilbur Schramm, et al. (eds.), *Handbook of Communication.* Chicago: Rand McNally.

McLeod, Jack M., and Garrett J. O'Keefe, Jr. 1972. "The Socialization Perspective and Communication Behavior." In F. Gerald Kline and Phillip J. Tichenor (eds.), *Current Perspectives in Mass Communication Research.* Beverly Hills, Ca.: Sage Publications.

McLeod, Jack M., and Lee B. Becker. 1974. "Testing the Validity of Gratification Measures Through Political Effects Analysis." In Jay G. Blumler and Elihu Katz (eds.), *The Uses of Mass Communications: Current Perspectives on Gratification Research.* Beverly Hills, Ca.: Sage Publications.

McLuhan, Marshall. 1964. *Understanding Media.* New York: McGraw-Hill.

McQuail, Denis. 1972. *Sociology of Mass Communications.* Harmondsworth, England: Penguin.

McQuail, Denis, Jay G. Blumler, and J.R. Brown. 1972. "The Television Audience." In Denis McQuail (ed.), *Sociology of Mass Communications.* Harmondsworth, England. Penguin.

Mendelsohn, Harold. 1973. "Some Reasons Why Information Campaigns Can Succeed." *Public Opinion Quarterly* 37:50–61.

Mendelsohn, Harold. 1974. "Behaviorism, Functionalism, and Mass Communications Policy." *Public Opinion Quarterly* 38:379–389.

Menzel, Herbert. 1971. "Quasi-Mass Communication: A Neglected Area." *Public Opinion Quarterly* 35:406–409.

Merrill, John C. 1968. *The Elite Press: Great Newspapers of the World.* New York: Pitman.

Merton, Robert K., with Marjorie Fiske and Alberta Curtis. 1946. *Mass Persuasion.* New York: Harper.

Merton, Robert K. 1949. "Personal Influence." In Paul F. Lazarsfeld and Frank N. Stanton (eds.), *Communication Research, 1948–49.* New York: Harper.

Minow, Newton N., John B. Martin, and Lee M. Mitchell. 1973. *Presidential Television.* New York: Basic Books.

Molotch, Harvey, and Marilyn Lester. 1974. "News as Purposive Behavior: On the Strategic Use of Routine Events, Accidents, and Scandals." *American Sociological Review* 39:101–112.

Molotch, Harvey, and Marilyn Lester. 1975. "Accidental News: The Great Oil Spill as Local Occurrence and National Event." *American Journal of Sociology* 81:235–260.

Mott, Frank Luther. 1962. *American Journalism,* 3d ed. New York: Macmillan.

Movement for a New Congress. 1970. *Vote Power: The Official Activist Campaigner's Handbook.* Englewood Cliffs, N.J.: Prentice-Hall.

Nimmo, Dan D. 1964. *Newsgathering in Washington.* New York: Atherton.

Noelle-Neumann, Elisabeth. 1959. "Mass Communication Media and Public Opinion." *Journalism Quarterly* 36:401–409.

Noelle-Neumann, Elisabeth. 1973. "Return to the Concept of the Powerful Mass Media." In H. Equchi and K. Sata (eds.), *Studies of Broadcasting,* No. 9.

Ostlund, Lyman E. 1973–74. "Interpersonal Communication Following McGovern's Eagleton Decision." *Public Opinion Quarterly* 37:601–610.

Paletz, David L., Peggy Reichert, and Barbara McIntyre. 1971. "How the Media Support Local Governmental Authority." *Public Opinion Quarterly* 35:80–92.

Parker, Edwin B. 1974. "Implications of New Information Technology." In W. Phillips Davison and Frederick T.C. Yu (eds.), *Mass Communications Research.* New York: Praeger.

Payne, David E. 1974. "Newspapers and Crime: What Happens During Strike Periods." *Journalism Quarterly* 51:607–611.

Peled, Isiyona, and Elihu Katz. 1974. "Media Functions in Wartime." In Jay G. Blumler and Elihu Katz (eds.), *The Uses of Mass Communications.* Beverly Hills, Ca.: Sage Publications.

Penrose, Jeanne, et al. 1974. "The Newspaper Non-reader Ten Years Later." *Journalism Quarterly* 51:631–638.

Peterson, Theodore. 1964. *Magazines in the Twentieth Century,* 2d ed. Urbana: University of Illinois Press.

Pool, Ithiel de Sola. 1973a. "Communication Systems." In Ithiel de Sola Pool and Wilbur Schramm (eds.), *Handbook of Communication.* Chicago: Rand McNally.

Pool, Ithiel de Sola. 1973b. *Talking Back: Citizen Feedback and Cable Technology.* Cambridge, Mass.: M.I.T. Press.

Pool, Ithiel de Sola. 1974. "The Rise of Communication Policy Research." *Journal of Communication* 24(2):31–42.

Pool, Ithiel de Sola, and Irwin Shulman. 1959. "Newsmen's Fantasies, Audiences, and Newswriting." *Public Opinion Quarterly* 23:145–158.

Pred, Allan R. 1973. *Urban Growth and the Circulation of Information: The United States System of Cities, 1790–1840.* Cambridge, Mass.: Harvard University Press.

Pye, Lucian W. (ed.). 1963. *Communication and Political Development.* Princeton, N.J.: Princeton University Press.

Quotations from Chairman Mao Tse-tung. 1967. New York: Bantam Books.

Rarick, Galen. 1973. "Newspaper Subscribers and Nonsubscribers." *Journalism Quarterly* 50:265–270.

Research Program on Communications Policy. 1974. *Report on First Half Year.* Cambridge, Mass.: MIT Press.

Riley, Matilda W., and John W. Riley, Jr. 1951. "A Sociological Approach to Communications Research." *Public Opinion Quarterly* 15:445–460.

Rivers, William L. 1973. "The Press as a Communication System." In Ithiel de Sola Pool and Wilbur Schramm (eds.), *Handbook of Communication.* Chicago: Rand McNally.

Roberts, Donald F. 1973. "Communication and Children." In Ithiel de Sola Pool and Wilbur Schramm (eds.), *Handbook of Communication.* Chicago: Rand McNally.

Robinson, John P. 1974. "The Press as King Maker." *Journalism Quarterly* 51:587–594.

Robinson, Michael J. 1974. "The Impact of the Televised Watergate Hearings." *Journal of Communication* 24(2).

Rogers, Everett M. 1969. *Modernization among Peasants: The Impact of Communication.* New York: Holt, Rinehart and Winston.

Rogers, Everett M. 1973. "Mass Media and Interpersonal Communication." In Ithiel de Sola Pool and Wilbur Schramm (eds.), *Handbook of Communication.* Chicago: Rand McNally.

Ronneberger, Franz (ed.). 1971. *Sozialisation durch Massenkommunikation.* Stuttgart: Enke.

Roper, Burns W. 1975. *Trends in Public Attitudes toward Television and Other Mass Media 1959–1974.* New York: Television Information Office.

Roshco, Bernard. 1975. *Newsmaking.* Chicago: University of Chicago Press.

Rosnow, Ralph L. 1974. "On Rumor." *Journal of Communication* 24(3):26–38.

Rosten, Leo C. 1937. The *Washington Correspondents.* New York: Harcourt.

Salcedo, Rodolfo N., et al. 1974. "A Successful Information Campaign on Pesticides." *Journalism Quarterly* 51:91–95.

Salisbury, Harrison. 1965. *Russia.* New York: Atheneum.

Sasser, Emery L., and John T. Russell. 1972. "The Fallacy of News Judgment." *Journalism Quarterly* 49:280–284.

Schiller, Herbert I. 1969. *Mass Communications and American Empire.* New York: Augustus M. Kelley.

Schiller, Herbert I. 1973. *The Mind Managers.* Boston: Beacon.

Schlesinger, Arthur M. 1958. *Prelude to Independence: The Newspaper War on Great Britain, 1764–1776.* New York: Knopf.

Schramm, Wilbur. 1957. *Responsibility in Mass Communication.* New York: Harper.

Schramm, Wilbur (ed.). 1960. *Mass Communication,* 2d ed. Urbana: University of Illinois Press.

Schramm, Wilbur. 1964. *Mass Media and National Development.* Stanford, Ca.: Stanford University Press.

Schramm, Wilbur. 1965. "Communication in Crisis." In Bradley S. Greenberg and Edwin B. Parker (eds.), *The Kennedy Assassination and the American Public.* Stanford, Ca.: Stanford University Press.

Schramm, Wilbur. 1973. *Men, Messages and Media.* New York: Harper.

Schramm, Wilbur. Forthcoming. "Ten Years of Communication Development in the Developing Regions." To be published in Wilbur Schramm and Daniel Lerner (eds.), *Communication and Change: The Past Ten Years—and the Next.* Honolulu: University Press of Hawaii.

Schramm, Wilbur, and Janet Alexander. 1973. "Broadcasting." In Ithiel de Sola

Pool and Wilbur Schramm (eds.), *Handbook of Communication*. Chicago: Rand McNally.

Schramm, Wilbur, and Richard F. Carter. 1959. "Effectiveness of a Political Telethon." *Public Opinion Quarterly* 23:121–126.

Schurmann, Franz. 1966. *Ideology and Organization in Communist China*. Berkeley and Los Angeles: University of California Press.

Schwartz, Benjamin. 1965. "Modernization and the Maoist Vision." In Roderick MacFarquhar (ed.), *China under Mao*. Cambridge, Mass.: M.I.T. Press.

Schwartz, David A. 1973–74. "How Fast Does News Travel?" *Public Opinion Quarterly* 37:625:627.

Schweitzer, John C. 1974. *The Newspaper and Its Community*. Ph.D. dissertation, University of North Carolina.

Sears, David O., and Jonathan Freedman. 1967. "Selective Exposure to Information." *Public Opinion Quarterly* 31:194–213.

Seiden, Martin H. 1974. *Who Controls the Mass Media?* New York: Basic Books.

Selected Works of Mao Tse-tung. 1954. London: Lawrence & Wishart.

Servan-Schreiber, Jean-Louis. 1974. *The Power to Inform: Media: The Information Business*. New York: McGraw-Hill.

Sherrod, Drury R. 1971–72. "Selective Perception of Political Candidates." *Public Opinion Quarterly* 35:554–562.

Shibutani, Tamotsu. 1966. *Improvised News*. Indianapolis: Bobbs-Merrill.

Shils, Edward A., and Morris Janowitz. 1948. "Cohesion and Disintegration in the *Wehrmacht* in World War II." *Public Opinion Quarterly* 12:280–315.

Shosteck, Herschel. 1973–74. "Factors Influencing Appeal of TV News Personalities." *Journal of Broadcasting* 18:63–72.

Siebert, Fred, Theodore Peterson, and Wilbur Schramm. 1963. *Four Theories of the Press*. Urbana: University of Illinois Press.

Sigal, Leon V. 1973. *Reporters and Officials*. Lexington, Mass.: Lexington Books, 1973.

Sigelman, Lee. 1973. "Reporting the News: An Organizational Analysis." *American Journal of Sociology* 79:132–151.

Smith, M. Brewster. 1949. "The Combat Replacement." In Samuel A. Stouffer et al. (eds.), *The American Soldier: Combat and Its Aftermath*. Princeton: Princeton University Press.

Snipes, Ronald L. 1974. "News Value and News Decisions of High and Low Authoritarian Editors." Ed.D. dissertation, Oklahoma State University.

Sommerlad, E. Lloyd. 1966. *The Press in Developing Countries*. Sydney, Australia: University Press.

Star, Shirley A., and Helen MacGill Hughes. 1950. "Report on an Educational Campaign." *American Journal of Sociology* 55:389–400.

Starr, Louis M. 1954. *Bohemian Brigade: Civil War Newsmen in Action*. New York: Knopf.

Stipp, Horst M. 1975. "Validity in Social Research: Measuring Children's Television Exposure." Ph.D. dissertation, Columbia University.

Stone, Vernon A. 1973–74. "Attitudes toward Television Newsmen." *Journal of Broadcasting* 18:49–62.

Stott, William. 1973. *Documentary Expression and Thirties America.* New York: Oxford.

Stouffer, Samuel A. 1955. *Communism, Conformity, and Civil Liberties.* New York: Doubleday.

Swanberg, W.A. 1961. *Citizen Hearst: A Biography of William Randolph Hearst.* New York: Scribner's.

Swanberg, W.A. 1967. *Pulitzer.* New York: Scribner's.

Tebbel, John. 1974. *The Media in America.* New York: Crowell.

Terrou, F., and L. Solal. 1951. *Legislation for Press, Film and Radio.* Paris: UNESCO.

Tichenor, Phillip J., G.A. Donohue, and C.N. Olien. 1970. "Mass Media Flow and the Differential Growth of Knowledge." *Public Opinion Quarterly* 34: 159–170.

Tichenor, Phillip J., Jane M. Rodenkirchen, Clarice N. Olien, and George A. Donohue. 1973. "Community Issues, Conflict, and Public Affairs Knowledge." In Peter Clarke (ed.), *New Models for Mass Communication Research.* Beverly Hills, Ca.: Sage Publications.

Tipton, Leonard, Roger D. Haney, and John P. Baseheart. 1975. "Media Agenda-Setting in City and State Election Campaigns." *Journalism Quarterly* 52:15–22.

Travers, Jeffrey, and Stanley Milgram. 1969. "An Experimental Study of the Small World Problem." *Sociometry* 32:425–443.

Truman, David B. 1951. *The Governmental Process.* New York: Knopf.

Tuchman, Gaye. 1972. "Objectivity as a Strategic Ritual." *American Journal of Sociology* 77:660–679.

Tunstall, Jeremy. 1970. *Media Sociology: A Reader.* Urbana: University of Illinois Press.

Turow, Joseph. 1974. "Talk Show as Interpersonal Communication." *Journal of Broadcasting* 18:171–180.

UNESCO. 1961. *Mass Media in the Developing Countries.* A UNESCO report to the United Nations, Reports and Papers on Mass Communication, No. 35.

UNESCO. 1964. *World Communications.* Paris.

UNESCO, 1975. *National Communication Systems.* Reports and Papers on Mass Communication, No. 74. Paris: The UNESCO Press.

U.S. Government, Surgeon General. *Television and Growing Up: The Impact of Televised Violence.* 1972. Washington, D.C.: Government Printing Office. (Report of the Surgeon General's Scientific Advisory Committee on Television and Social Behavior, plus five volumes of reports and papers.)

Vidmar, Neil, and Milton Rokeach. 1974. "Archie Bunker's Bigotry: A Study in Selective Perception and Exposure." *Journal of Communication* 24(1):36–47.

Wade, Serena E. 1973. "Media Effects on Changes in Attitudes toward the Rights of Young People." *Journalism Quarterly* 50:292–296.

Wade, Serena, and Wilbur Schramm. 1969. "The Mass Media as Sources of Public Affairs, Science, and Health Knowledge." *Public Opinion Quarterly* 33:197–209.

Waples, Douglas, Bernard Berelson, and Franklin D. Bradshaw. 1940. *What Reading Does to People.* Chicago: University of Chicago Press.

Ward, L.S. 1971. "Effects of Television Advertising on Children and Adolescents." In E.A. Rubinstein et al. (eds.), *Television and Social Behavior,* vol. 4. Washington, D.C.: National Institute of Mental Health.

Warner, Malcolm. 1968. "TV Coverage of International Affairs." *Television Quarterly* 7:60–75.

Weiss, Carol. 1974. "What America's Leaders Read." *Public Opinion Quarterly* 38:1–22.

Weiss, Walter. 1968. "Effects of Mass Media of Communication." In Gardner Lindzey and Elliot Aronson (eds.), *Handbook of Social Psychology,* 2d ed. Reading, Mass.: Addison-Wesley.

White, David Manning. 1950. "The Gatekeeper: A Case Study in the Selection of News." *Journalism Quarterly* 27:383–390.

White, W. James. 1969–70. "An Index for Determining the Relative Importance of Information Sources." *Public Opinion Quarterly* 33:607–610.

Wiebe, Gerhart D. 1969–70. "Two Psychological Factors in Media Audience Behavior." *Public Opinion Quarterly* 33:523–536.

Wilson, C. Edward. 1974. "The Effect of Medium on Loss of Information." *Journalism Quarterly* 51:111–115.

Wintour, Charles. 1972. *Pressures on the Press.* London: Andre Deutsch.

Wolf, Frank. 1972. *Television Programming for News and Public Affairs.* New York: Praeger.

World Statistical Annual. Published by the United Nations.

Wright, Charles R. 1975. *Mass Communication: A Sociological Perspective.* New York: Random House.

Yu, Frederick T.C. 1964. *Mass Persuasion in Communist China.* New York: Praeger.

Zajonc, Robert B. 1960. "The Concepts of Balance, Congruity, and Dissonance." *Public Opinion Quarterly* 24:280–296.

Zielske, Herbert E. 1959. "The Remembering and Forgetting of Advertising." *Journal of Marketing* 23:239–243.

INDEX